LITERACY COACHING IN THE SECONDARY GRADES

The Guilford Series on Intensive Instruction

Sharon Vaughn, Editor

This series presents innovative ways to improve learning outcomes for K–12 students with challenging academic and behavioral needs. Books in the series explain the principles of intensive intervention and provide evidence-based teaching practices for learners who require differentiated instruction. Grounded in current research, volumes include user-friendly features such as sample lessons, examples of daily schedules, case studies, classroom vignettes, and reproducible tools.

Essentials of Intensive Intervention
Rebecca Zumeta Edmonds, Allison Gruner Gandhi, and Louis Danielson

Intensive Reading Interventions for the Elementary Grades
Jeanne Wanzek, Stephanie Al Otaiba, and Kristen L. McMaster

Intensifying Mathematics Interventions for Struggling Students
Edited by Diane Pedrotty Bryant

Literacy Coaching in the Secondary Grades: Helping Teachers Meet the Needs of All Students
Jade Wexler, Elizabeth Swanson, and Alexandra Shelton

LITERACY COACHING IN THE SECONDARY GRADES

Helping Teachers Meet the Needs of All Students

Jade Wexler
Elizabeth Swanson
Alexandra Shelton

Series Editor's Note by Sharon Vaughn

THE GUILFORD PRESS
New York London

Copyright © 2021 The Guilford Press
A Division of Guilford Publications, Inc.
370 Seventh Avenue, Suite 1200, New York, NY 10001
www.guilford.com

All rights reserved

Except as indicated, no part of this book may be reproduced, translated, stored in a retrieval system, or transmitted, in any form or by any means, electronic, mechanical, photocopying, microfilming, recording, or otherwise, without written permission from the publisher.

Printed in the United States of America

This book is printed on acid-free paper.

Last digit is print number: 9 8 7 6 5 4 3 2

LIMITED DUPLICATION LICENSE

These materials are intended for use only by qualified professionals.

The publisher grants to individual purchasers of this book nonassignable permission to reproduce all materials for which photocopying permission is specifically granted in a footnote. This license is limited to you, the individual purchaser, for personal use or use with students. This license does not grant the right to reproduce these materials for resale, redistribution, electronic display, or any other purposes (including but not limited to books, pamphlets, articles, video or audio recordings, blogs, file-sharing sites, Internet or intranet sites, and handouts or slides for lectures, workshops, or webinars, whether or not a fee is charged). Permission to reproduce these materials for these and any other purposes must be obtained in writing from the Permissions Department of Guilford Publications.

Library of Congress Cataloging-in-Publication Data

Names: Wexler, Jade, author. | Swanson, Elizabeth, author. | Shelton, Alexandra (Alexandra Elizabeth), author.
Title: Literacy coaching in the secondary grades : helping teachers meet the needs of all students / Jade Wexler, Elizabeth Swanson, Alexandra Shelton.
Description: New York : The Guilford Press, 2021. | Series: The Guilford series on intensive instruction | Includes bibliographical references and index.
Identifiers: LCCN 2021011908 | ISBN 9781462546695 (paperback) | ISBN 9781462546701 (hardcover)
Subjects: LCSH: Reading (Secondary) | Reading—Remedial teaching. | Response to intervention (Learning disabled children) | BISAC: EDUCATION / Special Education / Learning Disabilities | EDUCATION / Secondary
Classification: LCC LB1632 .W44 2021 | DDC 418/.40712—dc23
LC record available at *https://lccn.loc.gov/2021011908*

About the Authors

Jade Wexler, PhD, is Associate Professor in the Department of Counseling, Higher Education, and Special Education at the University of Maryland. Her current research focuses on designing reading interventions to support adolescents with reading difficulties and disabilities in the content-area and supplemental intensive intervention settings. She also designs and evaluates professional development and schoolwide service-delivery models to support the implementation of evidence-based literacy practices in middle schools. Dr. Wexler has published over 45 articles focusing on adolescent literacy interventions. She is a former high school special education and reading teacher.

Elizabeth Swanson, PhD, is Research Associate Professor at The University of Texas at Austin, and has served the field of education since the 1990s as a special education teacher, researcher, public speaker, and writer. Currently, she focuses on improving educational opportunities for struggling readers and students with disabilities. Dr. Swanson has worked closely with teachers to co-create and test the effects of multiple sets of instructional practices focused on infusing the content areas with vocabulary and comprehension practices to improve outcomes for struggling readers. She has published more than 55 articles in peer-reviewed journals.

Alexandra Shelton, PhD, is a Faculty Specialist and Project Director in the Special Education Program within the Department of Counseling, Higher Education, and Special Education at the University of Maryland. She focuses on professional development for middle school teachers aimed at improving literacy instruction and intervention for students with and at risk for reading disabilities. Dr. Shelton is the author of multiple publications related to secondary literacy instruction and intervention. A former high school special education teacher, she served students in general and special education settings in English language arts and science.

Series Editor's Note

Welcome to the latest volume in The Guilford Series on Intensive Instruction, aimed at providing evidence-based practices that have been tested in schools and classrooms with educators just like you. The authors of *Literacy Coaching in the Secondary Grades: Helping Teachers Meet the Needs of All Students* present a feasible method for implementing a schoolwide coaching approach that supports school leaders, teachers, and students. I think you'll agree that the comprehensive approach outlined in this book provides a real platform for meeting the literacy needs of students in secondary settings effectively.

You are likely aware that there is a serious problem in secondary schools with the high numbers of students who are unable to read and learn from texts. To help these students make gains, we need to provide literacy instruction to all students across *all* content areas and intensive intervention for students with and at risk for disabilities. Providing this type of instruction and intervention requires secondary school leaders (e.g., instructional coaches) to build a coordinated schoolwide literacy model. Leaders will need to select and adopt evidence-based literacy practices and ensure that teachers receive high-quality professional development and ongoing coaching support as they implement such practices.

You may have wondered, as we have, how school leaders can make informed decisions to enhance literacy outcomes for students in the secondary grades. Or, how can secondary school leaders promote opportunities for all content-area teachers to infuse their lessons with literacy-supporting practices? I am excited to say that this book provides the type of practical solutions that will allow school leaders and teachers to implement a successful literacy platform centered on a strategic coaching approach.

Of course, building a schoolwide literacy model can be rewarding, but it is also complicated for a variety of reasons. For example, just as students have a range of needs, so do teachers. You are likely familiar with the resistance that leaders can face from teachers in their building who do not "buy in" to the overall schoolwide literacy model mission. Some teachers might perceive that they are not literacy experts and the literacy challenges that their students demonstrate fall to the elementary teachers. They might feel strongly that their focus should be teaching the content—whether it be history, science, or English language arts. Other teachers might be enthusiastic about adopting and implementing literacy practices but still require a lot of support to implement the practices effectively.

The fact of the matter is that most content-area learning in secondary and post-secondary settings requires students to read and learn from print. Whether this text is a traditional textbook, other print sources, or reading materials online, students are expected to be able to read and learn from a range of text types. So, how can we build schoolwide adolescent literacy models to address the dilemma of secondary students with significant reading difficulties and disabilities?

In this book, the author team provides empirically validated and practically implemented approaches to meeting the challenges associated with the variation in students' needs in secondary schools as well as the range of teachers' needs. The Adaptive Intervention Model for Coaching (AIM Coaching) is designed to be a realistic approach to recognizing that teachers have a variety of needs related to implementing literacy practices. AIM Coaching factors in the realities of teaching in secondary settings and provides a framework that is readily implemented and built on success. Of high importance in this coaching approach is the understanding that effective coaching involves identifying the needs of teachers. Rather than providing the same amount of support and resources to all teachers, AIM Coaching provides school leaders with a plan to understand the needs of teachers and facilitate their success by identifying target activities aligned with their skills, real-life challenges (e.g., time constraints), and needs of their students. This approach increases substantially the likelihood that teachers will make a shift to include literacy instruction in content areas as well as literacy intervention to meet the needs of all students.

This volume is a perfect addition to The Guilford Series on Intensive Instruction. All of the books in this series provide innovative ways to improve learning outcomes for students, addressing their unique academic and behavioral needs. The authors emphasize evidence-based practices that address differentiated instruction and include user-friendly features, such as sample lessons, case studies, and visuals to describe how the practices can be introduced in the school and classroom settings. I am confident that this book will support your literacy solutions at the secondary level.

Sharon Vaughn, PhD

Preface

Too many of our nation's students—32% of fourth graders and 24% of eighth graders—cannot read a text at a basic level (McFarland et al., 2019). This means they cannot identify the main idea, make simple inferences, and use the text to identify details that support their conclusions. They cannot read a story and identify the problem. They cannot gather information from various sections of informational text to support a conclusion. This happens in spite of the fact that, for example, identifying the main idea of a text is an expectation written into the Common Core State Standards (National Governors Association Center for Best Practices & Council of Chief State School Officers [NGACBP & CCSSO], 2010a) included at every grade level from kindergarten through 12th grade. Students as young as kindergarten are taught to look for "basic similarities in and differences between two texts on the same topic" (NGACBP & CCSSO, 2010b) as a foundation to the 12th-grade standard that requires students to "integrate and evaluate multiple sources of information presented in different media or formats (e.g., visually, quantitatively) as well as in words in order to address a question or solve a problem" (NGACBP & CCSSO, 2010c).

If standards require that students as young as 5 years old begin to learn these important literacy skills and if the standards repeat and expand as students move through the grade levels, then why are a quarter of our eighth-grade students still considered to be "struggling readers"? Some students have disabilities, but this accounts for only 14% of all public school students (Hussar et al., 2020), many of whom perform at or above basic levels on the national literacy assessment (U.S. Department of Education [USDOE], Institute of Education Sciences, National Center for Education Statistics, National Assessment of Educational Progress, 2019). Other students are English learners, but this accounts for only 9.5% of all public school students. Many of these students are proficient readers as well. There must be another reason why so many of our nation's middle school students struggle with basic literacy skills.

Several researchers have systematically observed content-area classrooms across the nation (e.g., Ness, 2016; Swanson et al., 2016; Wanzek et al., 2017). Through these studies, we catch a glimpse of the frequency and type of literacy instruction that takes place within middle school content-area classrooms. A substantial finding of note is that little reading of connected text takes place within social studies (10.4% of observed time), science (2.2% of observed time), and English language arts (14.8% of observed time; Swanson et al., 2016; Wexler et al., 2017). Even worse, observers reported that comprehension supports are rarely provided, with less than 1% of observed time in science classrooms spent on reading comprehension supports like previewing, asking/answering questions, or identifying the main idea (Wexler et al., 2017). While there was more reading comprehension support observed in social studies and English language arts classrooms, the type of support was overwhelmingly comprehension monitoring by asking questions (Swanson et al., 2016).

Many middle school leaders across the country are beginning to recognize this trend and are answering the call to build schoolwide adolescent literacy models in an effort to impact student literacy outcomes. It was with this goal in mind that our team of literacy experts and teachers partnered with several middle schools to implement a schoolwide literacy initiative (Vaughn, Swanson, Wexler, & Roberts, 2015–2019). We proposed a twofold effort to intensify literacy instruction for all students, including struggling secondary readers and students with disabilities:

1. *Instruction:* For all students in the school, we proposed an evidence-based vocabulary and text-reading routine that teachers in all subject areas could implement with ease and little time commitment.
2. *Intervention:* For struggling secondary readers and students with disabilities, we proposed a highly focused and intensive set of evidence-based instructional practices focused on multisyllabic word reading, vocabulary development, and reading comprehension strategy use.

This effort was well received by district and school leaders. Leaders were dedicated to improving student literacy and shared our vision that this feasible set of instructional practices could improve middle school literacy if woven into every content area, combined with more intensive intervention designed for struggling secondary readers and students with disabilities. We left these leadership meetings filled with enthusiasm and optimism.

When we received carte blanche to work with middle school teachers, we faced a different atmosphere. We shared with them the vocabulary procedures that required choosing three essential words and spending 2 minutes per word engaged in a routine to encourage a deep understanding. Many in the room voiced concern. Some were worried about their ability to choose words and prepare materials. Others were concerned about maintaining student engagement. We were told many times, "I'm not a reading teacher!" We wondered whether teachers were unwilling to implement the new practice or if they felt underprepared to deliver the vocabulary routine effectively. To help identify the issue, we conducted an anonymous survey. Teachers agreed that the initial professional development was of high quality. Every single teacher expressed his or her willingness to try the new routine. However, 85% of teachers were worried that they could not deliver the vocabulary routine in an effective, engaging way.

This finding helped us realize that our professional development should be both intensive (like our vocabulary workshop) and also sustained over time in order to influence teacher adoption of the practices in classrooms (Yoon, Duncan, Lee, Scarloss, & Shapley, 2007). Our new goal became to integrate professional development into the daily work of teachers (Joyce & Showers, 2002) through instructional coaching. This type of work required that instructional coaches work with teachers closely and over extended periods of time. The problem then became that our budget allowed for two instructional coaches to address the needs of over 60 science, social studies, and English language arts teachers. The challenge was indeed steep! Every teacher needed help of some kind. We predicted that some would require careful and time-consuming instructional coaching, whereas others would require only check-ins and motivational votes of confidence in their skills. How would we identify teacher needs? Furthermore, how would we identify teachers most in need of instructional support who were also willing to join an instructional coach during the learning process? We needed a systematic, streamlined instructional coaching model so that we could facilitate the instructional coaching of large numbers of middle school teachers with a variety of backgrounds, job descriptions (i.e., science, social studies, English language arts), ability, and enthusiasm. It was from this challenge that Adaptive Intervention Model (AIM) Coaching was developed.

PURPOSE OF THIS BOOK

Our goal for this book is to provide instructional coaches with a feasible format for implementing an intensive schoolwide adolescent literacy model that is focused on:

- Bolstering literacy instruction within every middle school content-area classroom to provide a platform of services that benefit all students, and
- Providing struggling secondary readers and students with disabilities with an intensive, evidence-based intervention that is based on their needs.

For the purpose of this book, we consider an instructional coach to be a literacy coach, some type of specialist (e.g., reading specialist or special education teacher), or even an assistant principal who is capable of providing professional development and ongoing instructional coaching support to teachers. The driving force behind the model is AIM Coaching that offers a structure for providing ongoing professional development and support to teachers across the entire school. Therefore, this book is designed for several audiences:

- For the school administrator or district leader who has a desire to adopt a schoolwide literacy model driven by AIM Coaching, it provides parameters for the model, desired qualifications for instructional coaches, and materials that can be used campuswide to encourage buy-in.

- For the novice instructional coach, it provides a presentation of evidence-based adolescent literacy practices and instruction in using AIM Coaching to reach the needs of all teachers.
- For the experienced instructional coach who may be knowledgeable about evidence-based adolescent literacy practices, it provides AIM Coaching explanations and also materials that can be used tomorrow morning with teachers.

Whether you are a middle or high school principal tasked with improving literacy for all of your students or a high school reading specialist asked to coach content-area teachers on how to infuse evidence-based literacy practices into content-area classes, this book is for you. We will review the latest evidence on adolescent literacy practices, walk you through AIM Coaching, and give plenty of examples from our real-life experiences providing instructional leadership in middle schools across the nation. We'll also offer tools to help you organize the process of AIM Coaching as well as materials you can use to present the model to your colleagues. Indeed, adopting a new instructional coaching model to support a schoolwide adolescent literacy model is not easy. Implementing AIM Coaching will be a challenge, but one worth accepting.

We live in an increasingly information-oriented society where literacy is key to social and educational mobility. With the Internet, information is at our fingertips and we must read to access it. The other day, my (E.S.) 5-year-old wanted to know how far a man could jump. I said, "Let's look it up!" And then he asked me where prairie dogs live. We "looked that up," too. From a very young age, children learn that (1) information is readily available and (2) accessing the information requires reading. Young adults do a lot of daily online reading, too. In 2018, adults in the United States between age 18 and 24 received an average of 128 text messages per day (Burke, 2018) that were, on average, 20 words long (Alan, 2013). That's a daily reading load of 2,560 words—equivalent to 3.4 college textbook pages per day (*http://cte.rice.edu/blogarchive/2016/07/11/workload*).

Consider also post-high school reading demands. In our nation's highly competitive colleges and universities, 92% of students report taking at least one class that requires more than 40 pages of reading per week (Arum & Roksa, 2011). Most college professors agree that students should study outside of class for twice the number of hours spent in class. Under these conditions, for each class, students could read as few as 15 very difficult to understand pages (e.g., in biology) to 120 easier to understand pages (e.g., in history) of text per week (*http://cte.rice.edu/blogarchive/2016/07/11/workload*).

We looked up the five most common jobs in the United States. The top three jobs (retail salesperson, cashier, and food preparer) require little reading. However, the number 4 and 5 jobs—office clerks (with 2,808,100 people employed) and registered nurses (with 2,633,980 people employed)—require a great volume of daily reading (Thompson, 2013).

How can we best prepare our students to participate in this information-based society that demands literacy? According to Michael Pressley, "If we can infuse literacy practices into every content classroom, maybe there's hope" (2004, p. 426).

TEACHER TRAINING IN LITERACY-BASED PRACTICES

Once teachers are in the field, the most common type of teacher training is the one-shot professional development session (Darling-Hammond, Wei, Andree, Richardson, & Orphanos, 2009; Hill, 2007). It serves an important role in teacher development. Evidence points to the fact that professional development sessions are effective in improving teacher knowledge of content and instructional techniques (Barlow, Frick, Barker, & Phelps, 2014; Penuel, Fishman, Yamaguchi, & Gallagher, 2007). However, additional ongoing efforts are necessary if teachers are to operationalize knowledge into classroom practice (Kraft, Blazar, & Hogan, 2018). One way to involve teachers in ongoing professional development is to engage instructional coaches and teachers in a professional dialogue focused on skill development (Lofthouse, Leat, Towler, Hallet, & Cummings, 2010).

Within the past 7–10 years, the number of studies investigating the efficacy of instructional coaching has flourished. Take, for example, Yoon and colleagues' review of professional development literature published in 2007. In this review, only 9 studies qualified for inclusion. A mere 11 years later, Kraft and colleagues (2018) located 60 studies of coaching that allowed for effects to be calculated. This awakening in the literature provides us with evidence that instructional coaching largely works across all subject areas and impacts not only teachers' practices but also student achievement (Kraft et al., 2018).

THE CHALLENGES OF INSTRUCTIONAL COACHING

The potential effectiveness of instructional coaching should not overshadow the challenges inherent in professional development models that require close communication and collaboration among professionals. After all, challenges exist related to the instructional coach, the teachers, and the students.

Instructional Coach-Based Challenges

Instructional coaches at the secondary level must possess a variety of skills. First, it is essential that instructional coaches have the ability and knowledge to analyze student data to identify areas of need, select evidence-based practices that fit student need, and then communicate the need and solution to not only administrators but also teachers. Next, instructional coaches must provide professional development that aligns with best practices in adult learning. Once evidence-based practices are in place within the classroom, instructional coaches must understand the critical role of fidelity to the intended practice and how to use formal and informal methods to determine fidelity. Instructional coaching methods that will encourage teachers to implement new practices with fidelity represent another essential area of knowledge. Finally, interpersonal relationship building is a skill critical to the success of teacher–coach relationships. With this long list of necessary knowledge and skills, it is no wonder that instructional coaching ability varies greatly from one instructional coach to the next (Blazar & Kraft, 2015). The sheer volume and variety of skills necessary for a successful instructional coaching experience are daunting.

Teacher-Based Challenges

When you, as an instructional coach, propose infusing middle school classrooms with literacy practices to benefit all learners, consider carefully not only what you are asking of teachers but also their possible responses. At the most basic level, you are asking them to shift their practices—to change what they do in some way. Change is exceedingly difficult for most human beings. Consider dieters. Even highly motivated people intent on losing weight or improving their health are able to maintain a diet different from their norm for an average of only a few weeks (Pelletier, Dion, Slovinec-D'Angelo, & Reid, 2004). Dieters are far more successful when the change to their diet is slight; and when there is built-in accountability and ongoing support in making changes to eating habits and exercise. It is no different among teachers. Among a group of middle and high school teachers who were asked to adopt new instructional practices, 82% reported discomfort and anxiety (Cantrell, Burns, & Callaway, 2008). In order to change, teachers must understand the benefits of infusing their classrooms with literacy practices, be given highly feasible instructional practices that can be implemented with relative ease, and receive ongoing support as they try the new practices and receive feedback for improvement.

Instructional coaches should also be aware of secondary classroom culture (Lee & Spratley, 2010). Within the structure of middle and high school, there are content-area subcultures that value different forms of knowledge and ways of teaching. For example, in social studies classes, teachers most often lecture, provide students with definitions, and administer formal tests of isolated content knowledge (Swanson et al., 2017). In English language arts, more text reading takes place, but instruction largely remains teacher-centered (Swanson et al, 2017). In science, the focus is on content delivery independent of text reading (Wexler et al., 2017).

As the instructional coach begins to train content-area teachers in more student-focused evidence-based literacy practices (e.g., explicit vocabulary instruction or text-based discourse), expect some hesitation. After all, many content-area teachers not only believe reading instruction is someone else's duty (i.e., "I'm not a reading teacher!"), they also question their skills and ability to deliver meaningful literacy instruction (Lester, 2000). When we approached a group of 8th- and 11th-grade U.S. history teachers and asked them to increase text reading, many said, "My students can't read well enough," or "I need to cover so much content. Reading slows my students down." In response, we showed them research evidence that pointed to student improvements when they engaged in text reading. We provided supports by way of on-grade-level text sources with discussion questions. We paired this with extensive training in ways to guide student text reading in the classroom setting. Over the course of 10 weeks, we taught teachers to read aloud with their students and engage them in rich discourse. We taught them how to structure partner reading with paired student discussions. We also taught them to use short stints of silent reading followed by text-supported discourse sessions. With these ongoing supports in place, we saw text reading increase from consuming only 10% of class time to 20% of class time (Swanson et al., 2016). We also detected student increases in not only knowledge of U.S. history but also broader reading comprehension (e.g., Vaughn, Swanson, et al., 2013; Vaughn et al., 2014). By the end, teachers said things like the following: "I was afraid I'd lose control of my students. Your modeling helped me understand how to engage in partner reading without losing control of the class," and "At first, I didn't like all of the noise involved in partner reading. But then I realized that every student had a chance to discuss the text and that is beneficial." Finally, "The students enjoyed reading primary historical documents. Ben Franklin's letters really brought his voice into my classroom."

Student-Based Challenges

Teachers are faced with ever-increasing student diversity in their classrooms. In many large urban or suburban school districts, as many as 147 different languages are spoken across students' homes (District of Columbia Public Schools [DCPS], 2017). Many middle school and high school newcomers to the United States sit in content-area classes with little to no second-language supports to help them understand instruction in English. Consider also students who struggle with reading. These students are almost always included in content-area classes. In fact, the majority of students with disabilities spend at least 80% of their school day in general education classes (Hussar et al., 2020). Struggling secondary readers and students with disabilities often require intensive reading instruction in order to make progress in the curriculum. Other students may not arrive at school with their basic needs met. Some didn't receive dinner at home the night before or any breakfast that morning. Approximately 1.3 million school-age children in the United States are considered homeless (USDOE, 2017). It is no wonder that teachers cite classroom diversity as a major consideration when adopting new instructional practices. They wonder, "Will it work for all of my students? What about my struggling readers?"

Students, too, are resistant to changes in instructional procedures and their teachers are keenly aware of this. In fact, 29% of teachers surveyed expressed skepticism of new practices if their students didn't like the instruction (Cantrell, Burns, & Callaway, 2008). During our partnership with a large urban school district in the mid-Atlantic United States, we surveyed students' perception of a new vocabulary routine at two points—once right after it was introduced and again after 6 weeks of instruction. Immediately after its introduction, students were more likely to rate the instruction as "not very" enjoyable and less helpful. However, just 6 weeks later, student perception improved, with almost all students expressing agreement that the vocabulary routine was enjoyable, helpful, and effective. A majority of students reported that they "think their teacher should keep using the vocabulary routine."

The Bottom Line

Expect a variety of responses to new instructional coaching efforts. Some teachers will be eager and willing to support new literacy initiatives. Others will not be so eager.

Understanding the challenges prior to engaging in instructional coaching will help instructional coaches better reach the resistant teachers in creative ways.

Here is a summary of key challenges in the instructional coaching of secondary teachers:

- Instructional coaches must possess a variety of skills, including identifying student needs, selecting evidence-based practices to meet student need, communication skills, presentation skills, and interpersonal skills.
- Change is difficult for all human beings, and it is no different among teachers who are asked to change their practices.
- Secondary classroom culture is subject-specific. Preferred instructional practices differ by subject area (Lee & Spratley, 2010).
- Teachers may be unwilling or perceive themselves as unable to infuse literacy practices into their subject area.
- Classrooms contain exceedingly diverse groups of students.
- Students are sometimes resistant to changes in classroom practice.

In this book, we will share the following practices to help you manage such challenges:

- Part I provides instructional coaches with a broad view of the state of adolescent literacy, commonly found secondary schoolwide service delivery models, and implications for instructional coaches.
- Part II focuses on the knowledge and skills that all instructional coaches should master. They include how to use data to make instructional decisions, how to choose text for students who receive intensive instruction, features of effective instruction, evidence-based literacy practices that can be implemented in all content-area classrooms, and an overview of the role of fidelity within a schoolwide literacy model.
- In Part III, we show instructional coaches how to use a multi-tiered system of support (MTSS) instructional coaching model to improve intensive literacy instruction for all students. Chapter 13 contains a series of case studies designed to bring the MTSS instructional coaching model to life. These case studies can help instructional coaches consider the essential question "How can I use the instructional coaching model effectively in my school?"

A NOTE ON LANGUAGE

In an effort to maintain gender balance throughout the book, we alternate between using masculine and feminine pronouns. For example, we may refer to an instructional coach as "she" in one chapter and "he" in the following chapter.

Contents

PART I. INTRODUCTION

PART II. INSTRUCTIONAL PRACTICES EVERY SECONDARY LITERACY COACH SHOULD KNOW

PART III. AN ADAPTIVE COACHING MODEL TO IMPROVE LITERACY INSTRUCTION FOR ALL STUDENTS

Purchasers of this book can download and print the reproducible figure and appendices and access online-only supplemental lesson plans and other resources at *www.guilford.com/wexler-materials* for personal use or use with students (see copyright page for details).

PART I

INTRODUCTION

CHAPTER 1

The State of Adolescent Literacy

Many adolescents enter middle or high school after struggling with reading for years. Some students struggle with decoding **multisyllabic words**, which they encounter frequently in secondary-level text (Bhattacharya & Ehri, 2004). Others may be able to decode fluently, but they continue to face comprehension challenges. Their poor reading performance can be attributed to a variety of factors. Some students never received sufficiently intensive, explicit **evidence-based** instruction. Others may have received instruction that did not adequately target their needs. Others may have a reading disability that was either not identified early or was not remediated effectively. The consequences of poor reading ability are glaringly apparent, resulting in frustration and less independent reading over time. Ultimately, reading less leads to a rapidly widening gap between secondary struggling readers and their typically achieving peers. When students read less, they profit less. In other words, students who do not read often acquire less vocabulary, background, and content knowledge (Gelzheiser & Meyers, 1991; Hairrell, Rupley, & Simmons, 2011). Without explicit instruction and practice, we also deprive students of a "toolbox" of strategies that they can apply to make sense of text when their comprehension breaks down (Smith, Doabler, & Kame'enui, 2016; Snow, Porcehe, Tabors, & Harris, 2007). Stanovich (1986) described this phenomenon as the **Matthew effect**. Put simply, we can think of it as "the rich get richer and the poor get poorer." Figure 1.1 depicts this phenomenon. You can see that the trajectory for students who *do not* receive sufficiently powerful explicit instruction and **intervention** in foundational-level reading skills from an early age is fairly flat, whereas the trajectory for their peers who *do* receive explicit instruction in foundational-level reading skills is much more promising.

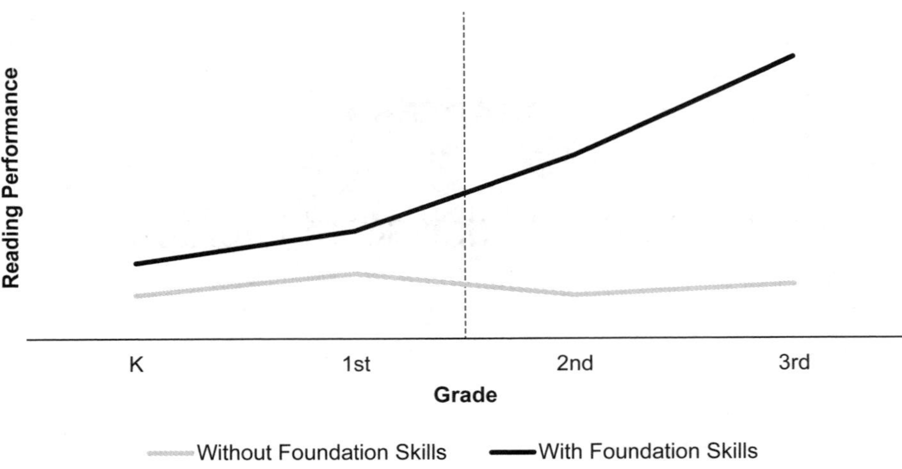

FIGURE 1.1. The Matthew effect in reading that occurs between students with and without foundational reading skills.

RIGOROUS EXPECTATIONS FOR STUDENTS

Regardless of students' ability to read and comprehend text proficiently, the secondary setting is replete with challenging demands. Middle and high school students are expected to learn a range of difficult content by reading and comprehending complex content-specific text (Lee & Spratley, 2010). This requires students to be able to proficiently navigate text that is laden with challenging multisyllabic words, unfamiliar text structure, confusing graphics, and unknown vocabulary (Gersten, Fuchs, Williams, & Baker, 2001; Sáenz & Fuchs, 2002). Even when students do have proficient word-reading skills, reading comprehension can still be compromised because elements of linguistic comprehension (e.g., vocabulary) contribute significantly to reading comprehension in the secondary grades (Chall, 1996; Chall & Jacobs, 1983).

Take a look at Figure 1.2. This figure depicts a common plot diagram for narrative text. There is a predictable beginning, middle, and end to narrative text. Students in elementary school most often encounter narrative text (Duke, 2000), so at a young age, students learn that narrative text includes characters who face some sort of conflict, climax, and resolution. Knowing this narrative text structure can support one's overall comprehension. However, as students enter middle and high school, they encounter increasing amounts of expository text.

Expository text does not follow the predictable narrative pattern, making it even more complex to comprehend. We will discuss the challenges of text in greater detail in Chapter 5, but let's take a quick look at a sample text to get a general sense of the challenges students face. See Figure 1.3 for an example of a text adapted for eighth-grade social studies: *General Correspondence: George Washington to George Clinton, February*

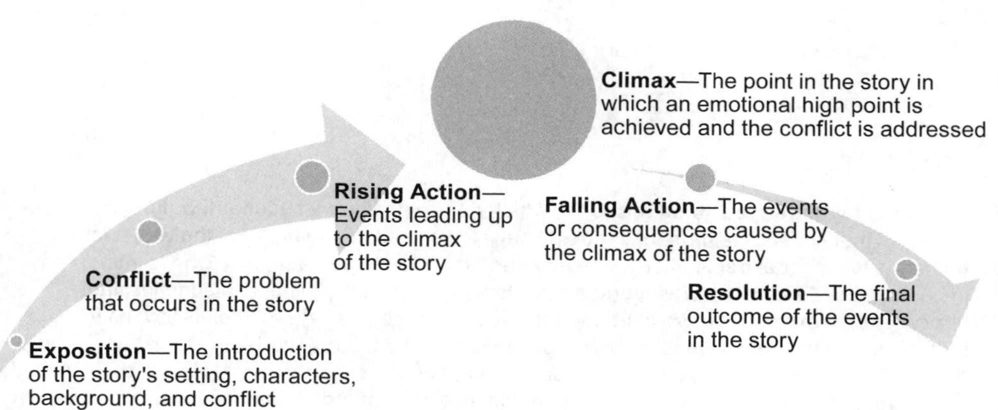

FIGURE 1.2. The common story pattern structure found in narrative text.

16, 1778. This one page alone is challenging for a number of reasons. For example, the text contains:

- A large number of multisyllabic words
- Sophisticated vocabulary and difficult content-specific technical terms
- Dense conceptual content

The challenging words, vocabulary, and text structure can make comprehending text that secondary students frequently encounter even more daunting. Many secondary students who struggle with reading are simply unprepared to approach this type of complex, conceptually rich text.

RIGOROUS EXPECTATIONS FOR TEACHERS

To help secondary students become proficient readers who can efficiently navigate narrative *and* expository text to learn content, content-area and special education teachers need to better understand how to integrate evidence-based adolescent literacy practices into their daily routines. We classify these practices in two ways: (1) **teacher-led instructional practices** and (2) **student-led instructional practices**. Both types of practices share the same goal: to enhance students' ability to comprehend text. Teacher-led instructional practices include preteaching important concepts (e.g., background knowledge and vocabulary) prior to students reading text. To ensure students can enhance their own comprehension and be independent learners, teachers need to also provide students with explicit instruction in student-led practices, literacy practices that they can employ on their own (e.g., how to use **context clues** to determine the meaning of words teachers have not pretaught or how to break down and decode multisyllabic words). Providing students with a "toolbox" of strategies can help them become

Headquarters, Valley Forge, February 16, 1778

To George Clinton

Dear Sir:

I don't like to trouble you about this topic, which does not fall under your authority; but it is a subject that causes me more upset than I have felt since the beginning of the war. It loudly demands the most extreme energy of every person of weight and authority who is interested in our success. I mean the present dreadful situation of the army in need of supplies and our miserable future. It is more alarming than you can probably believe because to really understand, you would have to be here. For some days past, there has been starvation in camp. A part of the army has been a week without any kind of meat and the rest for 3 or 4 days. Naked and starving as they are, we cannot enough admire the outstanding patience and loyalty of these soldiers because their suffering has not caused general rebellion or for soldiers to run away. Strong symptoms of discontent have appeared, and nothing but the most active efforts everywhere can prevent a shocking disaster.

Our current sufferings are not all. There is no plan made for any acceptable help in the future. All the storehouses provided in the states of New Jersey, Pennsylvania, Delaware, and Maryland, and all the immediate additional supplies they seem capable of providing, will not be enough to support the army more than a month longer, if that. Very little has been done to the eastward and as little to the southward. We cannot expect much from them. When the supplies are exhausted, what a terrible crisis will follow, unless all the energy of the continent is used to provide a solution in time.

Motivated by this thought, I am doing everything that I can possibly think of to prevent the fatal consequences we have so great a reason to fear. I am calling upon everyone who has a position of power or influence to help us. Because of your well-known enthusiasm, I expect you to do everything within your power. I am aware that you might be drained of resources since you have been so long at war. But, although you may not be able to contribute supplies to our relief, you can perhaps do something to help; and any assistance, however small, will be of great help at this important time. It will also help the army to stay together until something more permanent can be arranged. What methods you use is up to you; but if you can devise any means to get a quantity of cattle, or other kind of meat, for the use of this army, to be at camp in the course of a month, you will provide a really important service to the common cause. I have the honor to be with very great esteem & Respect, Sir.

Your most obedient servant.

George Washington

FIGURE 1.3. *General Correspondence: George Washington to George Clinton, February 16, 1778,* a sample expository text. Adapted from *George Washington Papers, Series 4, General Correspondence: George Washington to George Clinton, February 16, 1778*. George Washington Papers, Manuscript Division, Library of Congress, Washington, DC.

independent learners who will ultimately be able to synthesize information and use sophisticated reasoning (Berkeley & Riccomini, 2011).

Indeed, as discussed in the prologue of this book, there has been a renewed focus on rigorous literacy expectations in the Common Core State Standards (CCSS; National Governors Association Center for Best Practices & Council of Chief State School Officers [NGACBP & CCSSO], 2010a), a set of K–12 college- and career-ready standards in English language arts/literacy and mathematics that have been adopted by 42 states and the District of Columbia. Other recent initiatives align with the CCSS as well. For example, the nationwide science standards (i.e., Next Generation Science Standards [NGSS]; NGSS, 2013) affirm that reading in science is an important skill that requires students to have the ability to read and synthesize complex information and use textual evidence to make arguments. Bulgren, Graner, and Deshler (2013) argued that to meet these standards, content-area classes should include "high leverage learning strategies (e.g., comprehension monitoring)" (p. 24). In fact, some researchers have even recommended that teachers need to engage students in approximately 2 to 4 hours of literacy instruction and practice on a daily basis (Biancarosa & Snow, 2006). You are probably thinking, "Two to four hours of literacy instruction is a lot of literacy instruction! How can we ever fit that in when students are already taking social studies, science, math, etc.?" The simple, yet somewhat jarring, answer is that in order to meet this expectation, we expect *all* teachers, including content-area teachers (i.e., English language arts, social studies, science, and math), to become literacy teachers. This is particularly critical for secondary students with disabilities who spend a majority of their day in the general education content-area setting. In fact, more than 60% of students with disabilities spend 80% or more of their day in this setting (Hussar et al., 2020), and current estimates are that approximately two-thirds of students with disabilities receive instruction in general education for at least one content area (Newman, 2006). This represents an increase from 47% over a decade ago (Cortiella & Horowitz, 2014).

These rigorous expectations can, understandably, make some teachers feel anxious. Content-area teachers might feel unprepared or that they do not have time to provide such instruction while also meeting their content objectives (Wexler, Mitchell, Clancy, & Silverman, 2017). However, it is important for content-area teachers to understand that they do not need to teach the most basic foundational-level skills to students. On the contrary, they should be integrating evidence-based vocabulary and comprehension instruction into their lessons. Ideally, this will help students acquire the content. Furthermore, although students with the most intensive needs spend a majority of their instructional day within content-area general education classes (Kaldenberg, Watt, & Therrien, 2015), many of these same students will also require supplemental intensive intervention delivered by a specialist (e.g., special education teacher). This specialist can provide explicit instruction in the most foundational-level skills these students may lack in addition to more support in evidence-based vocabulary and comprehension practices.

These rigorous literacy expectations place demands on schools to be strategic about the ways in which they use their resources to ensure effective delivery of this critical instruction and intervention. School instructional coaches must carefully consider schoolwide adolescent literacy practices that they will adopt and have a plan in place to support this effort. When considering which vocabulary and comprehension practices to adopt to intensify instruction schoolwide, we recommend just a handful of evidence-based before-, during-, and after-reading practices that can be used across the curriculum in each content area. We will further address the issue of selecting practices in Chapter 4.

Regardless of the practices your school adopts, you might be wondering how you will provide professional development and ongoing support to ensure teachers are implementing these practices with **fidelity of implementation**—that is, delivering practices in the manner in which they were intended to be delivered. Relying on an instructional coach is one way to provide this support for teachers. The instructional coach can support content-area teachers who provide intensive instruction and intervention teachers (e.g., special education teachers, reading specialists) who provide intensive intervention. We will provide more in-depth information about evidence-based adolescent literacy practices that schools can adopt in Part II, and we will present a model that an instructional coach can follow for supporting literacy across the secondary setting in Part III.

POOR LITERACY OUTCOMES

Have these high expectations influenced trends in literacy and achievement outcomes for secondary-level students? Unfortunately, despite the current rigorous expectations for enhancing literacy instruction and intervention across the content areas and in supplemental intervention settings for students with the most intensive needs, we continue to face a crisis characterized by low literacy and poor achievement scores for students with and without disabilities. The National Assessment of Educational Progress (NAEP), or the Nation's Report Card, reveals data showing that more than 60% of eighth graders currently score below the proficient level in reading achievement (U.S. Department of Education, Institute of Education Services, National Center for Education Statistics, NAEP, 2019). Matters are worse for students of color. Only 18% of African American students and 23% of Latinx students read at a proficient level (USDOE, IES, NCES, NAEP, 2019). Additionally, only 21% of both students from low-income households and students whose parents did not attend college are able to read proficiently (USDOE, IES, NCES, NAEP, 2019). These trends show that many students of color and students from low-income homes are at risk for poor reading outcomes.

You might also be wondering about students' growth over time. In 2008, Howard Bloom and his colleagues from the Georgetown Public Policy Institute and Vanderbilt University conducted a study to determine the amount of academic growth students make in content areas across the span of K–12 (Bloom, Hill, Black, & Lipsey, 2008). Refer to Figure 1.4 and consider secondary students' performance in reading over time. The *y*-axis shows us effect sizes (ES), which help us interpret gains from the beginning to end of each school year. We consider an ES of 0.20 a small effect, 0.50 a moderate effect, and 0.80 a large effect (Cohen, 1988). What we are tempted to believe is that

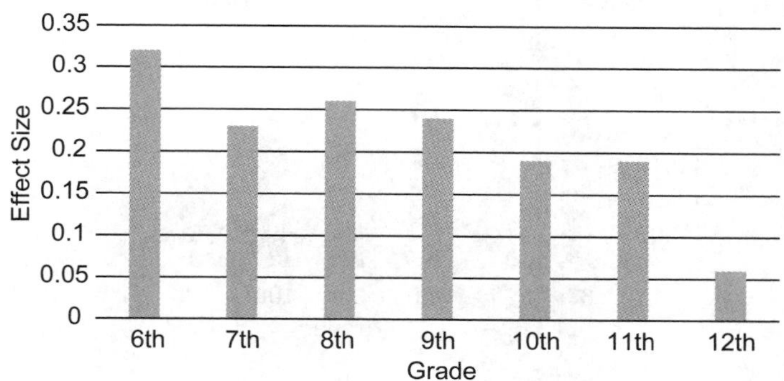

FIGURE 1.4. Effect sizes of expected reading growth for students in secondary grades.

students achieve the same amount of growth every year. Unfortunately, this isn't so. What does happen is that, in reading, students make generally small to moderate gains in middle and high school. Even more alarming is the trend of the scores over time: They decrease.

Is this pattern the same for science and social studies knowledge? Take a look at Figures 1.5 and 1.6. Indeed, the same trend of decreasing gains is present in science and social studies. Put simply, adolescents face a plethora of challenges (e.g., challenging text) in the secondary grades that make it difficult for them to maintain a positive trajectory.

What about students with disabilities? How do they fare on national literacy assessments? Unfortunately, matters are generally worse for students with disabilities as compared to students without disabilities. On the 2019 NAEP reading test, 70% of fourth graders and 63% of eighth graders with disabilities scored below the basic level, whereas only 28% of fourth graders and 22% of eighth graders without disabilities scored below the basic level (USDOE, IES, NCES, NAEP, 2019). The **achievement gap** between students with and without learning disabilities increases over time, and there has been

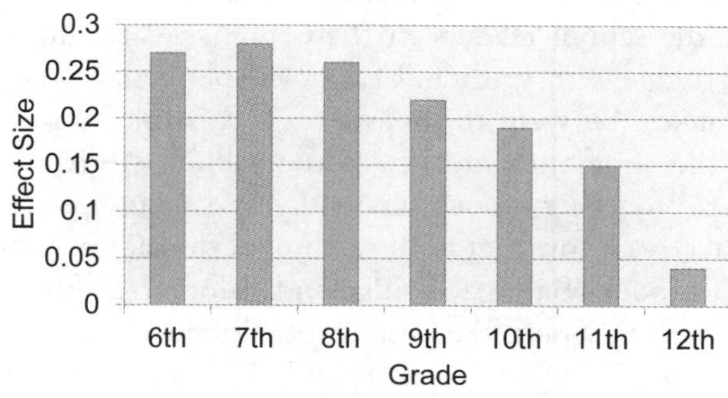

FIGURE 1.5. Effect sizes of expected science growth for students in secondary grades.

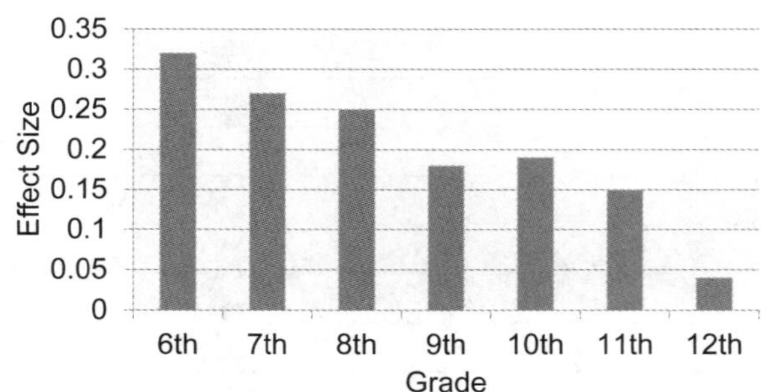

FIGURE 1.6. Effect sizes of expected social studies growth for students in secondary grades.

no significant improvement seen in the NAEP achievement scores for students with disabilities in the last several years (USDOE, IES, NCES, NAEP, 2009, 2011, 2013, 2015, 2017). By the secondary level, students with learning disabilities are, on average, 3 years behind in reading (Cortiella & Horowitz, 2014). Many students with disabilities also demonstrate difficulties with writing as well. For example, students with learning disabilities consistently produce essays that are judged to be of poorer quality than those written by students without disabilities (Baker, Gersten, & Graham, 2003). These data demonstrate the necessity of finding ways to support teachers (e.g., coaching support from instructional coaches) so that they can implement evidence-based instruction and intervention for all students.

CONSEQUENCES

As previously mentioned, it is likely that students who are not provided explicit reading instruction from a young age will continue to struggle in the secondary grades. Struggling readers are likely to demonstrate frustration, disengagement, and misbehavior (Lane, Carter, Pierson, & Glaeser, 2006). Can you think of any students in your school who demonstrate similar issues? Denton, Wexler, Vaughn, and Bryan (2008) asked struggling middle school readers in their intensive reading intervention study what it feels like to struggle with reading. One boy explained, "When I see a book, just to see those letters makes me want to go away. . . . I think 'Oh, this is frustrating' " (Wexler, 2009). By the time they are in middle school, students might be disconnecting from school all together—both physically and mentally (Balfanz, Herzog, & MacIver, 2007). In fact, we know that poor reading performance is one of the strongest predictors of school dropout (Balfanz, Bridgeland, Moore, & Fox, 2010; Hernandez, 2012). Results from a recently published report of a longitudinal study of nearly 4,000 students show that an inability to read proficiently by the end of third grade increases the likelihood students will not graduate on time. Furthermore, for students who live in poverty and who do not read proficiently, there is even more of a chance that they will not graduate on time, if at all (Hernandez, 2012). The bottom line is that the issue of school dropout goes hand in hand with the issue of improving the reading performance of struggling secondary readers (Vaughn, Roberts, Wexler, et al., 2015). Poor reading performance can lead to consequences for the individual (e.g., school dropout and the inability to progress professionally; Belfield & Levin, 2007) and for society (e.g., an increase in crime-related costs and a burden on society; August & Shanahan, 2006).

ARE STRUGGLING ADOLESCENT READERS MOTIVATED TO IMPROVE?

As described above, there is clearly a need to improve students' reading ability to avoid grave consequences. Exemplified in the Matthew effect (Stanovich, 1986), as previously explained, frustration and disengagement are some consequences that these students might experience. If you have ever worked with struggling secondary readers, you know what disengagement and frustration can look like. Some students demonstrate externalizing behaviors such as throwing papers on the floor and even storming out of the room. Others demonstrate more internalizing behaviors. They withdraw in class and can frequently be seen with their heads down on their desks, likely a result of depression and overall withdrawal. Such students' teachers may feel like broken records, asking these students to keep their heads up repeatedly throughout the day. After all, can we blame the students for exhibiting frustration and disengagement? After years of failure and frustration and, in many cases, not receiving the targeted, intensive instruction and intervention that they need, *wouldn't you feel the same way*?

Because many of these struggling secondary readers come across as frustrated and disengaged, it is easy for adults to question whether they are motivated to learn at all. Instead of wondering "*How* can we motivate them?," the question that often arises is "*Can* we motivate them?" In other words, is it even possible to motivate them? Can we essentially reverse the damage that has been done? This sentiment often brings up questions about resources. Should we spend resources, effort, and time trying to help support students who we think are likely unmotivated or, even worse, who we might not be able to motivate ever again?

Two decades ago, McCray, Vaughn, and Neal (2001) conducted a study to determine whether at-risk struggling secondary readers are indeed motivated to learn. Specifically, they investigated middle school readers with disabilities' perceptions of their own reading abilities and willingness to participate in explicit reading instruction. The authors revealed that the students were indeed motivated and willing to learn, but they could not describe much about their reading instruction, so the authors speculated that students were likely not receiving targeted, evidence-based reading instruction.

Over a decade later, Wexler, Reed, and Sturges (2015) replicated and extended this study with students with some of the most intensive needs: students who were struggling with reading and who were incarcerated in a juvenile justice facility. Many of these students can be considered victims of the Matthew effect: They were never provided sufficiently powerful reading instruction and intervention and thus never achieved growth. When the authors asked these students to describe their experiences in receiving explicit and systematic instruction that targeted their needs, they could not describe this kind of instruction. Instead, they spoke of the frustrating experiences that they had in school and how it affected their motivation and led them to disengage. Ultimately, many stopped going to school. One student said, "[I]n the class, like if I'm not receiving enough help or if it's too noisy . . . I'll be wanting to walk out of class . . . when a lot of people talkin', their voices bouncing off the wall . . . if you the only person in the classroom doin' work . . . I want to roam the halls" (Wexler, Reed, Barton, Mitchell, & Clancy, 2014).

Interestingly, in the juvenile justice facility where Wexler and colleagues (2015) conducted their study, there was a reading specialist who was providing very intensive, individualized reading support for students. When asked about this support as well as his evaluation of the importance of reading, one student who was working with the reading specialist explained:

> "I didn't care about reading or nothin' until I got locked up. Out on the other school I wasn't learning nothin' and I didn't have nobody pull me out. I don't have anybody like Miss B. [the reading specialist]. I was 15 last year and I didn't go to school since I was 14. I keep getting locked up. On the outside they need good people to help kids out and have them break words down and soon as kids do that they going to understand. I want my kid to go to school. You can't do nothin' if you don't know how to read. You gonna be a homeless person." (Wexler et al., 2014)

Furthermore, when asked about the purpose of reading, many students discussed functional reasons (e.g., reading a label); therefore, the authors speculated that no one ever explicitly told the students that the main purpose of reading is to learn and acquire new information. Overall, the findings aligned with those of the McCray et al. (2001) study over a decade ago. Struggling secondary readers wanted to learn, but their schools were not consistently providing instruction and intervention designed to meet their needs.

REVIEW AND PREVIEW

In this chapter, we addressed the fact that many secondary students continue to struggle with the rigorous expectations we have for them. While this poses challenges for students' teachers, it is essential that teachers address students' needs and that instructional coaches support teachers to do so. There are severe consequences for students who continue to struggle; however, most students *want* to learn. It is our job to provide instruction and intervention across a schoolwide adolescent literacy model. In Chapter 2, we will address the importance of providing evidence-based instruction and intervention across a schoolwide adolescent literacy model.

Terms to Know

Achievement gap: The discrepancy between the achievement of two groups of students (e.g., students with disabilities and students without disabilities).

Context clues: Hints within a text that assist readers in determining the meaning of words or phrases.

Evidence-based: Practices and programs that have evidence of effectiveness supported by rigorously conducted research.

Fidelity of implementation: Adherence to implementing instructional practices as they were intended to be implemented in order to maximize effectiveness.

Intervention: A practice, set of practices, or program intended to remediate the skills of students who are not demonstrating mastery of grade-level concepts (e.g., reading comprehension of grade-level texts).

Matthew effect: The principle that students who start out with proficient foundational-level skills increase their performance over time, while students with inadequate foundational-level skills tend to make less progress, causing the gap to widen between the performance of these two groups of students (see *achievement gap*).

Multisyllabic words: Words with multiple syllables frequently found in upper-level texts and that are difficult for some students to decode.

Student-led instructional practices: Practices that teachers instruct students on how to use in order to facilitate their own learning.

Teacher-led instructional practices: Practices that teachers lead in order to direct student learning.

Reflection Questions

1. What are some reasons students struggle with reading in the secondary grades?
2. What are consequences of having poor reading skills?
3. Describe the Matthew effect. What are the implications for struggling secondary readers and their teachers?
4. Can you list some challenging literacy demands that struggling secondary readers face?
5. How do text demands differ and impact comprehension in the elementary and secondary grades?
6. What is the difference between teacher-led and student-led instructional practices? Why is each important?

7. Students with disabilities spend a majority of their day in the general education content-area setting. What are the implications of this for all teachers?
8. We presented some challenging literacy demands and data that show how difficult it is for more students to make gains in the secondary grades. What are some implications of this for designing schoolwide adolescent literacy models?
9. What are some consequences of poor reading ability for the individual? For society?
10. Think about some of the students you work with now or have worked with in the past. When provided with targeted instruction or intervention, do they exhibit more motivation and engagement? What are some of the signs that students are motivated or engaged?

CHAPTER 2

What Do We Do about These Poor Outcomes?

We provided a lot of information in Chapter 1. To recap, struggling secondary readers and their teachers face a multitude of challenges. In fact, annual student growth in reading achievement is greatest during elementary school and declines considerably over time, with high school students making the least amount of growth (Bloom, Hill, Black, & Lipsey, 2008). The good news is that with the right instruction and intervention, even students with the most intensive needs express that they *want to learn.*

At this point, you might still be wondering: Is it even possible to improve outcomes or at least prevent students from falling further behind? Let's consider a study conducted by Vaughn, Wexler, and colleagues that was published in 2012 as part of the Texas Center for Learning Disabilities (*www.texasldcenter.org*). In this study, the research team investigated the effects of a yearlong, intensive, researcher-implemented supplemental reading intervention for eighth-grade students with serious reading difficulties who demonstrated low response to intervention in grades 6 and 7. The results revealed that students in the intervention condition demonstrated significantly higher scores than comparison students on standardized measures of comprehension (ES = 1.20) and word identification (ES = 0.49). However, the students did not close the gap with their typically developing peers and, therefore, continued to lack grade-level proficiency in reading despite 3 years of intervention. Notably, the research team in this study did *not* focus on enhancing literacy as a **schoolwide adolescent literacy model** approach. Instead, the research team provided intervention in place of an elective class for students who qualified for supplemental support. Therefore, the team members did not work extensively with the students' content-area teachers to also ensure that these teachers were integrating evidence-based adolescent literacy practices that would reinforce skills the students were practicing in the supplemental reading intervention class.

A subsequent study in 2015, led by some of the same researchers, also lends support for providing intensive supplemental reading intervention for students—this time for high school students with disabilities (Vaughn, Roberts, Wexler, et al., 2015). In this study, the authors implemented a reading intervention in place of each student's elective class (e.g., art) for students with disabilities who met criteria for low reading comprehension. Students received researcher-implemented intervention in a 50-minute reading class in place of an elective every day for 2 years. Notably, the students who were provided reading intervention demonstrated significant gains on reading comprehension compared with their peers who qualified for the intervention but were randomly assigned to a business-as-usual typical instruction comparison group. Like the study conducted in 2012, the authors of this study also did not provide professional development or ongoing instructional support (e.g., coaching) for the students' Tier 1 content-area teachers. Is it possible that the students would have made more gains had Tier 1 content-area teachers included key literacy practices in their instruction in addition to intensive intervention?

When answering the questions just posed, it is important to remember that students with disabilities spend a majority of their time in the content-area general education setting (Hussar et al., 2020). Therefore, providing evidence-based adolescent literacy instruction within this setting affords another opportunity to provide students with support. So, do we have any evidence that providing such instruction in the content-area setting is beneficial for students? Indeed, it is possible to positively impact outcomes for all students when providing feasible literacy-related instruction within the content areas. Swanson et al. (2017) meta-analyzed the effects of literacy instructional practices within the Tier 1 content-area setting on reading outcomes for students in grades 4–12, reporting an average effect size across 25 studies of $g = 0.09$, a small but statistically significant effect. They also synthesized results from a subset of 10 studies that focused on students with and at risk for reading disabilities, reporting that reading comprehension, vocabulary, and multicomponent interventions delivered in the Tier 1 setting positively impacted reading outcomes for students with or at risk for disabilities—with the ES ranging from –0.02 to 0.54 on standardized reading comprehension outcomes and 0.26 to 2.12 on proximal vocabulary outcomes. A series of three studies (Swanson, Wanzek, Vaughn, Roberts, & Fall 2015; Swanson et al., 2017; Wanzek, Swanson, Vaughn, Roberts, & Fall, 2016) were conducted investigating the effects of Promoting Adolescents' Comprehension of Text (PACT), a set of instructional routines focused on explicit vocabulary instruction and text comprehension through discourse delivered in Tier 1 middle school social studies classrooms. Students with disabilities performed well in these studies, with ES ranging from 0.05 to 0.59 on content reading comprehension. Finally, in a **meta-analysis** of Tier 2 and Tier 3 reading interventions delivered using social studies content (Swanson et al., 2014), students with disabilities performed well on reading outcomes (average ES = 1.02).

Taken together, the studies listed above provide evidence about the potential impact of providing students with evidence-based literacy *instruction* in the content-area setting *and* the supplemental intensive *intervention* setting for students who require more support. Providing these types of support in a schoolwide adolescent literacy model is critical for improving student outcomes; however, implementing such an integrated model is a challenge that many educators and researchers are still working on. One way to support this effort is with support from an instructional coach. This book is here to help.

So, you might agree with us that providing literacy instruction *and* intervention in a school is important. However, if you are reading this book, you are probably still wondering: How do we support a schoolwide adolescent literacy model that integrates instruction and intervention? In the 2012 and 2015 Vaughn studies presented above, researchers hired and trained their own team members to implement the interventions. This typically yields better results, likely due to higher fidelity of implementation, than if we relied on teachers in the school to implement the intervention (see Scammacca et al., 2007). This does not mean teachers are incapable of high levels of fidelity; however, expecting schools to hire and train researchers to implement instruction and intervention is not realistic. Who has the funding for that? So, if schools must rely on their own teachers to implement the instruction and intervention, how can instructional coaches support all of these teachers? What about schools made up of teachers with a variety of backgrounds, training, and experience? How do we differentiate our levels of support to meet the broad needs across a variety of teachers to ensure high levels of fidelity to the schoolwide adolescent literacy practices? We agree that this is an overwhelming thought, not to mention an incredible challenge. For this reason, we will suggest a model in Part III of this book that is designed to help instructional coaches differentiate support for all teachers to build a schoolwide adolescent literacy model that integrates evidence-based instruction in all content-area classrooms for all students coupled with evidence-based intensive intervention for students with substantial needs. For now, let's pause and focus on some more background information about the evidence-based practices we want teachers to implement in a schoolwide adolescent literacy model.

EVIDENCE-BASED: WHAT DOES IT MEAN AND WHY IS IT IMPORTANT?

We want teachers to implement evidence-based practices. *Why?* Well, we expect teachers to use evidence-based practices because they work (or at least have some evidence of working)! Their use is also mandated by a number of federal laws (e.g., the Every Student Succeeds Act [ESSA, 2015] and the Individuals with Disabilities Education Improvement Act of 2004). You might see the term *evidence-based* mentioned frequently in books, websites, and other education resources, but what does it actually mean? To clarify, **evidence-based practices** are practices that have "been shown to work in rigorous research studies" (Burns, Riley-Tillman, & VanDerHeyden, 2012, p. 2). **Evidence-based programs** are a "collection of practices that, when used together, have been proven to work through experimental research studies or large-scale research field studies" (IRIS Center, 2014).

So, how do teachers know which practices are evidence-based and should be considered for adoption? First of all, teachers may not even have a choice as many districts choose what practices or programs they want their teachers to use. Other times, when given more freedom to choose, teachers might select practices from a professional development opportunity they participated in or an interesting practice they came across on a website. How do they know these practices will work with the population they teach? In fact, while some practices that educators adopt are well known and even widely used, it is not uncommon for many of these practices to have virtually no evidence of effectiveness supporting their use.

Consider a series called "The Alerts" sponsored by the Council for Exceptional Children, the world's largest special education organization. Experts prepare each Current Practice Alert to provide informed judgments regarding prevalently implemented professional practices that focus on learning disabilities. Experts review the evidence behind each chosen practice and make a recommendation: "go for it" or "use caution." Practices that earn a caution rating are those for which the research evidence is preliminary, incomplete, mixed, or even negative! For example, let's think about a common service-delivery model many of us are familiar with: **co-teaching**. Co-teaching is a service-delivery model in which a general educator and special educator teach together in a general education classroom to enhance instruction for all students, including students with disabilities (Friend, 2000). In theory, it is a popular way to increase the effectiveness of inclusion and improve student outcomes (Murawski & Lochner, 2011). In a 2018 Current Practice Alert about co-teaching, experts assigned the practice a "use with caution" rating. Why? Despite schools' prevalent use of co-teaching, minimal evidence of its effectiveness for improving student and teacher outcomes from rigorously conducted research exists (Magiera & Zigmond, 2005; Murawski & Swanson, 2001; Welch, Brownell, & Sheridan, 1999). For example, Murawski and Swanson (2001) conducted a meta-analysis of co-teaching studies from 1989 to 1999 and reported a mean ES of 0.40 on student outcomes. However, only six studies were available for inclusion in the **synthesis**, none of which included random assignment. In a randomized experiment, researchers randomly assign participants to an intervention or a "business-as-usual" control group condition. Random assignment is an important rigorous research design feature that allows researchers to ensure that members of the intervention and control group are the same across important variables (e.g., gender, ethnicity, age). Because the group makeup is the same in the treatment and comparison conditions, any differences between the groups can be attributed to the intervention (i.e., the only difference between the two groups). As you can see, there is very limited data reporting the effectiveness of co-teaching on improving student outcomes (e.g., Bottge, Cohen, & Choi, 2018; Clancy & Wexler, 2017). Other practices listed under the "use with caution" rating include learning styles, cooperative learning, social skills instruction, and more. You can find the full list at *www.teachingld.org/alerts*.

Why do some continue to adopt practices that have limited or no evidence, and why is evidence so critically important? Simply put, middle school students who struggle with reading do not have time to sit in another reading class where they are unsuccessful. A group of middle school students who were long-time struggling readers reflected on their remedial reading class as follows (Reed & Wexler, 2014). One said, "I haven't learned anything in here"; another, "See, our teachers, they just throw you the work, step off, don't give us no help; no nothin'." But these students are still willing to persevere: "If you're sitting with me and helping me, teaching me ways that I can understand my reading, I'm gonna be willing." Students who enter the ninth grade in the lowest quartile (i.e., 25%) of their class are 20 times more likely to drop out of school than their highest-performing peers (Carnevale, 2001). According to the U.S. Bureau of Labor Statistics, the 2018 unemployment rate among high school dropouts was 5.6% (compared to 3.9% of the total labor force). For these reasons, what happens in the middle school reading class is of critical importance. We cannot waste time trying instructional practices that do not work with anyone. Instead, we must focus on only those that offer evidence of effectiveness with struggling middle school readers.

In other fields with high stakes (e.g., medicine), practitioners rely on evidence to provide exactly what is needed based on client needs. For example, for a pregnant woman with a diagnosis of gestational diabetes, doctors must consider what evidence-based intervention will make the most impact as quickly as possible. After all, gestational diabetes can lead to pre-eclampsia, preterm labor, and the baby's hospital admission for intensive neonatal care. With these serious consequences in mind, would you prefer and really insist that the doctor follow the most effective treatment plan? Evidence supports a multicomponent approach starting with medical nutrition therapy (i.e., calculating caloric allowance based on ideal body weight, carbohydrate intake reduction, and meals distributed across the day) and exercise. If these strategies do not work, insulin therapy is initiated—but not just any type of insulin—only those approved for use during pregnancy. Like teaching reading, (1) treating high-risk conditions requires a multicomponent approach; (2) as soon as the condition does not improve, the intervention changes and becomes more intensive; and (3) only evidence-based practices are utilized.

While we recommend that teachers choose practices that align with their students' needs and have the most rigorous level of evidence, sometimes evidence about a practice is lacking because the simple fact is that not much research has yet been conducted. Therefore, we acknowledge that as students still show up at school every day, teachers are faced with choosing practices to meet their needs. In these cases, we suggest that to the best of teachers' ability, they should choose practices with the highest levels of evidence. To do this, teachers can become what we refer to as **effective consumers of research** (Stanovich & Stanovich, 2003). This does not mean that teachers need to take several years of statistics courses and become researchers at top-tier universities. Instead, teachers must understand what questions to ask and what resources to consult to determine if the practices they are using need to be supplanted or supplemented with practices that have more levels of evidence.

See Figure 2.1 for a self-reflection checklist with sample questions teachers can ask themselves when considering whether they are selecting evidence-based practices that align with their needs.

To gather this information, we recommend that teachers consult a number of trusted sources. Two are particularly helpful: (1) the What Works Clearinghouse (*https://ies.ed.gov/ncee/wwc*) and (2) the National Center on Intensive Intervention (*https://charts.intensiveintervention.org/chart/instructional-intervention-tools*). These resources provide teachers with a summary of research findings for many interventions across the middle

- ✓ Has the practice or program been tested in a rigorous research study with students similar to mine (e.g., students with disabilities who struggle with decoding)?
- ✓ Has the practice or program been tested in a rigorous research study in a setting similar to the one where I will implement the practice or program (e.g., a supplemental intervention setting)?
- ✓ Are there particular resources that I will need to purchase to implement this practice or program?
- ✓ If there are particular resources that I will need to purchase to implement this practice or program, are they within my budget?
- ✓ Will I have to create particular resources to implement this practice or program?
- ✓ Do I need training to implement this practice or program?
- ✓ If I need training to implement this practice or program, how much time will it take?
- ✓ If I need training to implement this practice or program, how much will it cost?

FIGURE 2.1. A checklist that teachers can use to identify evidence-based practices. Adapted from the IRIS Center (2014).

school grades. After all, it is unlikely teachers have time to evaluate practices or programs themselves! For even more guidance on issues related to evidence-based practices, such as why they are not implemented frequently and how to evaluate them, we recommend you visit the IRIS Center's three-part modules on this topic. Specifically, see *https://iris.peabody.vanderbilt.edu/module/ebp_01* for Part I: Identifying and Selecting a Practice or Program (IRIS Center, 2014). This module will provide some foundational knowledge on how to become an effective consumer of research.

OVERVIEW OF EVIDENCE-BASED INTENSIVE LITERACY PRACTICES AT THE SECONDARY LEVEL

To implement evidence-based literacy instruction and intervention, teachers need an understanding of (1) evidence-based literacy practices that they can use in their content-area and intervention classes (Moje, 2008; Shanahan & Shanahan, 2008; Torgesen et al., 2007) and (2) evidence-based pedagogical approaches applied to intensify instruction and intervention (Archer & Hughes, 2011; Vaughn, Wanzek, Murray, & Roberts, 2012).

First, let's consider *how many* evidence-based literacy practices you should adopt. We want to highlight that teachers do not need to provide a "strategy du jour," or a new strategy every day. Consider, for example, the age-old practice of "word of the day" used often in a school. What happens during word of the day? An adult or another student reads a vocabulary word and its definition over the loudspeaker during the daily announcements. This word might be linked to some common theme in one of the content areas or might be drawn from a book indicating common words all students should know. First of all, if students are even able to listen and focus on this despite other distractions that might be occurring, providing superficial exposure to a new word every day by reading it once over the loudspeaker is not efficient or effective. We'll bet that if you asked students in the afternoon the word they heard that morning, they wouldn't be able to tell you! The same concept is true for teaching evidence-based literacy practices. Teaching a new strategy every day is counterproductive. You might have heard about this concept being referred to as the "spray and pray" method. In other words, just "spraying" a new practice a day at the problem is likely to "dilute" any positive effects. (Note that this is also true for introducing new initiatives in a school or district, and we will address this problem in Chapter 3.) Instead, adopting and providing repeated practice in a purposefully selected, relatively simple instructional routine before, during, and after reading should suffice (Swanson & Wanzek, 2014).

Second, think about *which practices* you should teach. A 2008 Institute of Education Sciences (IES) adolescent literacy practice guide by Kamil and colleagues provides a set of guidelines for practitioners about how to intervene with adolescents who struggle with reading. The authors of this guide synthesized the research base to identify evidence-based adolescent literacy practices and reflect findings from a broad body of work conducted with struggling adolescent readers. The guidelines are drawn from findings in studies that meet the highest standards for rigorous experimental research, supporting the trustworthiness of the practices presented in the guide. Although the guide is now over a decade old, findings from more recent syntheses (e.g., Berkeley, Scruggs, & Mastropieri, 2010; Edmonds et al., 2009; Flynn, Marquis, Paquet, Peeke, & Aubry, 2012; Gajria, Jitendra, Sood, & Sacks, 2007; Lee & Spratley, 2010) continue to align with the guidelines. See Table 2.1 for a listing of the IES guidelines as well as examples. Further examples and guidance regarding how to implement the practices recommended in the guide will be presented in more detail in Chapter 7.

Third, let's consider *how to implement* these practices. In addition to knowing what practices to implement, it is essential that teachers are skilled at implementing practices effectively. This requires teachers to use **features of effective instruction**. Table 2.2 lists these features for all classes, and Table 2.3 adds the features for intervention classes. We will review the features of effective instruction in depth in Chapter 6.

TABLE 2.1. IES Adolescent Literacy Practice Guide Recommendations and Examples

Recommendation	Example
1. Provide explicit vocabulary instruction.	Teacher introduces high-utility, high-frequency words before the unit, providing a student-friendly definition, example sentence as the word is used in the text, and a picture.
2. Provide direct and explicit comprehension strategy instruction.	Teacher teaches students how to generate a main idea statement for a portion of the text by modeling, providing guided practice, and independent practices.
3. Provide opportunities for extended discussion of text meaning and interpretation.	Students are provided time to discuss and interpret text with peers through peer-mediated practice.
4. Increase student motivation and engagement in literacy learning.	Teacher provides background information about the text to engage students in the high-interest article.
5. Make available intensive and individualized interventions for struggling readers that can be provided by trained specialists.	Teacher provides reteaching or preteaching to students who are struggling with grade-level text comprehension or foundational reading skills within the content-area setting or in a supplemental intensive intervention setting.

Note. Adapted from IES adolescent literacy practice guide (Kamil et al., 2008).

TABLE 2.2. Features of Effective Instruction for All Classes

1. Communicate clear expectations.
2. Model expectations with overt demonstrations of thoughts and actions ("I do").
3. Break the task into small steps and provide feedback after each step ("We do"). Gradually increase the number of steps or the length of work completed between feedback periods.
   - Offer feedback that specifically identifies what to continue and what to change.
   - Provide many opportunities for students to discuss their developing understanding.
4. Plan for follow-up instruction ("You do") to include:
   - Teaching self-monitoring and fix-up strategies.
   - Supplementing background knowledge.
   - Providing real-world applications.
5. Incorporate student engagement, such as:
   - Offering some choice in materials, activities, and/or products.
   - Making connections to other lessons and content.
6. Provide distributed practice.
7. Differentiate instruction by:
   - Utilizing different groupings of students.
   - Making the curriculum appropriately challenging across ability levels.

Note. Adapted from Reed, Wexler, and Vaughn (2012).

TABLE 2.3. Features of Effective Instruction for Intervention Classes

1. Adjust the pacing of instruction.
2. Redirect off-task behavior to maximize engaged time on task.
3. Teach students the "big ideas" and/or key concepts that you want them to learn, and provide multiple opportunities to apply them.
4. Provide immediate instructional feedback, with these characteristics:
   a. It is task-specific.
   b. It leads to self-regulated correction.
   c. It contains a clear and explicit indication of goals.
5. Build student's motivation and engagement.
6. Use ongoing assessment.

Note. Adapted from Reed, Wexler, and Vaughn (2012).

REVIEW AND PREVIEW

In this chapter, we addressed the need to provide instruction in the content-area setting in addition to intervention in the supplemental intervention setting using evidence-based adolescent literacy practices. It is essential for teachers to become effective consumers of research to ensure that the practices they adopt address their students' needs. We will provide more information on evidence-based practices in depth in Chapter 7. Finally, it is also important that teachers deliver these practices using features of effective instruction. Next, in Chapter 3, we will examine some common secondary schoolwide delivery models.

Terms to Know

Co-teaching: A service-delivery model in which a general educator and special educator teach together to provide instruction to students with and without disabilities in the general education setting.

Effective consumer of research: A teacher who consults available resources to select instructional practices that have high levels of supporting evidence.

Evidence-based practices: Practices that have been rigorously researched and determined to meet the academic or behavioral needs of students.

Evidence-based programs: Programs that have been rigorously researched and determined to meet the academic or behavioral needs of students.

Features of effective instruction: Practices that teachers should embed within student learning experiences in order to increase the effectiveness of instruction and facilitate student learning.

Meta-analysis: A systematic review that uses a statistical method to combine quantitative data from studies to answer an overarching research question(s).

Schoolwide adolescent literacy model: A model in which all content-area teachers (i.e., social studies, science, English language arts, math) within a school provide students with evidence-based literacy instruction and all special education teachers, reading teachers, or other specialists provide evidence-based literacy intervention in supplemental intervention classes to students who need more intensive support.

Synthesis: A systematic review of studies with a common theme (e.g., co-teaching intervention studies) and shared criteria conducted in order to summarize results and answer an overarching research question(s).

Reflection Questions

1. What are the findings and implications from the Vaughn, Wexler, et al. (2012) study and the Vaughn, Roberts, Schnakenberg, et al. (2015) study presented in Chapter 2?
2. Define evidence-based practices and programs. Why would we want to implement these types of practices?
3. We presented the idea that some commonly implemented practices are widely used but do not yet have a lot of supporting evidence. Can you think of any other practices like this?
4. What does it mean to be an effective consumer of research?
5. Why is providing new strategies or practices every day *not* a good idea?
6. What are the IES adolescent literacy practice guidelines (see Kamil et al., 2008)?
7. It is important to consider how to teach evidence-based literacy practices. Can you list some of the essential features of effective instruction?

CHAPTER 3

Common Schoolwide Support Models

To support efforts to raise the achievement level of all students and specifically those with intensive intervention needs, instructional coaches need to be knowledgeable about *what* evidence-based literacy practices teachers should implement and *how* to use features of effective instruction (e.g., explicit instruction) to implement them, as will be discussed in more detail in Part II. Instructional coaches also need to know what service-delivery models are conducive to the effective schoolwide delivery of these practices. Think about a seventh-grade English language arts classroom or a ninth-grade social studies class with which you are familiar. How many of these students struggle to read and comprehend text? As noted in Chapter 1, we know that secondary students with disabilities spend a majority of their day in the general education content-area setting. In addition to teachers' implementation of evidence-based vocabulary and comprehension practices in the content-area setting, would some of these students benefit from receiving supplemental intensive intervention support in more foundational-level skills (e.g., multisyllabic word reading)? In an ideal model, teachers in the content-area setting integrate literacy instruction and differentiated support into their content-area instruction, and special education teachers or other trained specialists provide more intensive supplemental support. Instructional coaches can ensure that their schools are structured in a manner to support delivery of these practices and put resources in place to support their teachers in this effort.

One approach that schools can adopt that supports the need to intensify instruction and intervention across a school is a **response-to-intervention (RTI) model** (Vaughn et al., 2008)—a commonly adopted service-delivery approach authorized by special education law (i.e., the **Individuals with Disabilities Education Improvement Act of 2004**). RTI has its roots in the elementary grades and is widely regarded as a model for preventing reading difficulties and disabilities (Fuchs & Fuchs, 1998;

Vaughn, Linan-Thompson, & Hickman, 2003; Vellutino, Scanlon, Small, & Fanuele, 2006). However, in the middle school setting, RTI takes on a different purpose and focuses almost exclusively on **remediation** of established difficulties (Fuchs, Fuchs, & Compton, 2010). In fact, Vaughn et al. (2008) note that the goal of any RTI approach is to "raise the achievement levels of all students, which requires a multi-tiered approach beginning in general education settings that provides increasingly intense and differentiated interventions for students who struggle with reading and learning from text" (p. 338).

An RTI model can be implemented in a variety of ways (Berkeley, Bender, Peaster, & Saunders, 2009); hence, the reason it is referred to as a model and not a program. However, despite variation in implementation, all RTI models share several essential components:

- **Universal screening** ensures that all students who are at risk for reading difficulties are identified as early as possible.
- **Progress monitoring** determines students' response to instruction to help teachers understand when instructional practices need to be adapted to meet students' goals.
- **Multi-tiered intervention** provides evidence-based instruction to all students in the general education setting (i.e., Tier 1) and increasingly intensive intervention to students who do not make progress in the general education classroom (e.g., Tiers 2 and 3).

Besides variation in implementation *within* elementary-level settings, implementation can also vary extensively *between* the elementary and secondary settings. Indeed, while models of RTI at the secondary level share the same essential components of RTI as conceptualized at the elementary level listed above, there are some unique challenges and logistics that make the model somewhat different for secondary-level implementation (Reed et al., 2012).

Before we delve into the differences between elementary and secondary models of RTI, let's take a step back and consider the idea of **prevention** and remediation, two central concepts of a schoolwide RTI model. Wexler, Wanzek, and Vaughn (2018) define these concepts in the following way: "Prevention—in an educational setting—refers to a course of action designed to keep something from happening. In contrast, remediation is the act of correcting or remedying an existing problem. Thus, with respect to reading difficulties, prevention refers to instruction aimed at keeping a reading difficulty from occurring or becoming worse" (p. 17).

The idea of prevention is typically associated with the elementary level. Intuitively, this makes sense as students at the elementary level are just beginning their school careers. Prevention efforts in the elementary grades should be focused on addressing any identified skills that students are at risk in and on preventing them from struggling with any other higher-level skills. With evidence-based core instruction in students' English language arts block (i.e., Tier 1), we can prevent many students from needing supplemental support (Wanzek & Vaughn, 2011). Table 3.1 offers sample elements

TABLE 3.1. Sample Elements of a Literacy Prevention Intervention

Lesson component	Focus
Phonological awareness	Blending and segmenting phonemes
Phonics and word recognition	Letter sounds, decoding words, building words with rimes, irregular words
Fluency	Sound fluency, word fluency, connected text fluency
Passage reading, vocabulary, comprehension	Text reading allowing application of reading practices taught, introduction to relevant vocabulary, comprehension monitoring

Note. From Wexler, Wanzek, and Vaughn (2009).

of a prevention intervention in the elementary grades. Keep in mind that time spent addressing each of these elements will need to be individualized based on student need.

Even with evidence-based strong core Tier 1 instruction, some students may be in need of an extra "boost," necessitating supplemental instruction (e.g., Tier 2 or 3). How do we identify who is in need of more support? Schools can use **curriculum-based measures (CBMs)** with well-established **psychometrics** to provide universal screening for all students. For a review of reliable and valid screening instruments, we recommend you visit the website for the National Center on Response to Intervention (*www.rti4success.org/essential-components-rti/universal-screening*).

Tier 2 at the elementary level is designed to supplement the core instruction. Teachers' focus of instruction for Tier 2 is often aligned with the content being covered in Tier 1, with an emphasis on more foundational-level skills. Furthermore, we know that multicomponent interventions (i.e., interventions that target more than one component of reading) focusing on several reading outcomes yield the strongest outcomes for students (Gersten et al., 2008; Wanzek, Wexler, Vaughn, & Ciullo, 2010). For elementary students, Tier 2 intervention is typically delivered 3 times a week for approximately 30 minutes a day *in addition* to the Tier 1 core instruction. Because students are not taking classes for credit as they do at the secondary level, it is usually possible to find supplemental Tier 2 intervention time throughout the elementary school day to provide this instruction (e.g., during a time when a student would ordinarily be engaged in her "specials," such as art or music). Once students are in Tier 2 intervention, it is necessary to monitor their progress on an ongoing basis to determine whether they are making adequate progress to meet their goals. We recommend that you visit the NCII website for a review of academic progress monitoring tools (*www.intensiveintervention.org/chart/progress-monitoring*).

Prevention efforts have been shown to dramatically reduce the number of students who struggle with reading (Wanzek & Vaughn, 2011). However, students who do not make adequate progress in Tier 2 will need Tier 3 remediation; therefore, a linear progression from Tier 2 to Tier 3 is common at the elementary level. Remediation at the Tier 3 level is for students who demonstrate very intensive needs that prevent them from making progress in reading and other content (Wanzek & Vaughn, 2007). How is Tier 3 different than Tier 2? In a nutshell, intervention aimed at providing remediation needs to be more intense than intervention designed for prevention purposes. Teachers can make interventions more intense in a variety of ways and can use progress monitoring data to adapt instruction on an ongoing basis (Vaughn et al., 2012). See Figure 3.1 for some suggested ways to make intervention more intense.

One approach to Tier 3, or intensive, intervention is data-based individualization (DBI). DBI is a multistep, systematic approach to intensifying *and* individualizing evidence-based interventions at the Tier 3 level on the basis of student data. Below, we provide a brief overview of the steps to DBI. Note that before DBI is implemented at the elementary level, a student's data should display insufficient progress at the Tier 2 level.

1. The Tier 2 intervention is intensified, using the methods we shared in Figure 3.1.
2. Progress monitoring data are collected frequently to determine the student's progress against a specific, measurable goal that has been set.
3. If the student has not adequately responded to the intervention (i.e., the student has not made adequate progress toward the goal), diagnostic assessment data are collected to identify the students' specific skills that are in need of remediation (e.g., decoding multisyllabic words).
4. The intervention is further intensified and individualized to meet the needs of the student, based on progress monitoring and diagnostic assessment data as well as the student's performance during intervention sessions.
5. Progress monitoring data continue to be collected and analyzed frequently, and intervention adjustments continue to be made.

For more information on DBI, you can explore the IRIS Center's DBI modules (*https://iris.peabody.vanderbilt.edu/module/dbi1* and *https://iris.peabody.vanderbilt.edu/module/dbi2*) as well as *Essentials of Intensive Intervention* (Zumeta Edmonds, Gruner Gandhi, & Danielson, 2019).

- Form small groups of students of the same ability.
- Provide targeted explicit instruction.
- Follow systematic routine that is clear and easy to follow.
- Provide many opportunities for students to practice skills.
- Provide students with immediate, corrective feedback.
- Provide instruction at an appropriate pace to increase engagement.
- Include frequent review of previously learned material.
- Use text that is at the students' instructional level.

FIGURE 3.1. Methods for intensifying interventions for students with intensive literacy needs. Data from National Center on Intensive Intervention (2014) and Weingarten, Bailey, and Peterson (2018).

With a typical RTI model in place as described above, we can expect that approximately 80% of students will be able to make adequate progress within Tier 1 evidence-based core instruction, 15% of the school population will need supplemental Tier 2 support, and 5% of the school population will require more intensive Tier 3 support. Figure 3.2 provides an image of a typical three-tiered model.

Now, let's shift our attention back to the secondary level. First, for a deeper discussion of RTI models at this level, we recommend that you read *RTI for Reading at the Secondary Level: Recommended Literacy Practices and Remaining Questions* (Reed et al., 2012). However, we acknowledge that you might not have time to pause and dive into another book right now. Therefore, because it is necessary for instructional coaches to understand some of the overarching issues presented in the Reed et al. book as they progress through this one, we provide an overview of some important issues to consider here.

Let's start with the idea of prevention. Is it possible to provide instruction aimed at prevention when students are already in the upper grades? While some might think that the idea of prevention sounds like an oxymoron at the secondary level, this is not necessarily the case. Especially because of the increasingly high expectations (e.g., heightened text demands) at the secondary level, instruction designed to assist students in comprehending text can be considered a form of prevention and this instructional support can be in place for all students. To provide this type of instructional support, teachers need to integrate vocabulary and comprehension practices across the Tier 1 setting (i.e., English language arts, social studies, science, and math). We will discuss ways to integrate evidence-based content-area literacy practices in Part II.

Still though, when students reach the secondary level and are continuing to struggle to read and comprehend text, many will need more intensive supplemental Tier 2

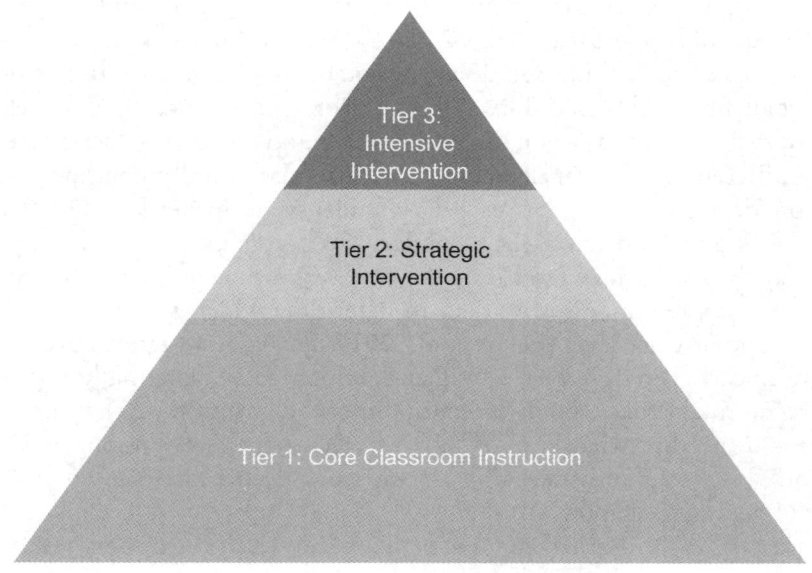

FIGURE 3.2. Elementary RTI model.

and Tier 3 support in foundational-level skills (e.g., word reading). Like the elementary level, Tier 2 intervention in the secondary setting is designed to provide a "boost" to students who are slightly below grade level. Tier 2 support can be considered as more prevention support in addition to the integration of evidence-based literacy instruction in Tier 1. Furthermore, Tier 2 intervention can be provided in groups of approximately 10–12 students (Vaughn et al., 2010) and can support Tier 1 instruction, with a focus on more support in vocabulary, comprehension, and advanced word reading skills (i.e., decoding multisyllabic words).

Adolescents only have so much time left before they are expected to graduate and become contributing members of society. The stakes are high. This means certain students will need intensive, supplemental Tier 3 support in an attempt to remediate some of the foundational-level skills they lack (e.g., word reading). Therefore, Tier 3 support is what we consider a form of remediation. We will discuss practices to support students in need of intensive intervention in Part II. Similar to Tier 3 at the elementary level, Tier 3 at the secondary level should provide more intensive individualized support than Tier 2.

You might be wondering when these interventions typically take place at the secondary level. Recall that at the elementary level, teachers provide interventions at a time convenient during the day, such as when students would be in their specials (e.g., art). Because secondary-level students are expected to earn credits for all their courses, it is much more difficult to find time during the day to provide these services. We can't just take them out of art 3 times a week when they are expected to earn an elective credit in art! Therefore, when secondary schools do provide interventions, they are typically offered in place of an elective class for credit. Notice that we stated, "*when* secondary schools do provide interventions." We say this because sometimes schools face resource challenges, making it difficult to provide intervention support both in general and especially in two different "levels" of support (e.g., Tiers 2 and 3). See the "Schoolwide Service-Delivery Model Challenges and Possible Solutions" section below for a deeper discussion of these common challenges. Also, see Tables 3.2–3.5 for comparisons between elementary and secondary Tier 2 intervention, and elementary and secondary Tier 3 intervention. Notice the differences between elementary and secondary implementation.

So, how do we know which secondary students are in need of Tier 2 or Tier 3 intervention? Should students at the secondary level progress linearly through the tiers as they do at the elementary level? On the contrary, we recommend that schools use screening and progress monitoring data to determine which students are in need of intervention and at what level (Fuchs et al., 2010; Fuchs & Vaughn, 2012). Instead of progressing linearly through Tier 2 to Tier 3, which could potentially waste precious time, we recommend that schools use cut points when examining their data to determine who is in need of what level of support: Tier 2 (i.e., prevention) or Tier 3 (i.e., remediation). Figure 3.3 illustrates this process. For a deeper discussion of issues related to the use of data, see Chapter 4.

Because DBI is not limited to a particular grade level, it can be used to intensify interventions for secondary students whose data indicate that they are in need of remediation. DBI at the secondary level shares many similarities with DBI at the elementary

TABLE 3.2. Key Elements of an Elementary Tier 2 Strategic Intervention

Focus: For students who have been identified with marked reading difficulties, and who have not responded to Tier 1 efforts

Curriculum: Specialized scientifically based reading curriculum (or curricula) emphasizing the five critical elements of beginning reading

Grouping: Homogeneous small-group instruction (1:5)

Time: 25–30 minutes a day, in addition to 90-minute core instruction

Assessment: Weekly progress monitoring on target skills to ensure adequate progress and learning

Interventionist: Research-provided interventionist, reading specialist, or classroom teacher

Setting: Appropriate setting outside classroom

Note. Adapted from Vaughn Gross Center for Reading & Language Arts (2005).

TABLE 3.3. Key Elements of a Secondary Tier 2 Strategic Intervention

Focus: For students who have been identified with marked reading difficulties, and who have not responded to Tier 1 efforts

Curriculum: Reading classes or small-group instruction designed to accelerate the reading growth of students with reading difficulties; this usually includes scientifically based program(s) emphasizing multisyllabic word recognition, fluency, vocabulary, and reading comprehension instruction.

Grouping: Homogeneous instruction provided within class sizes of 10–16 (typically)

Time: 30–50 minutes per day for two semesters

Assessment: Diagnostic assessment to determine the focus and pacing of instruction; progress monitoring with informal curriculum-based measures on target skills to ensure adequate progress and learning every 2–4 weeks; formal progress monitoring about every 6 weeks

Interventionist: Intervention provided by personnel determined by the school (usually a reading teacher or other interventionist)

Setting: Appropriate setting designated by the school (usually the reading class or supplemental tutoring)

Note. Adapted from Vaughn Gross Center for Reading & Language Arts (2005).

TABLE 3.4. Key Elements of an Elementary Tier 3 Intensive Intervention

Focus: For students who have been identified with marked reading difficulties, and who have not responded to Tier 1 and Tier 2 efforts

Curriculum: Individualized and responsive intervention emphasizing the critical elements of reading for students with reading difficulties/disabilities

Grouping: Homogeneous small-group instruction (1:3)

Time: 50 minutes a day, in addition to 90-minute core instruction

Assessment: Weekly progress monitoring on target skills to ensure adequate progress and learning

Interventionist: Research-provided reading specialist or classroom teacher

Setting: Appropriate setting outside classroom

Note. Adapted from Vaughn Gross Center for Reading & Language Arts (2005).

TABLE 3.5. Key Elements of a Secondary Tier 3 Intensive Intervention

Focus: For students with severe and persistent reading difficulties who do not make sufficient progress in Tier 2, or whom the school determines are so significantly behind that they initially require more intensive intervention than Tier 2 can provide

Curriculum: Specifically designed and customized reading instruction delivered in small groups or individually to students. Typically includes very individualized instruction in phonemic awareness, decoding, fluency, vocabulary, and comprehension; scientifically based reading program(s) emphasizing individual needs

Grouping: Homogeneous small-group instruction (no more than 4–5 students)

Time: 50–60 minutes every day for one or more school years

Assessment: Diagnostic assessment to determine the focus and pacing of instruction; progress monitoring with informal curriculum-based measures on target skills to ensure adequate progress and learning every other week; formal progress monitoring about every 4 weeks

Interventionist: Intensive intervention provided by personnel determined by the school (usually a reading teacher or other trained interventionist)

Setting: Appropriate setting designated by the school

Note. Adapted from Vaughn Gross Center for Reading & Language Arts (2005).

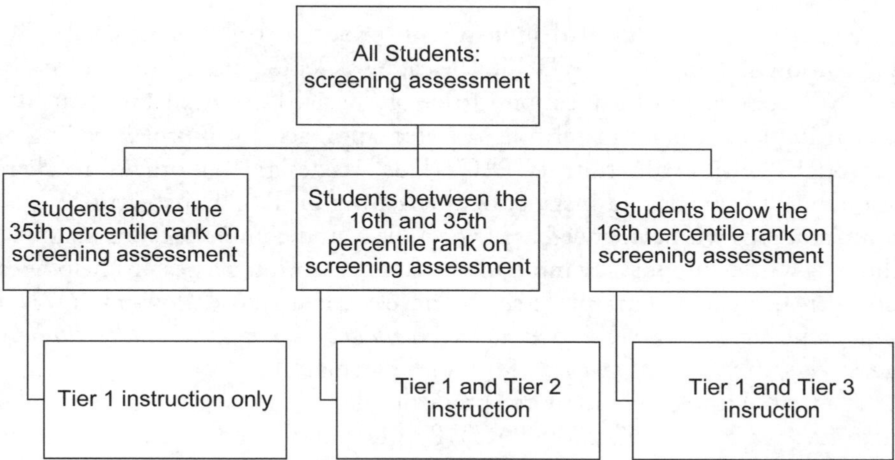

FIGURE 3.3. Sample cut points to determine the level of support each student needs. Adapted from Reed, Wexler, and Vaughn (2012).

level. For example, while students receive intensive intervention via the DBI process, they should still be receiving evidence-based Tier 1 instruction with high fidelity. The intervention that is intensified and individualized during DBI should also be evidence-based and implemented with fidelity. However, unlike in DBI for elementary students, DBI at the secondary level does not have to begin once a student has been inadequately responsive to a Tier 2 intervention. DBI can also begin when a student displays severe academic deficits, based on the Tier 3 cut point the school has established. Additionally, a unique structure needs to be in place for implementing DBI in secondary schools. Thus, secondary instructional coaches should ask themselves questions to guide DBI planning, including: What progress monitoring data will be collected, and what progress monitoring tools will they use to collect these data? What diagnostic assessment data will be collected for students who are not initially responsive to the Tier 3 intervention? When will the data be collected (e.g., how often, and in what class)? For a discussion about the use of data at the secondary level, see Chapter 4.

Overall, differences exist between elementary and secondary settings. Instructional coaches need to be knowledgeable about these differences so that they can ensure school structures and resources are in place to support these instruction and intervention efforts.

SCHOOLWIDE SERVICE-DELIVERY MODEL CHALLENGES AND POSSIBLE SOLUTIONS

Implementing adolescent literacy practices schoolwide is not without its challenges. To illustrate these challenges, consider an example from a school that recently participated in an adolescent literacy model demonstration project titled Promoting Adolescents' Comprehension of Text Plus (PACT Plus; Meadows Center, n.d.). This project, funded by the U.S. Department of Education Office of Special Education Programs (OSEP), focused on implementing and refining a tiered approach to improve reading among sixth- through eighth-grade students. PACT Plus was designed to provide teachers with professional development and instructional coaching on PACT instructional practices that equip students with evidence-based vocabulary and comprehension support across the school as well as support for more intensive intervention classes. To help with this, teachers were provided with professional development and follow-up instructional coaching support for 1 year. See *www.meadowscenter.org/projects/detail/promoting-adolescents-comprehension-of-text-pact* for more information.

After a year of implementation, the project leaders met with the teachers and school leaders to review progress. First, the PACT Plus team reviewed the typical RTI model. The team reminded them that 80% of the student population should make adequate progress with evidence-based Tier 1 instruction alone. Most students should not need supplemental Tier 2 or Tier 3 support. However, when the team showed the student data from a standardized measure of reading comprehension, the school staff realized they had their work cut out for them. See Figure 3.4 for pre- and posttest data on a standardized measure of comprehension.

The team explained the following:

> "At the beginning of Year 1, we group-administered a comprehensive screening measure. It gave us an idea of who was at risk for comprehension difficulty. It was also norm-referenced so when we look at the percentiles, we know that we are comparing the students to a nationally normative sample. When we look at these data, we can see that 78% of the schools' students scored lower than the bottom 25% of the nationwide sample. At the other end at pretest, 1.3% of the students

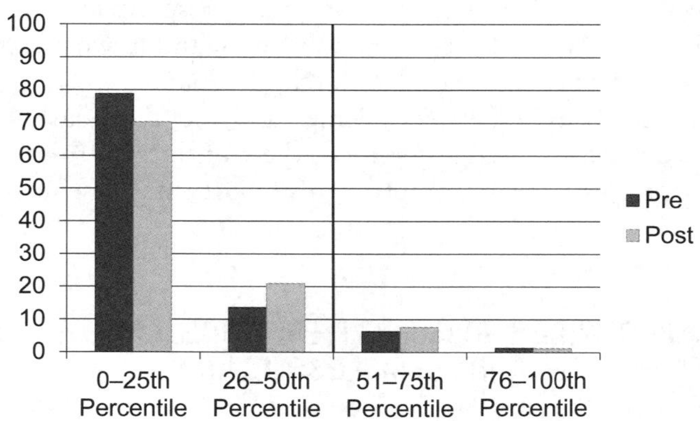

FIGURE 3.4. Sample school data from a standardized measure of reading comprehension.

scored higher than the top 75% of the nationwide sample. So, what can we take away from this information? First, the students in your school were in dire need of evidence-based literacy instruction and intervention. After a year of implementing such instruction and intervention, we would ideally like to see movement out of the lowest percentile categories and into the higher percentile categories. Second, we like to look at the dividing line at the 50th percentile. This gives us a 'pulse' reading to tell us how much need there is for some instruction to bolster comprehension. Now, let's examine what happened after a year of providing professional development and support while the teachers in your school implemented instruction and intervention. At the end of the year, nearly 90% of students at this middle school were considered at risk for comprehension difficulty. Therefore, a majority of these students need enhanced Tier 1 instruction and most of them need supplemental Tier 2 or 3 support."

Some teachers nodded their heads in agreement. They knew that many of their students were struggling already and didn't even need to see these data to prove it. One teacher was a little more skeptical. He raised his hand and asked, "You mean to tell me that after a whole year of this instruction, a majority of our students are *still* struggling readers?"

The PACT Plus team quickly reflected and thought about how to explain this. Before long, the teacher who posed the question exclaimed, "Just give it to me straight!" The team provided two potential reasons to the teacher that reflect common challenges for all secondary schools trying to implement this type of tiered support to improve adolescent literacy outcomes. First, the team revisited the idea that it is difficult for students to make progress when they have been struggling for years (Vaughn et al., 2012). The team referred the teachers to the findings from the 2006–2011 Texas Center for Learning Disabilities center study mentioned in Chapter 2 (see Texas Center for Learning Disabilities, 2012). Essentially, what we know is that students need enhanced Tier 1 instruction in the content areas across many years. In addition, numerous students will need supplemental instruction. This led the team to its second potential reason: fidelity. The team explained that even with the professional development and ongoing literacy instructional support (i.e., coaching) its members provided, implementation was poor. To put it bluntly, the teachers rarely implemented the PACT Plus instruction as intended and the school only implemented supplemental intervention to three classes of students! The instruction and intervention the teachers did implement were not implemented with fidelity. How can we possibly expect students to make gains when we do not implement evidence-based instruction and intervention with fidelity? (See Chapter 8 for more information about fidelity of implementation.) Needless to say, the PACT Plus team did not want to discourage the teachers and school leaders. The team understood that they were facing many challenges that made building a schoolwide adolescent literacy model challenging. See Table 3.6 for a description of some of these common challenges and possible solutions to focus on.

TABLE 3.6. Challenges of Schoolwide Adolescent Literacy Models and Possible Solutions

My challenge is . . .	Action item	Comments
In my school, a majority of students with reading difficulties and disabilities spend most of their day in the content-area classroom; we do not have resources to provide intensive supplemental intervention to all the students who need it.	Intensify Tier 1 instruction by providing professional development and ongoing instructional coaching support to your Tier 1 teachers.	Consider using some of the free resources that exist on enhancing your Tier 1 instruction. For example, administrators can share these free adolescent literacy IRIS Center modules with all of their teachers: *https://iris.peabody.vanderbilt.edu/module/sec-rdng* and *https://iris.peabody.vanderbilt.edu/module/sec-rdng2*.
	Intensify Tier 1 instruction by using a co-teaching model.	Co-teaching is a service-delivery model in which a general education teacher and special education teacher work together to provide instruction for students with and without disabilities in the general education setting (Cook & Friend, 1995). In theory, the teachers can combine their unique content and pedagogical expertise to provide opportunities for all students to access the general education curriculum. If you do choose to use a co-teaching model, make sure you provide professional development for the co-teaching pair about how to integrate literacy practices into instruction. For more information, we recommend that you visit *www.ProjectCALI.org*. This website provides information about how to implement a professional development model that some researchers developed with funding from the IES. The professional development model provides guidance for co-teachers about how to integrate literacy instruction and provide differentiated support to all students in the class.
	Consider integrating peer-mediated instruction into Tier 1 instruction.	Peer-mediated instruction is an evidence-based practice that, when implemented effectively, provides students with more opportunities to practice and receive feedback (Wexler, Reed, Pyle, et al., 2015). In other words, it is a service-delivery model that can help intensify Tier 1 instruction. Many free resources exist on peer-mediated instruction. For example, we recommend you review the following brief: *www.meadowscenter.org/files/resources/PartnerReadingBrief_final.pdf*.
The content-area teachers in my school do not think it is their responsibility to provide literacy instruction. It is common for teachers to say things like "I'm a science teacher—not a reading teacher!"	Find out what the barriers are for teachers in a sensitive way. For example, is it possible they have never participated in training on how to provide literacy instruction within their content area?	Review Part II of this book to learn about an adaptive intervention coaching model that helps instructional coaches determine the reason that teachers might feel hesitant about implementing literacy instruction.

Students have to earn credits. It seems like there is limited time to provide supplemental intensive reading intervention.	Find creative alternatives to scheduling intervention time.	Some schools let students take a supplemental intensive reading intervention class in place of an elective class. It might even be possible to provide credit for this class so students feel they are not only working on their literacy skills but also earning credit toward graduation. For example, do you have an advisory block or homeroom time when students can participate in intervention and earn credit for doing so? To review some sample middle school schedules that include time for intervention, see Reed et al. (2012).
My school does not have a lot of money to purchase intervention materials or programs.	Consider adopting a set of evidence-based practices that do not require a lot of extra materials beyond text that your school likely already has access to.	It is possible to adopt evidence-based word study, vocabulary, and comprehension practices without buying a program that costs money. (Note that we do recommend that you use a systematic scope and sequence for word study/decoding interventions; this might require purchasing a program depending on the expertise of your staff.) For more guidance on practices that are possible to integrate into your instruction and intervention, see Part II of this book. You might also consider reviewing practices in the following website and modules: *http://toolkit.csrcolorado.org/Login?ReturnUrl=%2f* Tier 1: *www.texasgateway.org/course/texas-adolescent-literacy-academy-tier-i-content-area-instructional-routines-support-academic* Tiers 2 and 3: *www.texasgateway.org/course/texas-adolescent-literacy-academy-tiers-ii-iii-assessment-and-instructional-routines-reading*
My school faces a lot of student behavior challenges.	Consider adopting positive behavioral interventions and supports (PBIS) for your entire school.	A great deal of information about PBIS exists. See this website, funded by the USDOE OSEP, for more information: *www.pbis.org/school/mtss.*
	Utilize a functional behavioral assessment (FBA) with particular students.	An FBA can help you identify the reason for the problem behavior and develop a behavior plan for individual students. See this IRIS module for more information: *https://iris.peabody.vanderbilt.edu/module/fba.*
We have so many other initiatives in our school. We are confused about what to focus on.	Consider limiting the number of initiatives you are focused on to avoid initiative fatigue.	While it is tempting to adopt initiatives that will potentially address several different priorities, adopting too many initiatives can confuse and frustrate teachers. Examine your school's data to determine where your greatest needs are and build a multiyear plan to slowly incorporate new initiatives. This will help your entire staff stay focused.

(continued)

TABLE 3.6. *(continued)*

My challenge is . . .	Action item	Comments
We provide professional development to the teachers, but they do not consistently implement the practices with fidelity after the professional development is over.	Use an instructional coach to support teachers on an ongoing, individualized basis. Also, by limiting the number of initiatives you are focusing on (see above), teachers may feel less overwhelmed and more inclined to incorporate the practices they learn during professional development.	The combination of initial intensive professional development followed by ongoing instructional coaching support can successfully affect both teacher practice and student learning (e.g., Hairrell et al., 2011; Simmons et al., 2010). See Chapter 8 for more information about fidelity of implementation. See Part II of this book for more information about how to provide systematic, ongoing professional development and instructional coaching support to teachers.
The teachers in our school tend to disengage during professional development and instructional coaching sessions. Sometimes they grade papers. Sometimes they take other calls. Sometimes they talk to each other. They do not always ask questions.	Determine the reason for their disengagement.	Is your professional development misaligned with what teachers perceive to be their needs? Does the professional development include active learning opportunities for teachers, or is it more of a "sit and get" session? Does your instructional coach target teachers' individual needs, or does she try to provide the same type and amount of support for teachers regardless of needs? To learn about how to make your professional development and ongoing instructional coaching sessions more engaging, review Part III of this book. As noted above, in Part II, we present an adaptive intervention coaching model that helps instructional coaches determine teachers' individual needs so that instructional coaches can target those needs appropriately. Chapter 9 reviews best practices for professional development and ongoing instructional coaching that align with Adult Learning Theory.
	Involve members of your administrative leadership teams in all professional development and ongoing instructional coaching opportunities.	Involving administrators in your professional development is not an attempt to catch teachers who are not being compliant. Strong leadership matters. We know your administrative leaders are busy, but it can be a powerful reinforcer when they participate in or at least attend professional development and even some instructional coaching sessions. Participating in professional development and ongoing instructional coaching can help your leaders fully understand the practices their teachers will be implementing. It will also give them an idea of some of the barriers their teachers face by listening and observing teachers' feedback. These efforts can support teachers and strengthen your schoolwide literacy model.

ARE THESE SCHOOLWIDE SERVICE-DELIVERY MODEL CHALLENGES UNIQUE?

It might be tempting to think that the challenges the PACT Plus school faced are unique. Is the teachers' lack of implementation of evidence-based practices with fidelity particularly unusual? On the contrary, data converge from recent observation research reveals that many teachers miss key opportunities to integrate evidence-based literacy and text reading practices into their instruction (Swanson et al., 2016; Wexler et al., 2017; Wexler et al., 2018). For example, from observations of vocabulary and reading comprehension practices implemented in secondary social studies (Swanson et al., 2016) and science classes (Wexler et al., 2017), authors reported that comprehension strategy instruction and comprehension monitoring were rare and previewing text was absent in more than 80% of classrooms. Even more concerning was that less than 15% of the observed time included text reading. Most recently, Wexler et al. (2018) conducted an observation study of literacy and co-teaching practices in co-taught middle school classrooms that include students with disabilities. Co-teachers provided a minimal amount of literacy instruction using connected text. In all three studies, the most common grouping structure was whole-class and independent work, depriving many students of opportunities to practice and receive immediate corrective feedback. Furthermore, in one of the observation studies that included teacher interviews, teachers cited a wide range of barriers (e.g., lack of time) to implementing literacy instruction in their Tier 1 classrooms, impacting their will to do so (Wexler et al., 2017). In sum, teachers have not been consistently implementing evidence-based literacy practices in Tier 1 secondary classrooms.

Is there a similar trend in middle school intervention classrooms? Ciullo et al. (2016) conducted a study to observe educators who were responsible for delivering literacy intervention in middle school districtwide RTI frameworks to provide initial understanding of the frequency and types of evidence-based practices used. The authors reported that educators rarely provided explicit comprehension instruction. For example, graphic organizers, an evidence-based tool that students can use to assist in comprehension of text (Dexter & Hughes, 2011), were minimally used for text comprehension or vocabulary purposes. Finally, Ciullo et al. reported that teachers rarely provided writing instruction, which enhances comprehension or independent reading practice. In sum, the trend of minimal provision of evidence-based literacy instruction and intervention remains the same for instruction in content-area Tier 1 classrooms and intervention in supplemental intervention classrooms.

IMPLICATIONS FOR INSTRUCTIONAL COACHES

Despite the fact that we have confirmed evidence-based practices that teachers should implement across a schoolwide adolescent literacy model, observation research reveals that secondary teachers struggle to incorporate evidence-based literacy practices in their classes. Yet, we know that content-area literacy instruction is essential for all students at the secondary level, and students with more intensive reading needs require intensive intervention as well. Teachers must receive training on how to support the language and literacy of secondary students across content areas and in intensive intervention settings so that they have full access to the curriculum and are prepared for postsecondary success. Therefore, instructional coaches are a critical piece of building a schoolwide adolescent literacy model.

Secondary instructional coaches have two important purposes. First, instructional coaches *lead down* (Maxwell, 2011) in order to influence teachers' instructional practices. In other words, they are tasked with disseminating and translating information about evidence-based practices and, ultimately, helping teachers intensify literacy instruction and intervention in their content-area and supplemental intervention classes. After all, knowing what practices to implement is futile if teachers do not have guidance on how to translate this knowledge into practice. In fact, Cook, Cook, and Landrum (2013) explain that "despite tangible results in determining what works, using dissemination approaches that fail to resonate with or influence practitioners represents an important but often overlooked contributor to the ongoing research-to-practice gap in special education" (p. 163). Second, instructional coaches *lead up* (Maxwell, 2011) by supporting administrators—their own leaders—in creating and implementing schoolwide adolescent literacy models that maximize the literacy instruction and intervention that students receive during an entire school day. In this book, we will tackle both purposes of secondary instructional coaches, but first, let's take a quick look at what we do and don't know about the impact of instructional coaching.

Although there is a critical need for secondary instructional coaches, knowledge of effective instructional coaching models, especially at the secondary level, is limited. In 2010, Kretlow and Bartholomew reviewed 13 studies that examined interventions providing preservice and inservice teachers with instructional coaching support for implementing evidence-based practices that targeted students' academic performance or classroom behavior. Outcomes related to student behavior were most commonly reported. Additionally, only two of the studies included secondary students. Therefore, not only do we know little about the impact of instructional coaching on students' academic outcomes, but we also know little about secondary instructional coaching interventions specifically.

Despite what we don't know about instructional coaching, we do know that instructional coaching positively affects teacher outcomes. In Kretlow and Bartholomew's (2010) review, all 13 instructional coaching interventions reported positive effects on teacher behaviors. Many of these interventions included group training and individual observations of teachers with follow-up consultative feedback from the instructional coach. Therefore, we know that in order to lead down and improve teacher practices, the instructional coach should provide teachers with direct training as a group as well as individualized support and feedback based on classroom observation.

In Part II of this book, we will present the skills instructional coaches need to possess and the content they need to understand in order to promote school success. In addition, we will draw from the relatively small but existing research base on instructional coaching (and other related literature) to demonstrate how instructional coaches can implement an instructional coaching model for the secondary level.

REVIEW AND PREVIEW

In this chapter, we presented the idea that instructional coaches need to understand common schoolwide service-delivery models and the common issues that schools face when trying to implement these models. We then offered an example of a school in the PACT Plus project that faced some real challenges. One challenge was that the teachers in the school were not implementing the evidence-based practices with fidelity due to a variety of factors. We next summarized some of the data we have learned from observation studies conducted nationwide to illustrate how these challenges are not unique to the school we described in the PACT Plus project. We ended this chapter by describing some implications for instructional coaches. The next section of this book, Part II, will review the content a secondary-level reading instructional coach should know.

Terms to Know

Curriculum-based measures (CBMs): Brief curriculum-independent assessments used for universal screening and progress monitoring. CBMs can help teachers understand how students are progressing in literacy skills (e.g., reading multisyllabic words) over time.

Individuals with Disabilities Education Improvement Act of 2004: Federal special education law that mandates individualized education programs, free and appropriate public education, least restrictive environments, appropriate evaluation, parent and teacher participation, and procedural safeguards for all students with disabilities attending public schools.

Multi-tiered intervention: A systematic approach to providing evidence-based core instruction to all students and intensified instruction and intervention to students in need.

Prevention: Instruction and other supports intended to keep the skills of students from further declining.

Progress monitoring: The frequent assessment of students using brief assessments to determine their response to instruction or intervention.

Psychometrics: Testing to establish the validity and reliability of educational and psychological assessments.

Remediation: Intervention intended to minimize the deficits of students with intensive academic needs.

Response-to-intervention (RTI) model: A service-delivery approach that includes universal screening, progress monitoring, and multi-tiered intervention for all students.

Universal screening: A brief assessment of all students to identify those who may have lower than expected academic achievement.

Reflection Questions

1. What is the goal of an RTI model as it was conceptualized at the elementary level?
2. What are the essential components of RTI?
3. Explain prevention and remediation concepts in terms of literacy instruction. How do these concepts apply to the elementary and secondary levels?
4. What are some resources to consult for more information about reliable and valid screening tools?
5. Can you list some schoolwide service-delivery model challenges and possible solutions at the secondary level? How do these challenges align with the top three challenges you face at your school?
6. Can you describe the trend and implications of the nationwide observation research presented in this chapter?
7. Can you explain the two important purposes that secondary instructional coaches have?

PART II

INSTRUCTIONAL PRACTICES EVERY SECONDARY LITERACY COACH SHOULD KNOW

CHAPTER 4

Using Data

When more than 1,000 middle school students enter the building on the first day of school, chances are their new teachers know relatively little about them. Yes, some students are preceded by their reputations—good or bad—but useful information about their skills and knowledge is generally unknown at the beginning of the year. Granted, many students do "just fine" or excel within the general education classroom because their instructional needs are met there. However, too many students in middle school lack foundational reading skills that are essential for success and require intervention (McFarland et al., 2019). There are several efficient ways to identify these students and gather information on their instructional needs. In this chapter, we provide an overview of three important forms of data collection: **universal screening**, **diagnostic data collection**, and **progress monitoring**. We also discuss how to use data to make instructional decisions. Our hope is that you use this information to build your own knowledge and craft effective professional development for your teachers.

UNIVERSAL SCREENING

Identifying the academic needs of all students entering a school or grade level is becoming more commonplace. However, a variety of methods are used. Some schools use a records review process. Others favor vertical team meetings to learn about incoming students. Essential to any method used are efficiency and effectiveness. A few common data review methods are described in Figure 4.1. As you read about each method, reflect on the efficiency and effectiveness of each.

Perhaps you recognized that although reviewing cumulative student files may be effective, it takes a great deal of time. Meeting with last year's team and reviewing high-stakes assessment results may be efficient, but the practices leave important questions

Method	Description	Effective?	Efficient?
Review curriculum files.	During curriculum file review, the teacher sits and reads through each of more than 100 student files belonging to students assigned to her class. She decides to be systematic about her review and reads information about each child, then sorts the files into two stacks: students on target or those needing additional help. Along the way, for students assigned to the "needs additional help" stack, she makes notes about each student's instructional gaps. How much time would this task take? Assuming the teacher is very efficient, let's say that 5 minutes per file is needed. If she has 150 students, it will take 750 minutes—or 12.5 hours!	✓	✗
Meet with the previous year's team.	Sometimes, teams set 1-hour meetings to pass on information about students from one grade level team to another. During these meetings, the previous year's teachers review student lists, identify who struggled in their class, and pass on this information to the next teacher. These reports might sound something like this: "I see you have Paulina in your class. She really can't read very well, and she failed almost every test in social studies last year." While the new teacher now knows that Paulina struggles with reading, she has no information about *what* is causing her struggles.	✗	✓
Review high-stakes assessment scores.	Some school districts allow teachers to access high-stakes assessment data for their new students. Using this method, the teacher may sort students and identify those who failed the high-stakes assessment in the previous year. Keep in mind that the information is limited by the purpose of high-stakes assessments—to determine if the students mastered that year's standards in the subject area (Smarter Balanced Assessment Consortium, 2019). The teacher may be able to see whether a child passed the test or what standards and objectives the student did not master. However, because this information does not help identify gaps in foundational reading skills that contribute so substantially to students' success, it does not address *why* students failed the test.	✓	✗
Universal screening.	Universal screening measures and assessments have improved substantially over the past 10 years. Often, screening is conducted via computer. Classes visit the computer lab (or use classroom laptops) to take an assessment lasting only a few minutes. Within 30 minutes of class time, assessment data are collected on every single student. Even if a teacher must assess students one at a time (e.g., through a 1-minute ORF test), he can test 20 students in a 45-minute class period, meaning that he will be finished in two class periods or even less time. Add a paraprofessional's help, and he will be finished in one class period. In addition, the information gathered is highly useful for identifying students in need of support and planning intervention.	✓	✓

FIGURE 4.1. Common methods for collecting and reviewing data.

unanswered about students who struggle. On the other hand, universal screening is a highly effective and efficient method of collecting key data across a large group of students in order to identify those likely to experience reading difficulty. While it is an increasingly common data collection method, teachers may still have questions about why universal screening data are collected, how to collect the data efficiently, and how they can best use that information.

First, let's think about the purpose of universal screening and measures like oral reading fluency (ORF)—a common tool to detect reading difficulty. To illustrate, consider another common tool and procedure used to detect illness—the thermometer (see Figure 4.2). Imagine your child coming home and saying, "I don't feel well." He looks a little pale and is tired. You think, "He might be sick. Let's see." Using a thermometer, you measure your son's body temperature. The measure itself takes very little

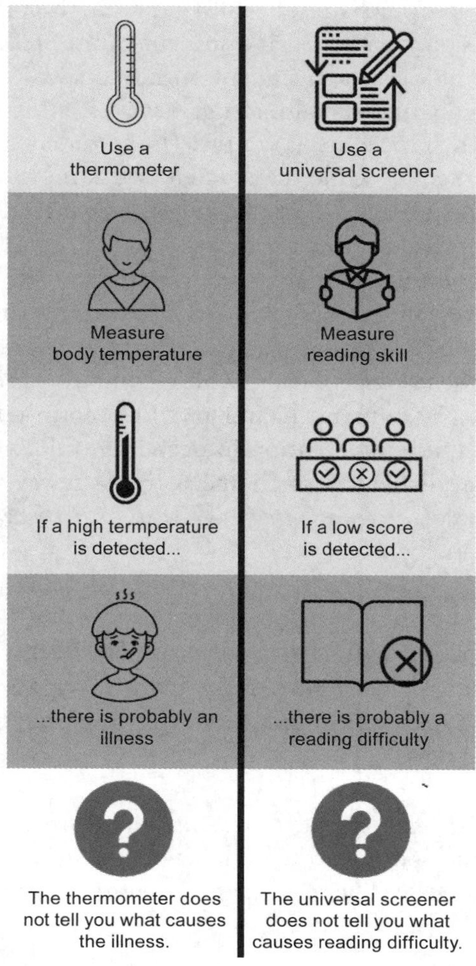

FIGURE 4.2. Similarities between a thermometer and a universal screener.

time—a few seconds. If the body temperature is high, then the tool (i.e., thermometer) has detected your son's illness. What the thermometer does not tell you is the cause of your son's illness. Likewise, universal screening measures like ORF can be administered very efficiently to students in about a minute. If the score is low on the ORF measure, then the tool has detected a possible reading difficulty. Like the thermometer, what the ORF measure cannot reveal is *why* the student is struggling with reading.

Using an ORF Measure for Universal Screening

One very efficient universal screener is an ORF measure. ORF has been shown both theoretically (Catts, 2018; Gough & Tunmer, 1986) and empirically (e.g., Fuchs, Fuchs, Hosp, & Jenkins, 2001) to be a powerful indicator of overall reading competence and is strongly correlated with reading comprehension—particularly among elementary and middle school students (see Fuchs et al., 2001). The high correlation between ORF and reading comprehension means that if a student cannot read with fluency at a rate expected of the average middle school student in their grade (i.e., the student has a low ORF score), they are highly likely to also struggle with reading comprehension.

The ORF assessment procedure is simple: (1) A student reads aloud an unpracticed passage for 1 minute; (2) while the student is reading, the teacher marks errors on an assessor copy of the passage; (3) at the end of 1 minute, the teacher subtracts the errors from the total number of words read to calculate the number of words correct per minute (WCPM). There are several valid and **reliable** ORF measures offered for a fee or free of charge. One valid and reliable ORF measure is the Texas Middle School Fluency Assessment (TMSFA), available free of charge at *https://meadowscenter.org/vgc/professional-development/detail/tala*. The TMSFA contains three measures: (1) word reading, (2) ORF, and (3) story retell and provides norm-referenced cut points to identify students who require intervention in decoding, ORF, and/or comprehension. Online training is also available free of charge at the Gateway Courses website (*www.texascourses.org/courses/course-v1:TexasGateway+TMSFA+2016/about*).

Who Should Be Screened and When?

Students enter middle school with a great deal of data from their elementary school years. Almost every student has results from high-stakes assessments, for example. These data can be used as part of a double-gate screening procedure to reduce the time teachers spend collecting data.

- *Gate 1: High-stakes assessment data review.* The instructional coach (or another educator) reviews students' scores on the high-stakes assessment to identify all students who failed or barely passed it. These students are more likely to have a reading difficulty.

- *Gate 2: Collect additional universal screening data.* Students who failed or barely passed the prior year's high-stakes reading assessment enter Gate 2 and are assessed using a measure like the TMSFA (i.e., ORF with retell). Two groups of students will likely emerge. One group of students will score within average to high ranges on the screening measure and therefore do not exhibit a reading difficulty. However, a second group of students will score within lower levels on the screening measure, indicating a need for intensive intervention to remediate reading difficulty.

• *Making a double-gate procedure work.* Let's consider how this works in a school with 300 students in seventh grade. During Gate 1, prior to school starting, the instructional coach reviews all of the high-stakes assessment data for the incoming seventh-grade students and notes that 14% of them (i.e., 42 students) failed the high-stakes assessment at the end of sixth grade. Another 5% of students (i.e., 15 students) passed—but just barely. These 57 students will now enter Gate 2. After reviewing available measures, the school chooses the TMSFA for the Gate 2 screener. During week two of the school year, a group of educators trained in TMSFA administration assesses the 57 students. Assessment takes approximately 10 minutes per student (i.e., get the student from class, walk to the testing location, explain the assessment, administer the assessment, and walk back to class), meaning that a team of four trained educators could each be assigned 14–15 students and complete assessment for all students in 2.5 hours. After data are collected, each assessor is tasked with organizing the data and identifying who is in need of intervention. An organized data sheet should list students and summarize the results. In this case, the data sheet includes the WCPM and retell accuracy of a sample of nine seventh graders (see Figure 4.3). Now that this information is organized, it is ready to be reviewed by key stakeholders to plan for intervention.

DIAGNOSTIC DATA COLLECTION

Using a double-gate universal screening procedure, about 10–15% of students may be identified as in need of Tier 3 intervention provided by a reading specialist. Remember: Universal screening measures—just like thermometers—don't tell us the cause of the problem. Therefore, it's time for the reading specialist, intervention teacher, or instructional coach to figure out what is causing the difficulty for these students through the use of diagnostic data collection.

One thing that helps instructional coaches select diagnostic assessments is an understanding of the component skills that, when added together, produce skilled reading. Skilled reading develops along a continuum (see Figure 4.4) starting with fundamental skills, like phonological awareness and word identification, and moving into more complex skills, like vocabulary and reading comprehension. In the elementary school grades, diagnostic data collection often takes place in a bottom-up manner, starting with phonological awareness and moving up the continuum with the goal of ensuring that foundational skills are well in place so that more complex reading skills may develop. However, this method of diagnostic data collection is time-consuming in middle school when students have likely developed many of the foundational skills (e.g., phonological awareness). Instead, consider a top-down approach to diagnostic

Name	WCPM	WCPM Level of Need	Retell	Retell Level of Need	Recommendation for Tier 2 Focus
Anna Barra	120	<89 = decoding, fluency, and comprehension	75%	>40% = Low	None
		90–118 = fluency and comprehension		<40% = High	
		>119 = comprehension			
Brett Allen	128	<89 = decoding, fluency and comprehension	80%	>40% = Low	None
		90–118 = fluency and comprehension		<40% = High	
		>119 = comprehension			
Anika Warren	112	<89 = decoding, fluency, and comprehension	70%	>40% = Low	Fluency
		90–118 = fluency and comprehension		<40% = High	
		>119 = comprehension			
Amanda Johnson	90	<89 = decoding, fluency, and comprehension	67%	>40% = Low	Fluency
		90–118 = fluency and comprehension		<40% = High	
		>119 = comprehension			
Paul Francis	96	<89 = decoding, fluency, and comprehension	30%	>40% = Low	Fluency Comprehension
		90–118 = fluency and comprehension		<40% = High	
		>119 = comprehension			
Alicia Vasquez	90	<89 = decoding, fluency, and comprehension	25%	>40% = Low	Fluency Comprehension
		90–118 = fluency and comprehension		<40% = High	
		>119 = comprehension			
Alice Chow	60	<89 = decoding, fluency, and comprehension	25%	>40% = Low	Decoding Fluency Comprehension
		90–118 = fluency and comprehension		<40% = High	
		>119 = comprehension			
Samantha Alex	50	<89 = decoding, fluency, and comprehension	23%	>40% = Low	Decoding Fluency Comprehension
		90–118 = fluency and comprehension		<40% = High	
		>119 = comprehension			
Varena Alama	75	<89 = decoding, fluency, and comprehension	20%	>40% = Low	Decoding Fluency Comprehension
		90–118 = fluency and comprehension		<40% = High	
		>119 = comprehension			

Summary of Screening Results

Tier 1 Only	Tier 2 Intervention Decoding, Fluency, and Comprehension	Tier 2 Intervention Fluency and Comprehension	Tier 2 Intervention Fluency
Anna Barra Brett Allen	Alice Chow Samantha Alex Varena Alama	Paul Francis Alicia Vasquez	Anika Warren Amanda Johnson

FIGURE 4.3. Sample universal screening ORF data sheet for a seventh-grade class.

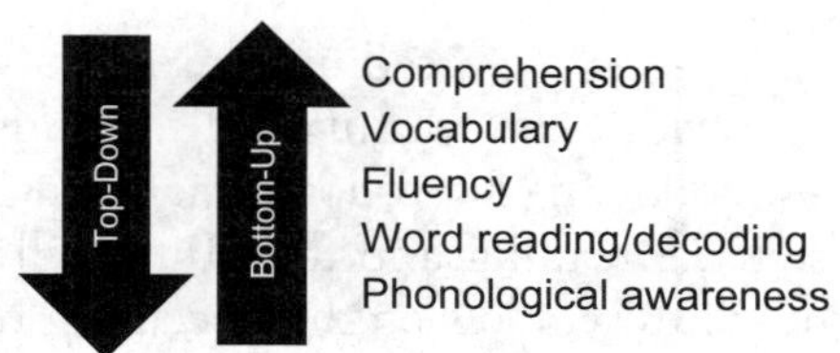

FIGURE 4.4. Reading skill development continuum.

data collection. Reading specialists begin by considering and collecting data on reading comprehension and then move down the continuum to help identify component skills that contribute to the difficulty.

Let's return to Figure 4.3 to apply this top-down diagnostic data collection model to our sample group of seventh-grade students. Each student's level of need is highlighted for WCPM and retell. We see that three students—Alice Chow, Samantha Alex, and Varena Alama—are all identified as having difficulty with reading comprehension, fluency *and* decoding. Let's look more closely at Varena's scores. Using the top-down diagnostic assessment model, we understand that comprehension difficulties might be caused by vocabulary difficulties, low rates of ORF, word reading/decoding gaps, and/or phonological awareness difficulties. Varena's teacher chose the diagnostic testing battery depicted in Figure 4.5.

Because the TMSFA signaled that fluency was an issue for Varena, the teacher wanted to know more about what caused the low ORF score. So, she administered a new, 1-minute passage fluency diagnostic assessment. This time, the teacher marked words that Varena mispronounced or could not read (i.e., accuracy) and made notes about the prosody (i.e., reading with inflection) and automaticity (i.e., pace of reading) with which Varena read. Also, because the TMSFA fluency score was so low (i.e., 75 WCPM), the teacher wondered whether or not word reading should be part of Varena's intervention. One measure used for diagnostic data collection is the CORE Phonics Survey (Honig, Diamond, & Gutlohn, 2000). The assessment is designed for use in grades K–8 and includes short assessments for alphabet skills (e.g., letter names and

Measure	Plan for Using the Measure	Time Needed for Administration	Where to Find the Measure
TMSFA	Closely examine issues related to ORF.	5 minutes	Gateway Courses. (n.d). Texas Middle School Fluency Assessment: Administering and Interpreting Results: *www.texascourses.org/courses/course-v1:TexasGateway+TMSFA+2016/about*
CORE Phonics Survey	Assess decoding and spelling skills.	10 minutes	Honig, B., Diamond, L., & Gutlohn, L. (2000). *Teaching reading sourcebook.* Novato, CA: Arena Press.

FIGURE 4.5. Sample diagnostic assessment plan.

sounds), reading and decoding skills (e.g., reading consonant–vowel–consonant [CVC] words through multisyllabic words), and spelling skills. Administering the entire measure takes about 15 minutes. Following a top-down model for assessing middle schoolers, teachers may administer the reading and decoding skills section along with the spelling section. If a student scores very low on these sections, the alphabet skills section may be administered. For additional training on how to use diagnostic data to plan for instruction, this booklet from the Institute of Education Sciences is helpful: *https://ies.ed.gov/ncee/wwc/Docs/PracticeGuide/dddm_pg_092909.pdf.*

Many teachers want a list of assessments that can be used for diagnostic purposes. This request is difficult to fulfill because of the breadth of assessments available, frequent updates to assessments, school budgets, time constraints, and teacher training. The National Center on Intensive Intervention (NCII) maintains a list of example diagnostic tools that can be found at *https://intensiveintervention.org/intensive-intervention/diagnostic-data/example-diagnostic-tools.* We suggest that in order to serve as a valuable resource to interventionists on your campus, instructional coaches should become familiar with a set of diagnostic measures that addresses each of the components of reading. Teachers need training in administering the measures and how to interpret the results. If instructional coaches maintain a "tool bag" of go-to diagnostic measures, supporting veteran teachers and training new ones becomes much easier, every struggling reader on campus receives the same high-quality set of diagnostic measures, and every struggling reader has a greater chance of remediating key skills that lead to academic success.

PROGRESS MONITORING

To this point, we have discussed the role of universal screening to identify students in need of support and diagnostic measurement to identify the causes of reading difficulty. Now, we turn our attention to the type of data teachers will collect during intervention to determine if students are making progress and, if not, when to change the intervention approach in some way. This approach to providing intervention has become commonly known as data-based individualization—a systematic way to review data to intensify and individualize instructional activities to align with student need. We will provide an overview of how to make instructional decisions based on progress monitoring data, but for extensive training in data-based individualization, we suggest visiting the NCII's Data-Based Individualization Training Series (*https://intensiveintervention.org/implementation-support/dbi-training-series*).

Choosing a Progress Monitoring Measure

As with other measures we've discussed, it is important to choose a progress monitoring measure that matches its intended use. This concept is called **validity** and is a very important metric when choosing a measure. In the case of progress monitoring, choose a measure that was designed to measure student gains (or lack thereof) over time.

Earlier, we discussed the TMSFA as a universal screening measure. In addition to the universal screening passages, the TMSFA offers a series of equated passages that can be used to monitor progress in ORF. When measuring ORF repeatedly over time, equated passages are particularly important. Let's consider several examples to illustrate this. In the first, a teacher pulls sixth-grade reading passages from the Internet to use for progress monitoring. Using these passages, he finds out that one of his sixth-grade students has oral reading fluency scores that increase over time. The teacher concludes that the fluency instruction he's been providing works. However, the teacher notices that, during instruction, the same student struggles with fluency when she reads many passages that are supposedly also on the sixth-grade level. In this case, the passages the teacher chose for progress monitoring differ in difficulty and have, in fact, become easier over time. The student's performance on ORF changed over time, not because her skills improved, but because the level of difficulty of the measure decreased over time. This resulted in an incorrect assumption that instruction is working, when truly, the student needs additional intervention.

In another example, consider the teacher who uses passages from the seventh-grade basal reader to assess ORF over time. She assumes that because the passages are in the seventh-grade basal, all of the selections are written on a seventh-grade reading level. Figure 4.6 shows a student's scores across a 10-week period using the seventh-grade basal passages. Notice the variability in scores—one week, the ORF score is low; the next, high. As a result, the teacher changes the fluency intervention. However, the student's ability did not create the pattern of variable scores. Instead, the passages the teacher used for progress monitoring varied in difficulty—one was easy, the next was difficult. The passage variability produced the variable scores. As a consequence, because the teacher used unequated passages, she made an error in her instructional decision as well.

Let's consider the same seventh-grade student, but in this case, the teacher uses the TMSFA progress monitoring passages. All of these passages are equated, meaning that they're all within a narrow band of difficulty. With the difficulty of the passages held standard, we can now "see" students' gains (or lack thereof) over time. See Figure

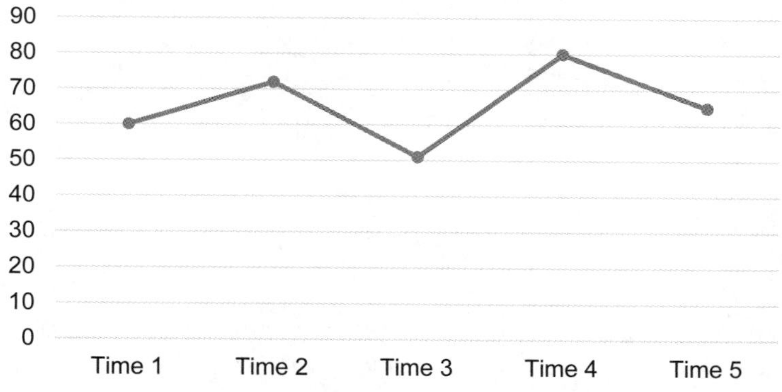

FIGURE 4.6. ORF scores (WCPM) with unequated passages.

4.7 for an example. In this scenario, the teacher may determine that the ORF lessons are working and, because the student may benefit from a larger dose of fluency lessons, decide to stick with them. This is a very different instructional outcome for the same student—all because the teachers used a set of equated passages designed for progress monitoring.

The TMSFA ORF progress monitoring passages for grades 6, 7, and 8 can be downloaded free of charge at *https://meadowscenter.org/projects/detail/building-capacity-for-response-to-intervention-rti-implementation-project*. Of course, ORF is not the only skill that may be monitored among struggling middle school readers. Teachers may want to monitor word reading or reading comprehension. A review of all available progress monitoring measures is beyond the scope of this book. We suggest you consider additional measures using the NCII's Progress Monitoring Tools Chart (*https://charts.intensiveintervention.org/chart/progress-monitoring*).

Using Progress Monitoring Data to Make Instructional Decisions

Using data to make instructional decisions should be a hallmark of both Tier 2 and Tier 3 intervention settings. We recommend measuring progress every 3–4 weeks. Evidence suggests that reading struggles are difficult to remediate at the middle school level and progress takes longer (e.g., Vaughn et al., 2011). Therefore, progress monitoring must be timed in such a way to detect changes that take place over a longer period of time.

Let's consider a case study to learn how to use data to make instructional decisions. First, take a look at Amanda Johnson's screening scores (see Figure 4.3). She scored 90 WCPM on the TMSFA ORF measure and 67% on the TMSFA retell measure. Diagnostic assessment uncovered a difficulty decoding multisyllabic words. Therefore, Amanda is placed with a Tier 2 reading intervention teacher who focuses on two things: (1) multisyllabic word reading and (2) ORF. To monitor Amanda's progress, the teacher uses the TMSFA progress monitoring passages. See Figure 4.8 for Amanda's scores over the course of 30 weeks.

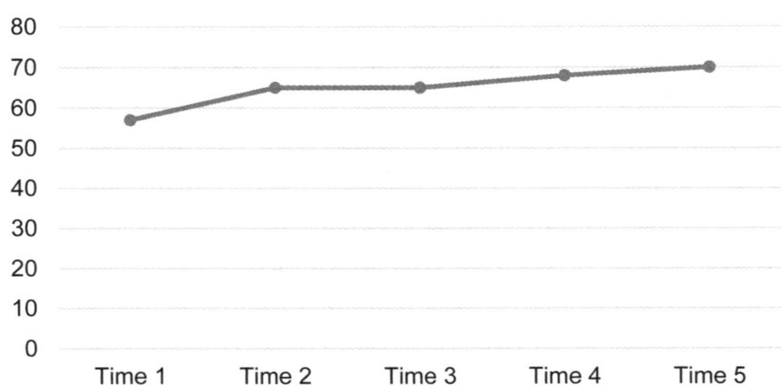

FIGURE 4.7. ORF scores (WCPM) with equated passages.

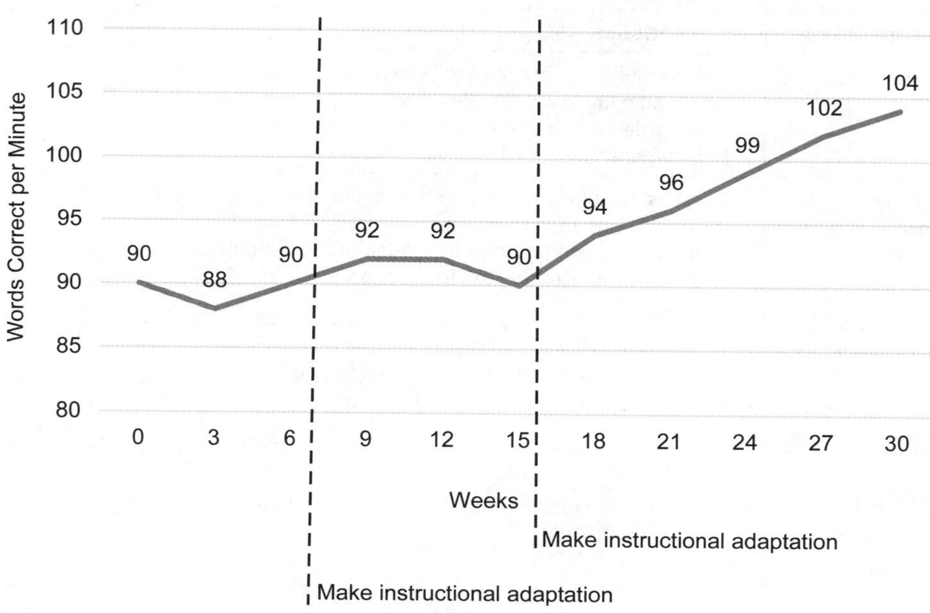

FIGURE 4.8. Student's ORF scores (WCPM) used to inform instructional adaptations.

After 6 weeks of intervention, Amanda's score remains largely unchanged. No gains occur. This signals a need to make an instructional adaptation (for more on instructional adaptations, see Chapter 7). An adaptation is made, and the teacher continues to collect data over three more data points. She realizes that after a small bump, Amanda's score returns to 90 (at week 15). This marks another point at which an instructional adaptation should be made. Notice Amanda's scores after 9 more weeks. She has made some very nice gains. Whatever instructional adaptation was made at week 15 worked. Amanda's scores continue to rise. Collecting data in a systematic way allowed her teacher to identify when teaching techniques worked and when they needed to be adapted, leading to Amanda's success (for more on instructional adaptations, see Chapter 7).

Instructional coaches should ensure that Tier 2 and Tier 3 teachers know (1) what measures to use that match the instructional goal, (2) the frequency with which they should collect data, (3) how to graph data, (4) how to interpret data to identify when instructional adaptations should be made, and (5) what instructional adaptations to try (see Chapter 7).

REVIEW AND PREVIEW

In this chapter, we provided an overview of systematic data collection starting with universal screening. We also explained how to collect diagnostic data for students who

Assessment Type	Characteristics
Universal screening assessments	• Assess skills that are related to reading comprehension. • Brief and easy to administer. • Takes little time to interpret. • Reliable and valid.
Diagnostic assessments	• Administered to students to show signs of reading difficulty on the universal screening measure. • Help teachers understand the cause of the difficulty. • Information is used to plan instruction. • Reliable and valid.
Progress monitoring assessments	• Administered every 3–4 weeks. • Sensitive to changes in students' performance. • Alternative forms are equal in difficulty. • Reliable and valid.

FIGURE 4.9. Characteristics of different types of assessments used at the middle school level. From Hanover Research (2016).

struggle with reading. Finally, we covered how to interpret progress monitoring data to make instructional adaptations so that students receiving intervention support make progress over time. A summary of the key components of each can be found in Figure 4.9. In the next chapter, we will discuss another issue that instructional coaches face—how to support teachers when their students are confronted with highly challenging texts.

Terms to Know

Diagnostic data collection: Collecting data with the purpose of identifying the skill deficiency that is causing the difficulty.

Progress monitoring: Data collection designed to examine students' progress over time so that changes to the intervention can be made if progress is not noted.

Reliable: The test produces the same results time and again. For example, if all is kept equal (e.g., the child doesn't receive any instruction) and you administer the same ORF passage 2 days in a row, the score will be the same (or about the same).

Universal screening: Assessing all students to identify those who are at risk for school difficulty.

Validity: The test actually measures what it claims to measure.

Reflection Questions

1. Reflect on your school's current universal screening procedures. What barriers does your school face?
2. How might the universal screening procedures be adapted at your school so they are more efficient?
3. Why is diagnostic assessment so important, and what improvements need to be made on your campus?
4. What training do Tier 2 and Tier 3 teachers need at your school in order to collect and examine progress monitoring data in a way that informs instructional adaptations?

CHAPTER 5

Challenges in Choosing Text for Intensive Instruction

Choosing text for adolescents isn't always easy. Teachers often try to accommodate adolescent's interests, choose texts that are motivating to students (e.g., magazines or comic books), and comply with the requirements of content-area curriculum. In this chapter, we provide instructional coaches with resources to use with teachers when guiding them to choose appropriate text for use in their classrooms. First, we share a simple measure for gauging student reading interests. Second, we discuss how adolescents' attitudes influence the type of text teachers choose. Finally, we provide teachers with some guidance on selecting text at appropriate levels of difficulty and complexity (Swanson & Wexler, 2017).

ADOLESCENTS' READING HABITS

Teachers may want to know more about adolescents' out-of-school reading habits to motivate their text reading during school hours. In 2007, a team of researchers (Hughes-Hassell & Rodge, 2007) surveyed 584 middle school students to learn more about their reading habits outside of school. Seventy-two percent of respondents said they read as a leisure activity, and 22% said they read only for school. In addition, as students move through grades 6–8, their attitude about digital and recreational print worsens, while their attitude about academic print-based text remains steady (McKenna, Conradi, Lawrence, Jang, & Meyer, 2012). When they do read recreationally, they most often read magazines, comic books, and sources from the Internet. Another group of researchers (Gabriel, Allington, & Billen, 2012) who interviewed middle school students explained that magazine reading can actually be rich in nature and noted that students could easily flip to a "page they would like to read" (p. 188). Students offered their own opinions of magazine content and why their opinion differed from the article writers. They also made inferences about the text based on what they observed in its images, which were frequently cited as a reason to "stop flipping" and read an article. Including text sources that are similar to those students are naturally drawn to may serve to increase motivation to read in school.

Figure 5.1 presents a short survey that students can complete in less than 10 minutes. This survey provides information about the types of materials students like to read, the fictional genres they enjoy, and the nonfiction text types that most appeal to them. Teachers may have students in their classes who do not read very often. In that case, there are questions related to movie genres, video games, and TV shows. The survey also asks questions with regard to how students learn about new reading materials. This information can be helpful when trying to inspire adolescents to read. For example, if most students in a class report that they follow recommendations from friends, the teacher may want to form a list of peer book recommendations. The information this survey provides is especially helpful when guiding the reluctant reader who may generally dislike reading and believe that there is nothing of interest for him in the library. Prior to a visit to the library, the teacher might meet briefly with the student and say something like, "I really want you to choose a book today that is interesting to you. I see on your reading survey that you play sports video games. Go to section Z of the library and you can find all kinds of video game playing guides. I'll bet you find one you like. Later today, show me what you found."

ADOLESCENTS' ATTITUDES ABOUT READING

Understanding information about student attitudes toward reading is also valuable. Several factors influence adolescents' reading habits, including their own identity as a reader (Hall, 2012; Henk, Marinak, & Melnick, 2012), their sense of independence in choosing what to read (Ivey & Broaddus, 2001), whether their friends and family read (Klauda, 2009), and whether they value reading (Guthrie & Coddington, 2009; Pitcher et al., 2007). Teachers may wonder how to gather information about students' reading attitudes and how to use that information when choosing texts. In 2013, Conradi and colleagues published a measure called Survey of Adolescent Reading Attitudes (SARA; Conradi, Jang, Bryant, Craft, & McKenna, 2013). Four different constructs are assessed in the survey: (1) attitude toward academic reading of print, (2) attitude toward academic reading in digital settings, (3) attitude toward recreational reading of print materials, and (4) attitude toward recreational reading in digital settings.

Teachers can use information from the SARA in two ways. First, teachers may be interested in student responses to single items. For example, you might be planning a research project where students will look up information to read online. You may choose to ask question 16 from the measure: "How do you feel about looking up information

1. What kinds of reading materials do you like? Mark all that apply.

- ☐ Magazines
- ☐ Newspapers
- ☐ Poetry
- ☐ Online magazines
- ☐ Novels
- ☐ Blogs
- ☐ Plays
- ☐ Informational books
- ☐ Biographies and autobiographies
- ☐ Online articles

2. When you choose to read a work of fiction, what types of stories do you like? Mark all that apply.

- ☐ Adventure and survival
- ☐ Mystery and suspense
- ☐ Romance and relationships
- ☐ Graphic novels
- ☐ Historical fiction
- ☐ Science fiction
- ☐ Realistic fiction
- ☐ Humor
- ☐ Fantasy
- ☐ Poetry
- ☐ Horror

3. What types and subjects of movies, TV shows, and video games do you like? Mark all that apply.

- ☐ Adventure and survival
- ☐ Mystery and suspense
- ☐ Romance and relationships
- ☐ Biography and autobiography
- ☐ Technology
- ☐ Historical fiction
- ☐ Science fiction
- ☐ Realistic fiction
- ☐ Humor
- ☐ Fantasy
- ☐ Science
- ☐ Horror
- ☐ History
- ☐ True crime
- ☐ Sports
- ☐ Politics
- ☐ War

4. When you choose to read nonfiction text, what do you like to read about? Mark all that apply.

- ☐ Biography or autobiography
- ☐ Health, wellness, or fitness
- ☐ Politics
- ☐ Other:
- ☐ True crime
- ☐ Technology
- ☐ War
- ☐ Science
- ☐ Art
- ☐ History
- ☐ Sports
- ☐ Religion
- ☐ Music

5. Whose recommendation would you follow when looking for a good book? Mark all that apply.

- ☐ Friend
- ☐ Other family member:
- ☐ Other person:
- ☐ Teacher
- ☐ Librarian
- ☐ Parent

(continued)

FIGURE 5.1. PACT Plus reading interest survey. This work was supported by the USDOE through Grant No. H326M150016 to The University of Texas at Austin and the University of Maryland. The opinions expressed are those of the authors and do not represent the views of the USDOE (Meadows Center for Preventing Educational Risk, 2018). Reprinted in *Literacy Coaching in the Secondary Grades: Helping Teachers Meet the Needs of All Students* by Jade Wexler, Elizabeth Swanson, and Alexandra Shelton (The Guilford Press, 2021). Permission to photocopy this material is granted to purchasers of this book for personal use or use with students (see copyright page for details). Purchasers can download enlarged versions of this material (see the box at the end of the table of contents).

6. Other than recommendations from others, how do you find good material to read? Mark all that apply.

   ☐ Browsing in a bookstore
   ☐ Browsing in a library
   ☐ Looking in an online catalog
   ☐ Surfing the Web
   ☐ Other:

7. What is the best book you ever read?

   Why did you like it?

8. What are your three favorite...

MOVIES	TV SHOWS

9. In your free time, what do you most like to do? Write three things.

Thank you for completing this survey!

FIGURE 5.1. *(continued)*

online for a class?" It would be rather easy to print one question on a slip of paper and hand it to students as they walk in or as an "exit ticket" before they leave. Then, thumb through the responses to learn more about students' attitudes toward the reading task you have planned. If attitudes are high, you'll be ready to use the text source. If they tend toward the low end, you might want to find out why students feel badly about the text reading task. Do they lack a certain skill (e.g., how to use a search engine) that you might preteach prior to your lesson? Are the low scores due to overall reading difficulty, in which case you might choose an easier-to-read text format?

A second way you may use the SARA is to administer the entire measure to learn more about students' general feelings on text reading. You might find that a majority of your students feel "bad" about reading text in class. When scores are low, we suggest reviewing the trends in answers to create a plan for addressing students' attitudes about reading. You may ask a few students to share the reasons for their low scores. It could be that many students in your class struggle with reading grade-level text. It might be that no one has ever taught them how to use a dictionary or encyclopedia. If students show a more positive attitude toward reading newspapers or magazines, consider requesting funds (or raising funds) for one of the many content-area resources published in newspaper or magazine format. Both the Reading Interest Survey (Meadows Center for Preventing Educational Risk [MCPER], 2018) and the SARA (Conradi et al., 2013) are designed to provide teachers with clues that they can use to identify text that is interesting and motivating to students. They also help teachers identify ways in which they might intervene when skill deficits are evident. Another guide for choosing appropriate text is included in the Common Core State Standards (CCSS; NGACBP & CCSSO, 2010a).

USING THE CCSS GUIDELINES TO CHOOSE TEXT

Teachers are encouraged by the CCSS to consider three sources of data: (1) **quantitative information**, (2) **qualitative information**, and (3) information about the students and the task. We wrote an article entitled "Selecting Appropriate Text for Adolescents with Disabilities" that shows teachers how to use the CCSS guidelines for text selection in their classrooms (Swanson & Wexler, 2017). Although the title indicates that the article is focused on students with disabilities, the practices and procedures can be used when selecting text for any adolescent. The guidance provided in that article is summarized below.

Use Quantitative Information

Quantitative information includes aspects—such as word length, sentence length, and text cohesion—that are most easily measured by computer software. The CCSS guidelines suggest using **Lexile** levels to quantitatively evaluate text (NGACBP & CCSSO, 2010c) and provide bands of Lexile difficulty for each grade level (see Figure 5.2). There are other text difficulty scales (e.g., Flesch–Kinkaid), but the authors of the CCSS recommend using Lexile levels because they are easy to calculate and interpret. Lexile

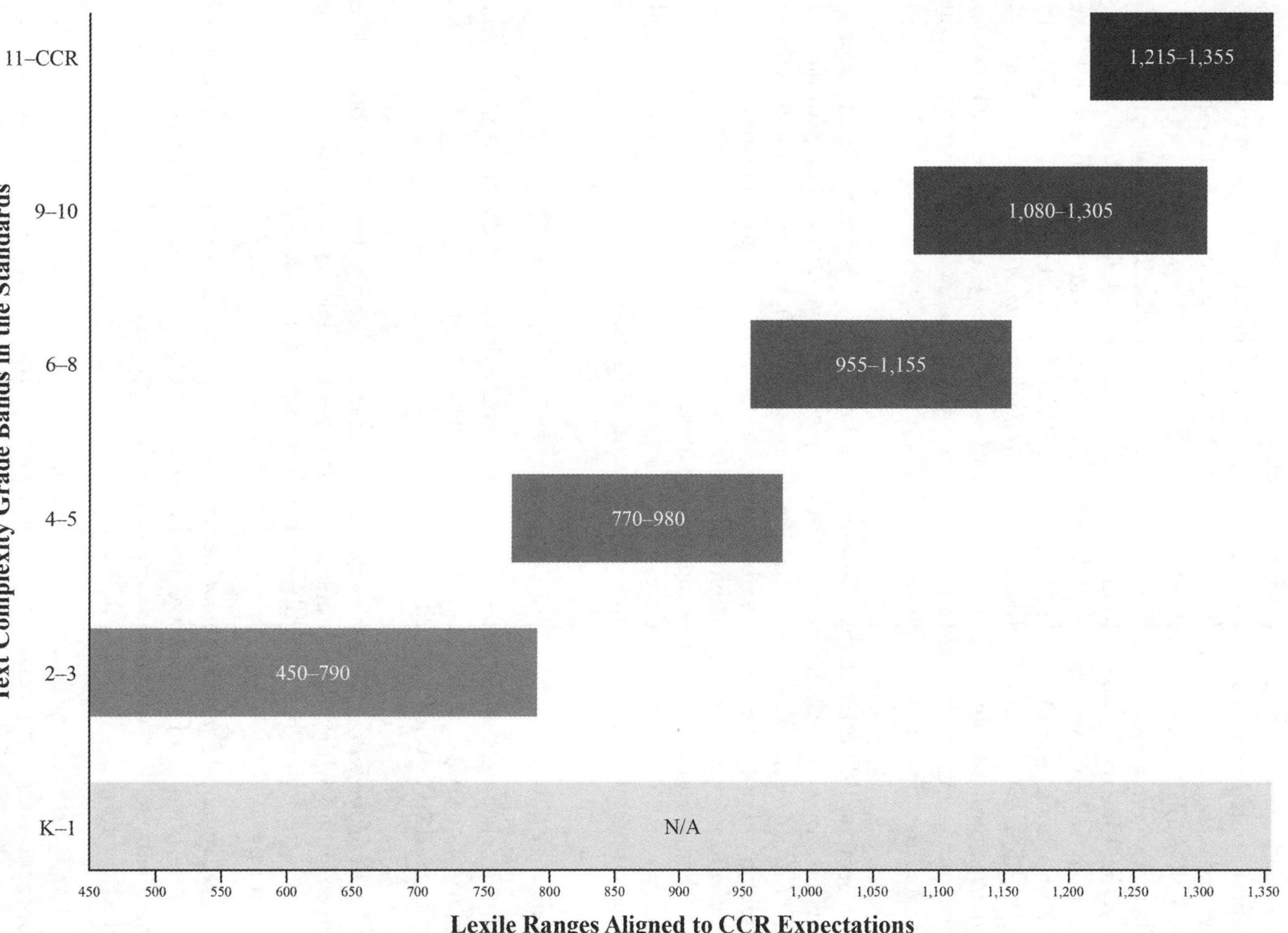

FIGURE 5.2. Lexile ranges aligned to CCSS expectations.

bands can be used by teachers to approximate the level of difficulty that should be targeted for students at each grade level. However, if a teacher finds that a text within the grade-appropriate Lexile band is too difficult, authors of the CCSS suggest moving into the lower adjacent Lexile band with the goal of moving up in Lexile level as quickly as possible (NGACBP & CCSSO, 2010b).

There are several online resources teachers can use to identify Lexile levels of published works. One of the easiest to use is the Lexile Framework for Reading: Matching Readers with Texts website (*www.lexile.com*). Here, teachers can type into a search box the title of a book and obtain the Lexile score. In addition, teachers may register to use the Lexile Analyzer free of charge (*https://hub.lexile.com/analyzer*). This tool allows teachers to submit files in Plain Text (.txt) format and receive a Lexile level. It is useful when measuring the Lexile levels of text excerpts, primary documents (e.g., legal documents, historical essays, historical letters), and original works (e.g., online essays or articles).

Teachers should be aware that current quantitative measures, such as Lexile scores, often underestimate the challenge posed by complex narrative fiction. For example, the novel *To Kill a Mockingbird* (Lee, 1982) is at Lexile level 790, which is in the fourth- to fifth-grade band of Lexile ranges established by the CCSS. The common language used in *To Kill a Mockingbird* is responsible for the low Lexile level. However, because of the complex themes in the book, it would not be advisable to assign *To Kill a Mockingbird* to elementary school students. For reasons such as this, the CCSS authors recommend also considering qualitative information when choosing texts.

Use Qualitative Information

Here, the teacher uses professional judgment to make informed decisions about text complexity. The CCSS authors describe several elements that make texts easy or challenging to read (NGACBP & CCSSO, 2010c).

- *Levels of meaning (literary texts):* Low-complexity literary texts have one single level of meaning, while high-complexity texts have multiple levels of meaning. One example of a text that has multiple levels of meaning is a satire, where there is both literal and figurative meaning.

- *Levels of purpose (informational texts):* Low-complexity informational text **explicitly** states the purpose of the passage. At the other end of the spectrum, high-complexity informational text has a more obscure or **implicit** purpose that is hidden somewhat from the reader.

- *Text structure:* Low-complexity structure is simple and conventional. Graphics are simple and either unnecessary or **supplementary**. Text structure in high-complexity text may make use of flashbacks, flash forwards, or other manipulations of time and sequence. Graphics are more complex, are essential to understanding the text, and may also provide an independent source of information.

• *Language conventionality and clarity:* Low-complexity text uses literal, clear, contemporary, conversational language. High-complexity text uses language that is figurative, ironic, ambiguous, purposefully misleading, archaic, or unfamiliar. It may include general academic or domain-specific vocabulary.

• *Knowledge demands:* Authors of low-complexity texts make few assumptions about the extent of students' background knowledge (cultural, literary, or discipline-specific). Little background knowledge is needed to read these texts with understanding. High-complexity texts require background knowledge of a cultural, literary, or discipline-specific nature.

Texts used in any grade level range in qualitative complexity. For example, in grade 1, the commonly known story *Frog and Toad Are Friends* (Lobel, 1970) is about two friends. The theme is very straightforward and little inference is necessary. However, consider another popular book, *The Giving Tree* (Silverstein, 1964). Although children may be able to read the words easily, the themes in *The Giving Tree* related to love, generosity, and comfort are complex. Again, no matter the quantitative complexity of a text, teachers should consider qualitative information when deciding if a text is adequately complex for use in a lesson or whether students might require additional support from a special educator to meet instructional goals. Even with quantitative and qualitative information about a given text, teachers must finally decide if it is appropriate for their students. This is where Step 3 is useful—considering the student and the task.

Consider Student Characteristics and the Task

The goal here is to choose a text level that is challenging to students but not frustrating, and is matched to the purpose of the reading assignment. Several sources of information should be used during this step. The RAND Reading Study Group (2002) identified several student-level factors that affect comprehension, including reading fluency, cognitive abilities (e.g., attention, memory, critical analytic ability, inference-making ability, visualization ability), knowledge (e.g., vocabulary knowledge, background knowledge, knowledge of how discourse works, knowledge of comprehension strategies), and prior experiences. It also named important variables related to the task of reading: the type of reading (e.g., skimming or studying) and intended outcomes (e.g., increase in knowledge, solution to a real-world problem, or entertainment).

Consider, for example, the student-level factor of ORF:

• What is the student's fluency score when reading text within the required Lexile band for the grade level? If fluency is too low to facilitate reading comprehension, in what Lexile band does the student have sufficient fluency to facilitate reading comprehension? If there is a text that meets the same instructional purpose but is written at a lower Lexile level, use it with the intention of working toward assigning more complex text.

In another example, consider students' background knowledge:

- Is this the first time a student will be exposed to a topic? If so, the teacher may need to provide some background knowledge-building instruction prior to reading. In this way, students may access more complex text.

- Is the reading set during a specific historical time, and is unique vocabulary used? Instead of decreasing the reading demand by choosing a simpler text, preteach vocabulary that is necessary to understanding the text.

Consider also the purpose of the reading assignment:

- Is this assignment for independent or supported reading? Assignments for independent reading may need to be at the lower end of a Lexile band to match students' reading ability.

- Will intensive teacher support be available? Assignments that allow for intensive teacher support may permit the use of text at the higher end of a Lexile band.

An Example Using the CCSS Guidance for Text Selection

In Figure 5.3, we provide a summary of quantitative information, qualitative information, and consideration of student characteristics used to determine the work's text complexity. We read the young adult historical fiction called *Five 4ths of July* by Pat Hughes (2011) and considered the quantitative measure of Lexile level, qualitative measures, and reader–task considerations.

Systematically using all of these suggestions to make decisions about text selections can seem overwhelming. However, providing all students with access to the content through text reading requires not only literacy support but also careful selection of high-quality texts that are well matched to student needs and requirements of the assignment. Although the task is complex, the process need not be cumbersome. Our description of CCSS text selection guidelines is coupled with a way for teachers to systematically apply these guidelines to choosing effective texts or evaluating texts for student support needs. Providing teachers with practical assistance in this complex task is important to make text selection choices that are appropriate for all students in a way that aligns with the CCSS.

REVIEW AND PREVIEW

In this chapter, we shared several resources that instructional coaches can share with teachers as they choose text for students to read in class. We also shared resources that can help students choose their own recreational text. In the next chapter, we will dive into evidence-based content-area literacy practices, providing not only a review of research but also several sets of instructional materials for instructional coaches that may be used in secondary content-area classes.

<table>
<tr><th>Qualitative Measures</th><th>Quantitative Measures</th></tr>
<tr><td rowspan="5">Levels of Meaning
The level of meaning is relatively literal throughout the book. There is some requirement to interpret characters' motives and actions, but most of these are explained in the book.

Structure
The events are told in chronological order.

Language Conventionality and Clarity
The language used is generally familiar. It is conversational with a good deal of extended dialogue that requires readers to remember who is talking. This may be a challenge to some readers. There is also historically significant vocabulary that may not be familiar to students (e.g., musket, fort, Red Coat). The author describes settings, but imagery is necessary to fully understand the events in the book.

Knowledge Demands
The themes are somewhat sophisticated, and characters' perspectives may be different from those of students. Knowledge of the Revolutionary War is helpful. Some knowledge of the geography on the East Coast of the United States would be helpful but not absolutely necessary.</td><td>The Lexile level of Five 4ths of July is 880, placing it within the grades 4–5 text complexity band. While sentence length is relatively long (average of 14 words per sentence), the syntax is relatively uncomplicated.</td></tr>
<tr><td>Reader–Task Considerations</td></tr>
<tr><td>Each teacher, while thinking about his or her group of students, should determine reader–task consideration. Consider students' motivation, knowledge, and experiences. Consider the purpose for reading the book and whether students are able to answer the types of questions necessary to achieve the target purpose.</td></tr>
<tr><td>Recommended Placement</td></tr>
<tr><td>While the Lexile Analyzer indicates this novel is relatively "easy" (grade 4–5), the novel conveys a sophisticated theme and content related to war. There are scenes conveying violence that make it more suitable for middle school (grades 7–8). In this case, qualitative measures have overruled the quantitative measures.</td></tr>
</table>

FIGURE 5.3. Summary of information to determine text complexity of *Five 4ths of July*.

Terms to Know

Explicit: Fully and clearly expressed or demonstrated, leaving nothing implied.

Implicit: Implied, rather than expressly stated.

Lexile: A numeric representation of a text's difficulty.

Qualitative information: Information about a text selection that requires professional judgment, such as text complexity, level of meaning, and text structure.

Quantitative information: Information about a text selection that can be counted, such as word length and sentence length.

Supplementary: Additional.

Reflection Questions

1. How might knowing students' reading habits help a teacher encourage text reading outside of school?
2. How can teachers use information gathered from the SARA to plan for text reading in the classroom?
3. Can you explain this statement from Swanson and Wexler (2017): "One of the most efficient ways of learning essential content in the curriculum is through reading" (p. 161)?
4. How can the instructional coach encourage teachers to engage students in more text reading in content-area classes?

CHAPTER 6

Features of Effective Instruction

If you perform an online search for "components of effective instruction," you will see more than 800,000 results naming a wide variety of components, leaving many wondering, "What components of effective instruction really impact student outcomes?" In this chapter, we provide a model for **intentional learning** (see Figure 6.1) that contains six components of effective instruction and can be used in any subject area to impact student outcomes. Instructional coaches can help teachers enhance student learning by incorporating these components of effective instruction into their lessons.

THE RESEARCH EVIDENCE

In a meta-analysis of 37 studies, Adams and Engelman (1996) reported that instruction including these six components had a large effect on outcomes for students with disabilities (d = 0.76), students without disabilities (d = 1.27), younger students (d = 0.87), and older students (d = 1.50). These large effects were also detected across subject areas:

- Reading d = 0.69
- Social studies d = 0.97
- Math d = 1.11
- Spelling d = 1.33
- Science d = 2.44

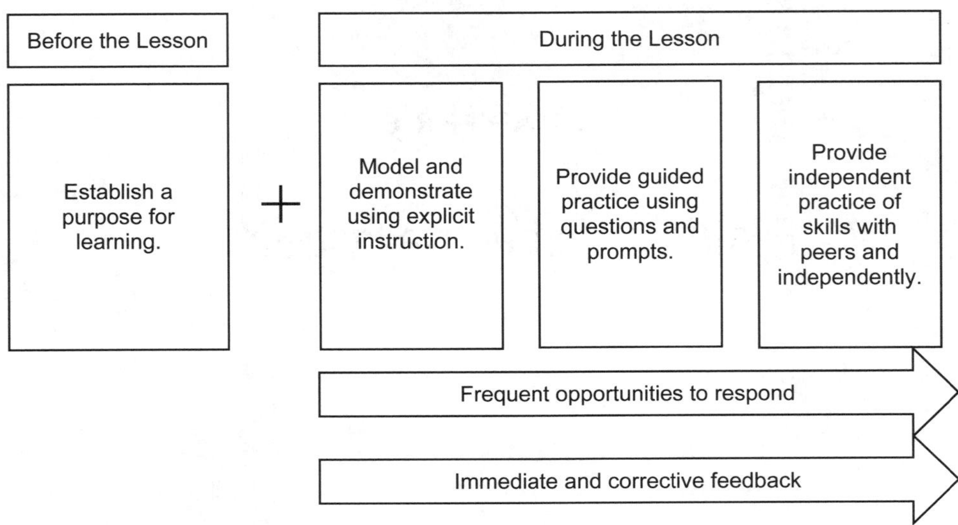

FIGURE 6.1. Evidence-based model for intentional learning.

In another meta-analysis by Alfieri and colleagues (Alfieri, Brooks, Addrich, & Tenenbaum, 2001), teaching approaches using these six components outperformed discovery-based approaches with a medium **effect size** of $d = 0.39$. When you compare these effects to the relatively small effects of problem-based learning ($d = 0.15$; Hattie, 2009), you see that including the six components of effective instruction in your daily classroom routines can really impact student learning outcomes.

UNPACKING THE MODEL FOR INTENTIONAL LEARNING

Before the Lesson: Establish a Purpose for Learning

What do you want 100% of your students to learn today? The answer to this question is your purpose for learning. Start by considering a state curriculum standard, national curriculum standard, or a specific objective. Then, enrich it even further to identify a purpose for learning that all of the students in your class will achieve by the end of the lesson. For example, the state-described objective may be to "identify the life cycle of a frog," but your purpose for learning can be richer than that. Consider making this the purpose: "Students will use signal words when explaining the life cycle of a frog to another person." In Table 6.1, find additional curriculum standards and enriched purposes for learning.

Now that you've identified a purpose for learning, it's important to communicate that information to students in a way that they can understand. This requires teachers to go beyond posting objectives in their classroom, writing them into their lesson plan

TABLE 6.1. Enriching the Purpose for Learning

Curriculum standard	Enriched purposes for learning
Compare and contrast potential and kinetic energy (middle school science).	Describe two ways in which potential and kinetic energy are alike and two ways they are different.
Classify rocks as metamorphic, igneous, or sedimentary by the processes of their formation (middle school science).	Draw a picture showing the process of formation for sedimentary rocks.
Explain the reasons for the growth of representative government and institutions during the Colonial period (middle school U.S. history).	Tell a partner two reasons more and more people agreed with the concept of representative government during the Colonial period.
Explain the causes of the European expansion from 1450 to 1750 (high school world history)	Choose the most influential reason for European expansion and provide text evidence.

books, and simply reading the curriculum standard to students. Instead, setting the purpose for learning should spark interest and provide a goal that all students can strive to attain. For example, a teacher might say something like, "Today, I will teach you about the life cycle of a frog. At the end of our lesson, you are going to use words like *first, second,* and *last* to tell your friend about how it grows from a tadpole into a frog. I'll teach you how!" In Table 6.2, we take the enriched purposes for learning and show you how to present them using student-friendly language.

TABLE 6.2. Communicating Enriched Purposes for Learning to Students

Enriched purposes for learning	What to say to students
Reveal two ways in which potential and kinetic energy are alike and two ways they are different.	"By the end of today's experiment, I want you to be able to tell your lab partner two ways that potential and kinetic energy are alike and two ways that potential and kinetic energy are different."
Draw a picture showing the process of formation for sedimentary rocks.	"Today, we are going to read about sedimentary rocks. We are also going to investigate them in a lab. By the end of the lesson, I want you to draw me a picture of the process by which sedimentary rocks are formed."
Give a partner two reasons why more and more people agreed to representative government during the American Colonial period.	"We've been learning about the newly formed U.S. colonies. Today, I will teach you more about what a representative government really is. Your job, by the end of this lesson, will be to tell your partner two reasons that more and more people during Colonial times agreed with the idea of a representative government."
Choose the most influential reason for European expansion and provide text evidence.	"We have spent a lot of time reading about and discussing the causes of European expansion. Today, I'm going to give you six cards that each list a reason. I want your team to identify the most influential cause for European expansion and provide text evidence to support your choice."

During the Lesson

There are five components of intentional learning that may take place during a lesson. When introducing a skill for the first time, teachers should model the skill carefully. Practice comes in the form of guided practice or independent practice. Two components run throughout all of these lesson types. They provide frequent opportunities to respond and immediate and corrective feedback. Each of these components is discussed below.

Model and Demonstrate

Modeling new skills in a step-by-step fashion is critical to **mastery**. At the most basic level, you are showing students what they are supposed to do. This is accomplished through two simultaneous actions (Archer & Hughes, 2011):

1. Demonstrate the skill: Show students how to complete the task.
2. Describe what is being done: Expose students to your thinking (i.e., a **think-aloud**) as you engage in the skill. This illustrates for them the decisions you make as the problem is being solved or the task is being completed.

Figure 6.2 provides an example from a lesson that we developed to show teachers how to model Get the Gist with middle school students. Get the Gist is a strategy used by students to identify the main idea of a section of text that includes three steps: (1) Identify the most important "who" or "what" in the section; (2) identify the most important information about the "who" or "what"; (3) write a short, complete sentence containing that information. Notice how the teacher demonstrates the skills and describes what she is doing as she uses the strategy. Within the sample in Figure 6.2, we pick up after the teacher introduces the lesson and begins to engage in modeling.

The key to a high-quality think-aloud during modeling is clarity. Being clear and concise means that students will more likely remember the steps to the new skill. Use as few words as possible and avoid straying away from your modeling exercise. Also, keep your wording consistent. Notice how in the example above, the teacher always uses the same language to describe the three steps (i.e., the most important "who" or "what"; the most important information about the "who" or "what"; a short complete sentence). In the following example, the teacher models how to spell out the word *disappointment* using a multisyllabic strategy. She uses concise, consistent language.

> "We have been learning about prefixes and suffixes. Today, I'm going to show you how to use that knowledge to spell multisyllabic words. Step 1: Hold up your hand and put a finger up for every syllable you hear. Step 2: Spell each syllable. Step 3: Check the word. Let's try disappointment. Step 1: I'm going to hold up my hand and put up a finger as a say the word *disappointment.* Four syllables. Step 2: Now, let's start with the first syllable and spell it: *dis*. This is a prefix that we know how to spell. Write it down. Next syllable: *ap*. I can sound it out and write the letters: *a, p*.

Next, *point*. I can sound it out and write the letters: *p, oi, n, t*. Last syllable: *ment*. That is a suffix that we know how to spell. Write it down. Okay, we have written the word *disappointment*. Let's check it. Read the word slowly and check that what you are saying matches what is written on the page. *dis-ap-point-ment*."

In this model, the teacher's language is concise and consistent. The three steps needed to spell a word are **explicitly** stated, then during the think-aloud, the teacher uses the same language over and again.

Let me show you how Get the Gist works. Follow along as I read the first paragraph about Mahatma Gandhi.

[Read the following paragraph.]

> Mahatma Gandhi was born on October 2, 1869, in Porbandar, Gujarat, India. His name was actually Mohandas Karamchand Gandhi, but he is known by the title Mahatma, which means "great soul." He went to college in London, England, to become a lawyer. After graduation, he moved to South Africa, where he worked to help the laborers from India who lived there. He lived his life with two goals: to set India free from England's rule, and to free Indians everywhere from prejudice.

A lot of information is in this paragraph. Let's see whether we can write a gist statement. The first step is to identify the most important "who" or "what." I think the most important "who" is Gandhi, because many of the ideas in the paragraph are about Gandhi.

[Write *Gandhi* on the board.]

The second part of Get the Gist is to write the most important thing about the "who" or the "what." I am going to make a list of all the important information in this paragraph about Gandhi.

1. **He was from India.**
2. **He was a lawyer.**
3. **He fought against injustice toward Indians.**

I made a list of important things about Gandhi, but for a gist, we need only the most important information. I think the most important information about Gandhi in this section is that he was a lawyer who fought against injustice toward Indians.

Now, I'm going to write a gist statement. A *gist* is a short complete sentence. The idea is to write a gist that is about 10 words long.

[Write *Gandhi was a lawyer who fought against injustice toward Indians.*]

Let's check our gist statement.

[Read and discuss the following questions.]

- **Does it name the most important "who" or "what"?**
- **Does it tell the most important information about the "who" or "what"?**
- **Is it a short, complete sentence?**

FIGURE 6.2. Modeling the Get the Gist comprehension strategy. Mahatma Gandhi passage from Shannon (2019).

In the following non-example, the teacher models how to spell out the word *disappointment* using the same multisyllabic strategy, but she gets off task and forgets to describe what is being done.

> "Today we're going to spell some words using our multisyllabic strategy. Our word is *disappointment*. I'm going to hold up my hand to count, say, the syllables. Remember that syllables are the beats or sections in the word. How many syllables are in disappointment? [Four.] Yes, four syllables. Okay, let's take that first syllable: *dis*. That's a prefix you know. Let's spell that first. Now what's next? *ap*. Yes. That is not a prefix or suffix, but you can sound that out. *a . . . p*. The next syllable is *point*. Let's spell that. Then we hear a suffix that we know: *ment*. So let's write that. Let's check it. Look and read: *disappointment*."

In this modeling non-example, the teacher gets off topic when she starts to talk about what syllables are and how many are in the target word. The teacher also doesn't clearly express the steps to writing a word. It is a little confusing to us. Imagine expecting a middle schooler to follow along.

A question we hear frequently is "How many times should I model the practice?" We acknowledge that it may be tempting to model a new skill once or twice and expect students to use that skill with proficiency. Depending on the complexity of the skill, model it as many times as needed with different reading passages, different lengths of text, and different subjects. More complex skills will require more modeling. Encouraging students to generalize a skill requires teachers to model its use in different settings and different scenarios. After a good deal of modeling, and as soon as students demonstrate understanding of the skill, move on to **guided practice**.

Provide Guided Practice

Now it's time for students to try the skill with your support. At first, this may mean providing a high level of support, but as time goes on and students begin to succeed in the skill, these supports should fade. Support can take the form of questions and prompts. The key here is to allow students to do all of the work but with your questions and prompts leading the way. As they begin to better understand the skill, you can pull back on these questions and prompts. Figure 6.3 offers an example of guided practice from Collaborative Strategic Reading Get the Gist strategy instruction.

Notice how the teacher still guides the lesson. She asks key questions using consistent language throughout so that students can memorize the steps to the skill. Students are doing all of the work, but the teacher is asking questions and giving prompts to guide them. As time goes on in guided practice, the teacher asks fewer questions and provides fewer prompts and increasingly turns the task over to the students. One way to scaffold this shift in responsibility is to distribute carefully designed practice pages that students can use to engage in the skill without as much teacher support. Instead, the support is built into a student learning log (Figure 6.4). Notice that the log includes

Let's practice Get the Gist together. Let's read the next paragraph.

> Gandhi spent years of his life in jail. Whenever he heard his followers were acting violently, he stopped eating. The hunger strikes worked. Not only did his followers stop using violence, but England also made concessions because they knew how important Gandhi was to the people of India. In 1947, England granted freedom to India.

What is the first step in Get the Gist?

[Identify the most important "who" or "what" in the section.]

Turn to your partner and tell him who or what this section is mostly about. [Gandhi.]

Raise your hand if you can tell me who or what this section is mostly about. [Gandhi.]

What is the second step in Get the Gist?

[Identify the most important thing about the "who" or "what."]

Let's list the most important things about Gandhi from this section.

[Write students' ideas on the chalkboard. Help students decide which of those ideas are most important. Possible ideas include the following.]

1. Gandhi spent a lot of time in jail.
2. He went on a hunger strike whenever his followers became violent.
3. Nonviolent resistance contributed to England's decision to free India.

Now, let's write a short complete sentence that contains the most important "who" or "what" and the most important thing about the "who" or "what." I will give you 2 minutes to come up with a sentence.

[After students write their gists, have some share their gists with the whole group. *Possible gist:* Gandhi convinced his followers to use nonviolent resistance, which led to India's freedom from England.]

FIGURE 6.3. Guided practice for the Get the Gist comprehension strategy. Mahatma Gandhi passage from Shannon (2019).

the same language used by the teacher during modeling and earlier stages of guided practice. Logs like these continue to provide supports for students who are not quite ready to engage in the practice independently.

We encourage teachers to engage in guided practice for quite some time until students are well able to complete the task or skill with ease. Move from (1) asking lots of guiding questions and providing many prompts to (2) providing the prompts on a learning log, and then (3) providing fewer prompts until you are confident students can perform the task on their own. Then, it is time to move into the final phase of intentional learning: independent practice.

Provide Independent Practice of Skills

After you have modeled the skill many times and after students have engaged in guided practice with your questions and prompts for another length of time, it is finally

Date: ________________

Studies Weekly, Week 7

Lesson 7: American Indian Society

Unit Big Idea	The early civilizations of Texas included Paleoamericans, American Indians, and European settlers.
Vocabulary	product, deflect

Gist 1

Gist Questions

Who or what is this about?________________

What's the most important idea about the main "who" or "what"?

____

Gist Statement

____

____

FIGURE 6.4. Guided practice for the Get the Gist comprehension strategy using a learning log. Copyright © 2015 STRIVE Project. This work was supported by Grant No. R305A150407 awarded to Elizabeth Swanson, Sharon Vaughn, and Greg Roberts at the Meadows Center for Preventing Educational Risk, The University of Texas at Austin, by the Institute of Education Sciences, USDOE. Reprinted by permission.

appropriate for students to practice independently. During this phase of intentional learning, students have an opportunity to try out new skills on their own and you have an opportunity to determine if students have mastered the skill. In the initial phases of independent practice, it is a good idea to practice one problem or task at a time followed by **feedback** from the teacher. This prevents students from making mistakes repeatedly before receiving feedback. Spelling new, short words might sound something like this:

> "Today, you're going to practice spelling some multisyllabic words on your own. Everyone, tell me the first step in spelling a multisyllabic word. [Hold up your hand and put a finger up for each syllable.] Good. Everyone, tell me the second step. [Say each syllable and spell it.] Good. Tell me the third step. [Check the spelling.] Here is our new word: *intolerable*. What is the word? [*Intolerable*.] Spell

intolerable on your paper. [Give students time to write. While they work, monitor their use of the strategy.] Let's check it. [Show students how you say each syllable and write the letters. Allow them to correct their word if needed.]"

As you monitor the use of the skill, provide feedback to students as soon as possible. Imagine walking through the class and noticing a student who did not do the first step for spelling a multisyllabic word (i.e., hold up your hand and put a finger up for each syllable). This is the perfect time to give a short prompt to remind him of the strategy—something like "Remember: syllables, write, check. Let me see your hand up."

Sometimes, teachers allow their students to enter into independent practice and then realize, "Whoa. My students are not quite ready. They can't actually do this skill without my prompting." That's okay! The wonderful thing about using an intentional learning framework is that the teacher may return to any of the prior levels of supports as needed. If most students are not able to perform the skill independently, return to modeling. If many students still need some prompts, return to guided practice. When teachers think flexibly about intentional learning by using modeling, guided practice, and independent practice based on student need, their students benefit greatly.

Frequent Opportunities to Respond

Throughout the modeling, guided practice, and independent practice phases of intentional learning, it is critical that students have frequent opportunities to respond. This is often difficult when there is only one teacher and 20-plus students. In typical classrooms, the teacher asks a question like, "What is the first thing we do when we Get the Gist?" Then, students raise their hands, and the teacher calls on one particular student. The teacher has some idea about who knows the answer, depending on how many hands went up, but in reality, she only knows for sure that one student in the class knows the first step. One way to increase the opportunities to respond is to use a turn-and-talk procedure. This requires teachers to pair students prior to the lesson—for example, those who are sitting side-by-side. Assign one student as "A" and the other student as "B." During the lesson, direct students to turn to their partner to reveal an answer. Using this technique, half of the students in the room are answering the question. The other half are listening to their partners. Every student is engaged. Instruction might sound something like this:

"Today, you're going to practice spelling some multisyllabic words on your own.

"Partner A, tell partner B the first step in spelling words. [Hold up your hand and put a finger up for each syllable.]

"What is the first step, everyone? [Hold up your hand and put a finger up for each syllable.] Good.

"Partner B, tell partner A the second step. [Say each syllable and spell it.]

"What is the second step, everyone? [Say each syllable and spell it.] Good.

"Partner A, tell partner B the last step. [Check the spelling.]

"What is the last step, everyone? [Check the spelling.] Good.

"Here is our new word: *drizzle.* What is the word? [*Drizzle.*] Spell *drizzle* on your paper.

"Let's check it. Look up here while I use the steps to spell *drizzle.* Correct your spelling if you need to do so."

Another way to increase opportunities to respond is to place students in small groups to practice skills. Students are assigned jobs, or roles, described on cue cards that contain prompts for the other students to follow. The Get the Gist strategy lends itself to this type of small-group practice. Refer to the sample job card in Figure 6.5 for a "gist expert." Notice that the job card contains a job description and a script for the gist expert to follow. As you read through the script, notice how the prompts encourage students in the group to actively engage in the Get the Gist strategy. For more cue cards and model lessons for the Get the Gist strategy, see the book *Now We Get It! Boosting Comprehension with Collaborative Strategic Reading* (Klingner, Vaughn, Boardman, & Swanson, 2012).

When engaging students in group work, it is important to use the intentional learning sequence (modeling, guided practice, and independent practice) to teach students

Job Description

The gist expert makes sure that all students in the group write their own gists. The gist expert also leads the group in sharing their gists and discussing the quality of the gists. High-quality gists contain the topic (the most important "who" or "what") and the most important information about the topic. Gists should be about 10 words.

DURING READING

Get the Gist

- What is the most important "who" or "what" in this section?

[Ask students to share.]

- Everyone, think of your own gist and write it in your learning log.

[When everyone is done:]

- Who would like to share their gist?

[Help your group come up with a gist that includes the most important information, leaves out the details, and contains about 10 words.]

FIGURE 6.5. Gist Expert job card.

how to engage in their assigned role. Below is an example of what intentional learning for the gist expert role might entail:

- *Modeling:* Provide the job description. Have students read it. Discuss it. Read the script and practice it with students. Point out the most important behaviors you will be looking for from the gist expert. Provide an example of a "good" gist expert who follows the script and includes everyone in the group. Provide a non-example of a "poor" gist expert who doesn't follow the script or doesn't include everyone in the group.

- *Guided practice:* Have students move into preassigned groups. The teacher begins the lesson and the entire class reads a portion of text. Then, ask the gist expert to provide the first prompt, allow for work or think time, and then stop the class for a check-in that might sound something like this: "Put your thumb up if the gist expert asked you to identify the most important 'who' or 'what.'" Continue the procedure with the remaining gist expert prompts. During this lesson, be sure to circulate around the room to make sure the gist experts are performing their job well.

- *Independent practice:* Have students move into preassigned groups. Practice the Get the Gist strategy and monitor groups closely. Make note of who is a proficient gist expert and who needs assistance. Spotlight a group that is functioning well. Have the spotlight group go through the gist procedure, while the rest of the class watches for specific behaviors (e.g., observing how this gist expert includes everyone in the group.) Stop the group periodically to point out what members are doing well. As a wrap-up, set a goal for the entire class: "For the next section of text, every group will participate. This time, I want your gist expert to focus on having each person in the group answer at least one prompt."

There are other very simple ways to increase student opportunities to respond. See Table 6.3 for more examples.

Immediate and Corrective Feedback

Feedback is a powerful instructional tool that can improve understanding and guide students in mastering skills. In fact, feedback has a more powerful effect on achievement than students' prior ability, socioeconomic status, and homework. It is ranked only slightly below explicit instruction (i.e., intentional instruction) in effect (Center on Instruction, 2008). The goal of providing feedback is to bring students closer to meeting the goal of the lesson. High-quality feedback has several key features:

1. *Feedback is timely.* It should be provided as close in time to the task as possible. This means that while students are writing gist statements, teachers are checking in to provide feedback during the activity. Providing feedback after an activity and far removed from the next time the task is assigned is particularly difficult for struggling secondary readers to remember and apply.

TABLE 6.3. Simple Ways to Increase Opportunities to Respond

Thumbs up, thumbs down	This is perfect for dichotomous answers that only have two possibilities: yes/no; A or B; Option 1 or Option 2
Sign language	Teach students some simple sign language and open up a variety of response opportunities. For example, teach students the letters *a, b, c,* and *d* in sign language. Then, they can answer multiple-choice questions you ask during your lesson. You can glance to see how many students understand the question.
PowerPoint add-ins	Many middle and high school teachers use PowerPoint presentations. Most students have a smartphone or access to a tablet with Internet access. You embed a survey or question into the PowerPoint presentation. Students follow a link and answer the question on their device; their answers then populate on your PowerPoint document in real time. This takes some planning, but it is a lot of fun for you and your students. Some options: • *Polleverywhere.com* • *Mentimeter.com* • *Participoll.com*

2. *Feedback is spoken.* Spoken feedback from the teacher is better than notes on a graded assignment. In fact, students report greater satisfaction when provided with narrative feedback (Ramani & Krackov, 2012). For struggling secondary readers, written feedback is especially difficult to understand and then apply at a later date.

3. *Feedback is specific.* Specific feedback is easier to incorporate into a task. The clearer your feedback is, the better the student will perform upon correction.

4. *Feedback is* **systematic.** Ultimately, the most effective feedback is clearly stated, reinforces what is well done, identifies what can be improved, and then provides a plan for improvement (Griffiths, Luhanga, McEwen, Schultz, & Dalgarno, 2016).

In one study where adolescents were asked what they liked and disliked about feedback they received from their teachers, several themes emerged (Taylor, 2008). Among the themes, students said that feedback made them feel respected in the classroom—that the teacher cared about their success. Students disliked feedback that simply took the form of grading with no explanation, and they consistently said they wanted more feedback. Finally, students were more likely to incorporate feedback when it was immediate or close to the task being completed. Table 6.4 offers some ideas for transforming common teacher phrases into more effective feedback.

REVIEW AND PREVIEW

In this chapter, we covered the components of intentional learning that consist of multiple elements with research evidence for effectiveness when teaching new skills, new

TABLE 6.4. Examples of Effective Feedback

Student action	Non-example	High-quality feedback
Correct: The student writes a gist statement that correctly identifies the main idea in 10 words or less.	"Great work!"	"I like how your gist statement included the 'who' and the most important idea. Nice work!"
Partially correct: Student identifies Christopher Columbus as the "who" in the paragraph, but is unable to identify the most important idea about Christopher Columbus.	"You're almost there, keep working!"	"You identified the correct 'who' of this paragraph—Christopher Columbus. Nice work with Step 1. Try rereading the paragraph to figure out the most important idea."
Incorrect: Student copies a detail sentence from the paragraph	"Try again!"	"You wrote a detail from the paragraph. A gist statement tells about the whole paragraph using your own words. Go back to your gist cue card and follow the steps to help you write a gist statement."

materials, and new tasks. Including these elements when planning lesson sequences is key to effective outcomes for all students, particularly those who struggle in school. In Chapter 7, we will go further and provide a variety of evidence-based literacy practices that can be infused into content-area instruction and supplemental intervention.

Terms to Know

Effect size: A simple way to quantify the difference between groups. Small effects are 0.10 or less; medium effect sizes are around 0.30; large effect sizes are anything larger than 0.50.

Explicit: Fully and clearly expressed or demonstrated, leaving nothing implied.

Feedback: Providing information about the operation or outcome of an action so that subsequent attempts can be altered or corrected.

Guided practice: A time for students to attempt a skill with teacher support.

Intentional learning: Persistent, continual process to acquire, understand, and use a variety of strategies to improve one's ability to attain and apply knowledge.

Mastery: Comprehensive knowledge or skill in a subject or accomplishment.

Systematic: Presenting information in a reasonable, step-by-step order.

Think-aloud: This is a modeling method used by teachers. As they teach students how to engage in a strategy or thought process, they talk about their thinking.

Reflection Questions

1. What are the six components of intentional learning?
2. What two components of intentional learning should be included in every lesson?
3. What is the purpose of modeling?
4. How can you determine when students are ready to move into independent practice?
5. What are two ways to increase opportunities to respond in the secondary classroom?
6. What is the purpose of providing feedback?
7. What are two different things you could say to a student instead of "That's not quite right" that align with the tenets of high-quality feedback?

CHAPTER 7

Evidence-Based Content-Area Literacy Practices to Support Students with Intensive Needs

Caroline is a seventh grader who plays clarinet in the band. She loves art and has won several awards for drawing. She also started struggling with reading in first grade and was diagnosed with a learning disability in second grade. Since then, she received reading intervention services, but at the beginning of sixth grade, she still reads at a fourth-grade level. In middle school, she is assigned to a special education teacher for English language arts (ELA) and participates in the general classroom in math, science, and social studies. The question we face when considering the appropriate education of adolescents with intensive instructional needs is: How can all of the teachers at Caroline's middle school contribute to her growth as a reader and as a learner?

Caroline is not alone. It is estimated that 24% of middle school students struggle with reading to such an extent that they are not able to locate information in a text; identify its main idea, theme, or the authors' purpose; or make simple inferences from the text (USDOE, IES, NCES, NAEP, 2019). For Caroline and almost one-quarter of middle school students, features of effective intensive reading instruction cannot remain isolated in a 1-hour-long special education class. Instead, the general education classroom can provide a solid foundation on which intervention may be built. This requires that high-quality literacy practices must be infused into content areas so that supportive instruction is provided throughout the day. In this chapter, we provide instructional coaches with an explanation of how teachers can apply rigorous instructional practices to the general education content-area classroom and how they may be further intensified for their readers who struggle the most.

Evidence is clear that once students enter middle school, remediating reading deficiencies becomes very difficult (Bloom et al., 2008; Scammacca, Fall, & Roberts, 2015). At the same time, reading requirements increase. Middle school students are expected to read a greater volume of information across multiple subject areas compared to students in upper elementary school (Gajria et al., 2007). In addition, middle school standards emphasize more rigorous forms of **reading comprehension**, including synthesizing information from multiple texts, interpreting authors' point of view, and analyzing authors' arguments for relevance and sufficiency (NGACBP & CCSSO, 2010a).

Academic rigor has become a modern buzzword in education. Not only is it evident in our standards, teachers use the concept to describe their instruction—"The instruction in my class is rigorous"—and many times, it simply means that the work is difficult (Williamson & Blackburn, 2010). Students in these classes complain of "mountains" of homework and brag that they are "ahead of grade level" in the class. Lori Ungemah (2012) has told of her time as a teacher trying to figure out the definition of "rigor." She came to this conclusion:

> I left that year with a vague idea that rigor is pushing the students *just* to the brink of the work being too hard, but not over the brink because then the students would get discouraged and give up, and definitely not under the brink, because—duh—that's not rigorous. Not a very clear working definition.

When rigor is defined by how much can be crammed into a school day, it leads to a belief that rigor is not for everyone—that some students simply cannot keep up with the "rigor" required by "this" school. That may certainly be the case when the definition of rigor is so off-target. Instead, let's define rigor in a way that is helpful to all students; in a way that challenges each middle schooler to stretch in his thinking, apply what he already knows to new learning, and help him think critically at very deep levels (Lynch, 2018). When this is the goal of rigor, then every student can participate in rigorous instruction.

The remainder of this chapter will be spent explaining three components of PACT (Promoting Adolescents' Comprehension of Text), a set of instructional practices designed by researchers and a group of middle and high school teachers. Researchers have tested PACT for efficacy in seven independent randomized control trials and two quasi-experiments. Three of these studies investigated the effects of PACT on struggling readers and students with disabilities. More than 100 teachers and 3,000 students have used the practices so far. A summary of these studies and findings can be found in Figure 7.1. Across studies, students who received the PACT instructional practices consistently outperformed their peers who did not on measures of content knowledge and reading comprehension (Vaughn, Swanson, et al., 2013; Vaughn et al., 2014; Vaughn et al., 2018; Wanzek et al., 2014; Wanzek et al., 2015). Students with disabilities included in these classes also performed well on the same measures (Swanson, Wanzek, et al., 2015; Swanson et al., 2017; Wanzek et al., 2015). Sample lessons and videos of a teacher implementing the lessons may be found at *www.meadowscenter.org/projects/detail/promoting-adolescents-comprehension-of-text-pact.*

Setting and Sample	Efficacy Trial	Content Knowledge	Content Reading Comprehension	Broad Reading Comprehension
In these studies, students in PACT classes received 6 weeks of PACT instructional practices. Students in the comparison classes receive typical social studies instruction that usually consisted of teacher lectures and note-taking.				
All students in the general education classroom	Vaughn, Swanson, et al. (2013)	.17*	.29*	.20*
	Vaughn et al. (2014)	.32* .29* .26*	.02	.01
	Wanzek et al. (2015)	.36* .22* .24*	.02	.04
	Wanzek et al. (2015)	.31*	Not tested	Not tested
	Wanzek et al. (2014)	.19*	Not tested	Not tested
All students in the general education classroom, the vast majority of whom were English learners	Vaughn et al. (2018)	.40*	.20*	.12
Efficacy for students with disabilities in the same classes				
Students with disabilities in the general education classroom	Swanson, Wanzek, et al. (2015)	.26*	.34*	.09
English learners with disabilities in the general education classroom	Wanzek et al. (2015)	.51*	.04*	.02
In the following study, struggling eighth-grade readers were provided with a full year's dose of PACT instructional practices.				
	Swanson et al. (2017)	.35*	.59*	.10

FIGURE 7.1. Summary of PACT studies and findings. An asterisk (*) indicates a statistically significant effect size. This means that the differences between the treatment and comparison groups were not due to chance; instead, they were due to the PACT instructional practices.

Three PACT instructional practices—Comprehension Canopy, Essential Words, and Critical Reading—are presented below, with a focus on how the practices can increase rigor in the content-area classroom. In the second half of the chapter, we discuss how these instructional practices can be intensified for use in the intervention setting.

PACT FOR THE CONTENT-AREA CLASSROOM

Comprehension Canopy

One way to increase rigor in the classroom is to build and access background knowledge in order to enrich learning. The Comprehension Canopy serves this purpose. The purpose of the Comprehension Canopy is to (1) motivate students to learn the coming content, (2) prime existing background knowledge, and (3) build critical background knowledge. It consists of three activities. In the first activity, the teacher introduces the unit of study with a short story or introduction. For an ELA on heritage, the teacher might begin like this:

> "Throughout American history, millions of people from around the world have left their home country for a chance to start a new life in this country—and people continue to come here to this day. People come to the United States for different reasons. The earliest settlers, the Pilgrims, sought religious freedom. More recently, people have come to America for job opportunities. All of these people bring with them their traditions, values and culture. In this unit we will explore the immigrant experience that is the foundation of the United States."

Second, teachers engage students in a motivational springboard activity using a video or compelling image. The goal here is to build interest and background knowledge. Figure 7.2 is used in the springboard example that follows.

Display the springboard image of the melting pot and tell students:

> "For many years, America has been referred to as a melting pot. The term came from a play written in 1908 that showed how immigrants from different nations 'melted' or blended together to become Americans."

Display the springboard image of the salad bowl and tell students:

> "More recently, a metaphor—a salad bowl—has been used to describe America. A salad is made of several ingredients mixed together in a bowl. The ingredients remain separate, but together, they form a salad."

Display the springboard images together and conduct a turn-and-talk session. Tell students:

"With a partner, discuss the two terms *melting pot* and *salad bowl.* How do they differ? How are they the same? Which term do you think best describes the United States today?"

Finally, teachers introduce a comprehension question that overarches the coming unit. An example might be: "How does heritage define us individually and as a nation?" The question cannot be answered after reading one selection or after one lesson. Instead, it guides learning throughout the unit. By its end, students should be able to synthesize information from all of the readings to answer the question.

FIGURE 7.2. Images used in the Comprehension Canopy instructional practice. Copyright © 2015 The Meadows Center for Preventing Educational Risk, The University of Texas at Austin. The PACT and PACT Plus research teams from The University of Texas at Austin, Florida State University, and Texas A&M University developed these materials with funding from the Institute of Education Sciences (No. R305F100013) and Office of Special Education Programs (No. H326M150016).

Essential Words

Another way to increase academic rigor is to improve background and content knowledge through the use of in-depth vocabulary instruction. This moves far beyond the most common type of vocabulary instruction—providing students with definitions (Swanson et al., 2016)—and propels students into a deep understanding of key concepts that are crucial to understanding content-area text. Our team has developed and tested the efficacy of a vocabulary instructional method that is multicomponent in nature. Teachers report that it is feasible to implement and that it improves students' ability to engage in text-based discussion. When it is paired with text-based discussion, the impact is impressive (see Figure 7.1).

Choosing Essential Words

In every content area, there are terms essential to understanding content. Teachers can follow a multistep process to identify these essential words. First, we encourage teachers to review the state or national standards, curriculum maps, and textbooks and make a list of all possible essential words. This process will result in a list that is far too long to allow in-depth examination of each word. Therefore, the second step involves identifying words that are of high utility. These words are (1) critically important to content learning; (2) high frequency, meaning that they show up many times across the year or across grade levels; and/or (3) applicable across subject areas. In Figure 7.3, we show a list of key terms from an eighth-grade U.S. history curriculum. The list is not complete—in fact, the original list was over 100 words long! This

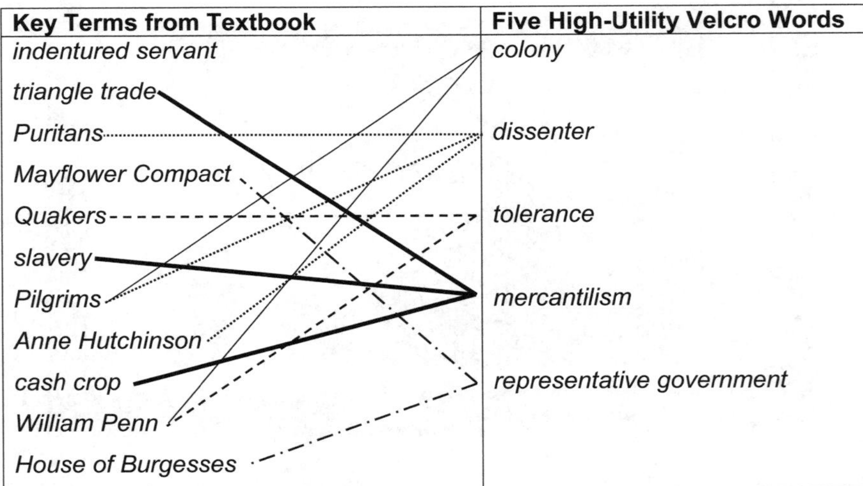

FIGURE 7.3. Key terms and the "high-utility Velcro words" that can be used to teach the terms using the Essential Words instructional practice.

is just a smaller collection of words taught during a unit on Colonial America. We asked teachers to examine this list of words to identify five high-utility Velcro words. These Velcro words enable the connection of related words. Note in Figure 7.3 that several words to the right were pulled aside as Velcro words—*colony, dissenter, tolerance, mercantilism,* and *representative government.* These are fantastic Velcro words since they are critically important to content learning and high frequency. Some are applicable across subject areas (e.g., tolerance). In addition, when a teacher uses the Essential Words routine to teach the term *colony,* she can also teach or review words like *Pilgrims* and *William Penn.* When *mercantilism* is presented, the teacher may also teach *triangle trade, slavery,* and *cash crop.* Identifying a few essential Velcro words maximizes instructional time and increases rigor by deepening one's understanding of vocabulary.

The Instructional Practice

For Essential Words instruction, we find it most helpful for teachers to use a one-page instructional guide like that shown in Figure 7.4. It contains several different components. In this chapter, we will explain how to use the instructional guide to engage students in explicit vocabulary instruction that increases the rigor of content-area lessons. There are seven different short activities on the instructional guide: (1) word, (2) student-friendly definition, (3) examine a visual, (4) related words, (5) example usage, (6) examples and non-examples, and (7) turn and talk.

WORD AND STUDENT-FRIENDLY DEFINITION

These first two activities should be very familiar to all teachers. After all, they represent the most often used instructional technique when teaching new vocabulary (Swanson et al., 2016). Here, the teacher pronounces the word for the students and asks them to repeat the word. It sounds something like this: "The first word is *assimilate.* What word?" Students say, "Assimilate." The teacher continues: "*Assimilate* is a verb meaning that it is a type of action." Next, the teacher reads the definition and underlines key words. At the beginning of implementation, the teacher will want to model how this is done. During the modeling lesson, the teacher's instruction might sound something like this:

> "Read the definition silently as I read it aloud. The definition is 'to adopt the customs, attitudes, and behavior of another culture.' Now, I want to underline key words that will help us remember what *assimilate* means. Remember that *assimilate* is a verb, so let's be sure to underline the action word in the definition: *adopt.* Everyone underline *adopt.* Now, what are they adopting? Mainly customs, so let's underline *customs.* Finally, it's not just any set of customs. It's customs from another culture. That is important. So, I've underlined: *adopt, customs,* and *another culture.*"

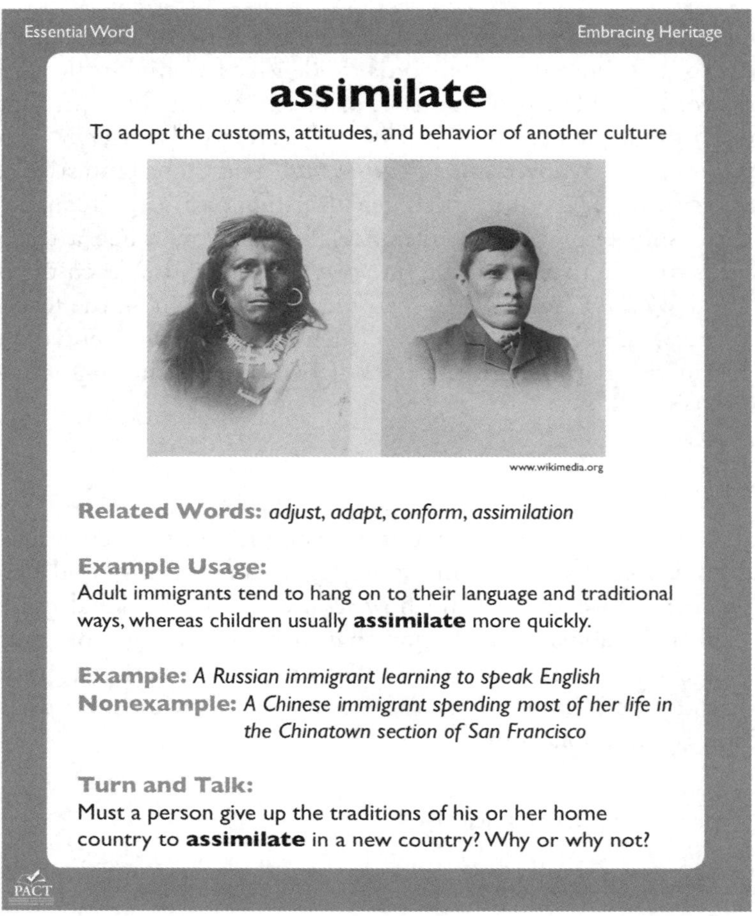

FIGURE 7.4. An example of the graphic organizer used to guide and enrich Essential Words instruction. Copyright © 2015 The Meadows Center for Preventing Educational Risk, The University of Texas at Austin. The PACT and PACT Plus research teams from The University of Texas at Austin, Florida State University, and Texas A&M University developed these materials with funding from the Institute of Education Sciences (No. R305F100013) and Office of Special Education Programs (No. H326M150016).

The teacher may choose to model this for a few words, but then move into guided practice that would sound more like the following:

> "Turn to your partner. Partner A, read the definition to Partner B. Partner B, follow along. [Allow 10 seconds or so.] Thank you. *Assimilate* means to adopt the customs, attitudes, and behavior of another culture. Now, the next step is to underline key words that will help us remember what assimilate means. *Assimilate* is a verb, so look for a key verb. Everyone, take 10 seconds to underline key words. [Allow 10 seconds.] Turn to your partners. Partner B, tell partner A what you underlined and why. [Allow 10 seconds.]"

After spending plenty of time modeling words and then engaging students in guided practice, independent practice of these two steps might sound something like this:

> "Turn to your partner. Read the definition and underline the key words. [Allow 20 seconds.]"

EXAMINE A VISUAL

The goal of this activity is to deepen understanding of the essential word by discussing a visual representation. The discussion should be short. It can be teacher-led, but should include mostly student talk. The discussion should start with a thought-provoking question that is focused on the essential word. In the Figure 7.4 example, the discussion might sound something like this:

> "On the left is a picture of a Native American man. What do you notice about his appearance? Turn to your partner and answer. [Give about 10 seconds; have a few groups share what they noticed.] Take a look at the picture on the right. This is the same man. What evidence do you see of assimilation? Turn to your partner and answer. [Allot about 20 seconds; have a few groups share what they noticed.]"

In this example, the teacher is playing a leadership role in the discussion because it needs to stay right on the topic of assimilation. However, students are doing most of the talking and discussing. By using discussion partners, every student in the class has the opportunity to contribute instead of only a select few.

RELATED WORDS

This is a perfect opportunity to use the essential word to learn additional related words. These may be common words that students have heard before. They may be other technical terms that are related and highly useful. This activity should move along quickly with the goal of always taking the discussion back to the essential word. Using Figure 7.4, the activity might sound like the following:

> "Here are four related words. They all have something to do with the word *assimilate.* The first two words are *adjust* and *adapt.* Everyone, say, 'adjust.' [Students: '*Adjust.*'] Everyone say, 'adapt.' [Students: '*Adapt.*'] In the photo above, the man adjusted or adapted his clothing to assimilate into American culture. Name one other thing he adjusted or adapted. Tell your partner. [Allow 5 seconds and ask a group or two to share; they might say, 'He changed his hair; he took out his earrings.'] Another word related to *assimilate* is *conform.* Say, 'conform.' [Students: '*Conform.*'] When you conform to something, you look around and try to be like others. This is also what a person does when she assimilates to another culture.

The last word is *assimilation*. Everyone say, 'assimilation.' [Students: '*Assimilation*.'] There is a suffix here. It is *-tion*. Remember when we add *-tion* to a verb like *assimilate*; this makes it a noun. So, think of a sentence about the man in the picture using the word *assimilation*. Give 5–10 seconds.] Tell your partner your sentence. [Allot 5 seconds and have a group or two share.]"

EXAMPLE USAGE

Sometimes, this activity is very short and simply involves reading the sentence. Other times, it is an opportunity for a short discussion about a topic related to the essential word. Just remember to keep the discussion short—about 1 minute in length. In Figure 7.4, the example usage is a perfect opportunity for a short discussion that might sound something like this:

"Will someone please read the example usage aloud? Everyone else follow along. [Student reads.] Why do you think children usually assimilate more quickly?"

EXAMPLE AND NON-EXAMPLE

This activity should be kept very brief. It ought to contain clear, extreme examples that are not ambiguous. This is not a time for debating whether it's an example or non-example. Instead, it's a time for students to solidify their understanding of the essential word. Here's what this section might sound like from Figure 7.4:

"Here is an example of *assimilate*. When a Russian immigrant learns to speak English, he is assimilating. He is changing his behavior to fit into another culture. Here is a non-example. A Chinese immigrant spending most of her life in the Chinatown section of San Francisco. Yes, the Chinese woman moved to the United States. However, she did not change any of her customs, attitudes, or behavior. Therefore, she did not assimilate."

TURN AND TALK

The purpose of this activity is to relate the essential word to students' lives. The question should be written in a way that prompts students to either think about their own lives or something very familiar to them. The turn-and-talk procedure is highly useful in a classroom. Think of traditional teacher questions and student answers. One teacher asks a question. One or two students answer. At best, the other students have answered the question to themselves. At worst (and probably closer to reality), students quickly learn passivity and don't think at all, hoping to avoid being called on to answer. Turn and talk does not allow this. In fact, every student in the class has the opportunity to answer the question posed. Here's how the turn-and-talk procedure works with Figure 7.4:

"Class, I will ask you the turn-and-talk question. I'll give you about 20 seconds to think about how you would answer the question. You may jot down a few notes in your note-taking guide. Then, I'll have you turn to your partner to share. Here is our turn-and-talk question: Must a person give up the traditions of her home country to assimilate in a new country? Why or why not? Answer the question first on your own. [Allow 20 seconds.] Now turn to your partner. Partner A, you go first with your answer. [Allow 30 seconds to 1 minute; then regroup and have partners share with the class.]"

Turn and talk is a fantastic classroom procedure that can be used in any subject area and for a variety of purposes. For additional information on how to instruct teachers to engage students in turn-and-talk activities, refer to *Turn and Talk: An Evidence-Based Practice Teacher's Guide* (Stewart & Swanson, 2019) available on this book's companion website (see the box at the end of the table of contents).

Student Record of Essential Words

Teachers may want students to keep a record of their essential words and associated notes. We've found that a simple form can be effectively used for this purpose (see Figure 7.5).

Multiple Exposures to Essential Words: Warm-Ups

It is important to not only teach the essential words directly during focused instructional time. Learning is enhanced when students experience multiple exposures to the information distributed over time (Benjamin & Tullis, 2010). We do this in two ways. The first way is through warm up activities that focus on the essential words. These warm-up activities vary in nature. Sometimes, they require students to interpret a figure (Figure 7.6). Other times, they require students to synthesize information (Figure 7.7). These warm-up activities can be used during the first 5–10 minutes of class while the teacher is taking attendance or preparing for the class period. They can be completed independently or with a partner. The goal of these is provide repeated exposure in a way that deepens students' thinking about the essential words.

Critical Reading of Text

Now that students have adequate background knowledge and a strong foundation in concept, or critical word knowledge, they're motivated to learn and it's time to tackle content-area text. Choosing text for students exhibiting a wide range of abilities and struggles is challenging. However, even students who struggle can learn content from silent text reading (Reed, Swanson, Petscher, & Vaughn, 2014), so don't underestimate the ability of students who struggle with reading. In addition, there are several different ways to engage students in reading that provides them with access to text in a supportive way. Figure 7.8 describes several of these reading procedures.

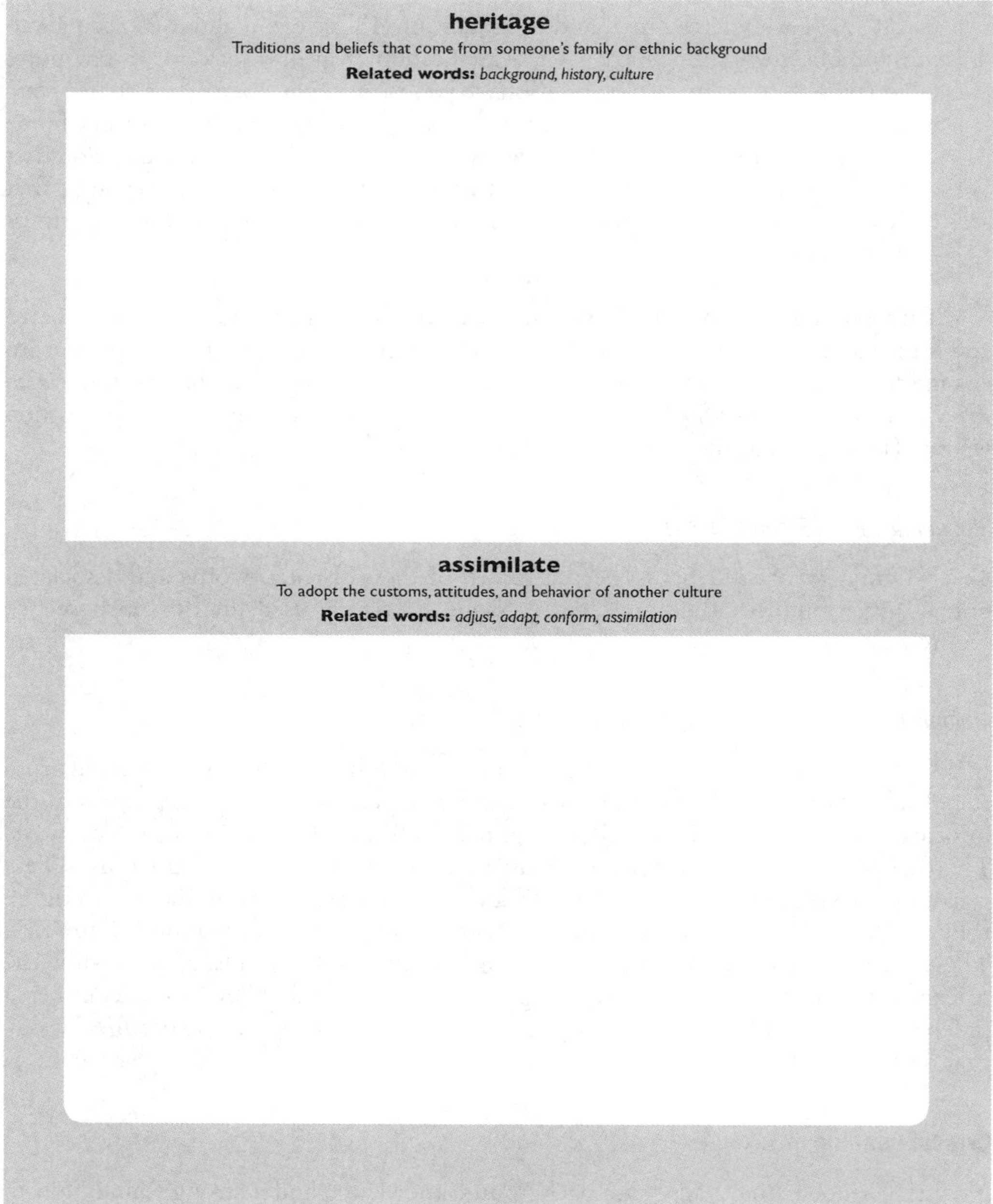

FIGURE 7.5. The student log used during the Essential Words instructional practice. Copyright © 2019 The University of Texas at Austin/The Meadows Center for Preventing Educational Risk Licensed under Creative Commons BY-NC-ND 4.0 International.

Warm-Up Colonial America • Lesson 5

mercantilism

The idea that if a country imports cheap raw materials and exports finished products, it will become rich

Look over the illustration of how **mercantilism** makes some people rich.

1. Colonists cut down trees and ship the lumber to the mother country. The colonists are paid very little.

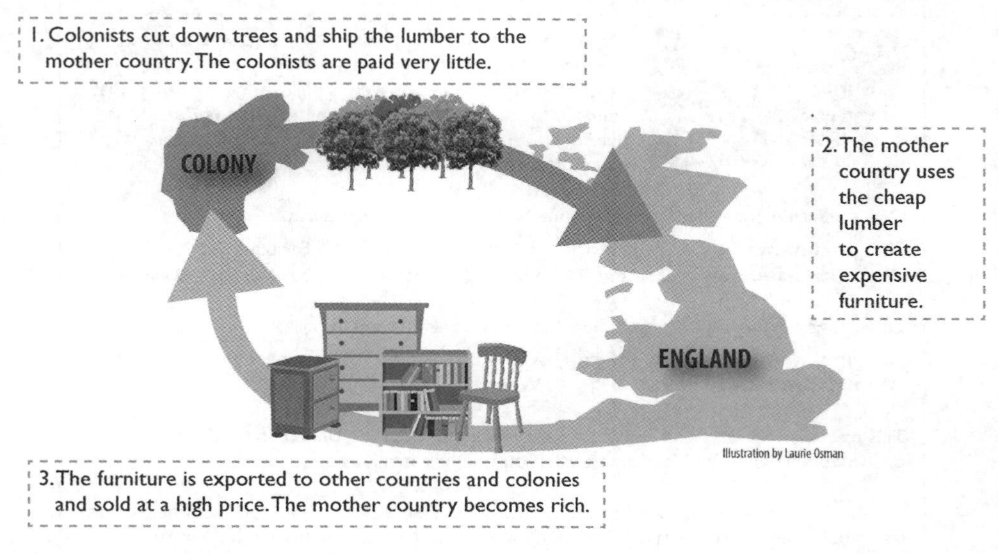

2. The mother country uses the cheap lumber to create expensive furniture.

3. The furniture is exported to other countries and colonies and sold at a high price. The mother country becomes rich.

Briefly answer the following questions:

1. Who benefits least in this process?

2. Why does this group benefit the least?

3. Is **mercantilism** fair?

FIGURE 7.6. Sample Essential Words warm-up activity with single word. Copyright © 2013 The Meadows Center for Preventing Educational Risk, The University of Texas at Austin. These materials were developed with funding from the Institute for Education Sciences (No. R305F00013) to The University of Texas at Austin. The materials were developed by members of the PACT research teams from The University of Texas at Austin, Florida State University, and Texas A&M University.

Warm-Up | Embracing Heritage

assimilate

To adopt the customs, attitudes, and behavior of another culture

heritage

Traditions and beliefs that come from someone's family or ethnic background

Read the text below.

One of the first things that many immigrants who arrived in America in the late 1800s and early 1900s did was change their names. Why? Their reasons were simple: Adopting names that sounded more American might help them **assimilate** more quickly. It might help them avoid ethnic discrimination. It might be better for the businesses they hoped to start in America.

Often, immigrants decided on a new name by altering their original name:

Original name	Petrasovich	Noblinski	Hrabko	Savitch	Madsen
Americanized name	Preston	Noble	Harbor	Savage	Madison

Other times, immigrants changed their name to its English translation:

Original name	Blau or Bleu	Weiss, Blanc, or Bianco	Weber	Schmidt
Translated name	Blue	White	Weaver	Smith

This trend has changed over the past several decades. Today, the United States is a more multicultural country and immigrants are proud of their **heritage**.

Lisa Chang's parents immigrated to the United States from Korea in 1976. She kept her Korean last name when she got married. "I felt like I would lose a part of myself and my Korean **heritage**," she said, "and like I was cheating on my family's name."

Adapted from Roberts, S. (2010, August 26). New life in U.S. no longer means new name. *The New York Times*, p. A1. Retrieved from http://www.nytimes.com/2010/08/26/nyregion/26names.html

Is it possible for an immigrant be proud of his or her **heritage** and to **assimilate**? Why or why not?

FIGURE 7.7. Sample Essential Words warm-up activity with multiple words. Copyright © 2015 The Meadows Center for Preventing Educational Risk, The University of Texas at Austin. The PACT and PACT Plus research teams from The University of Texas at Austin, Florida State University, and Texas A&M University developed these materials with funding from the Institute of Education Sciences (No. R305F100013) and Office of Special Education Programs (No. H326M150016).

Grouping Structure	Description
Whole-class reading	• The teacher reads aloud to the class. • One or two fluent readers read to the class. • Students listen to an audio recording of the text.
Small-group reading	• Students in groups of three to five read the text aloud to one another.
Paired reading	• Student pairs take turns reading the text aloud to each other.

FIGURE 7.8. Descriptions of three ways to engage students during text reading.

In addition, we covered the issue of choosing text for a variety of readers in Chapter 5. When planning for this portion of PACT, we suggest teachers choose two passages per week, which will take about 20 minutes each to cover. Therefore, passages should be short, compelling, and tied closely to the Comprehension Canopy question. Let's consider one example from an ELA unit on heritage.

Using "Letter from M. Goodstein to His Aunt in Poland" (see Figure 7.9), the teacher begins with a short introduction to the reading that accomplishes two things: (1) a compelling introduction to the reading and (2) a purpose for reading. The teacher might say something like this:

> "Even after settling in the United States, some immigrants felt caught between their new American lives and the 'old country' they left behind. Some kept in touch with their relatives back home by exchanging letters with them. The letter we will read is a primary source. It is an actual letter from a young Jewish man who moved from Poland to San Bernardino, California, in the late 1800s. As you read, pay attention to the author's feelings about his heritage as he assimilates in America. As we read, we'll stop periodically to answer questions and take notes about what we've read."

Students begin reading using the teacher's chosen method (see Figure 7.8). After a compelling section of text, stop and ask a question that encourages in-depth thinking. Continue reading and keep the following in mind:

1. As needed, clarify vocabulary. Point out connections to the essential words where applicable.
2. At each stopping point (including the final one), facilitate discussion and teach students to locate and cite text evidence. Note the first question in Figure 7.9. There is a discussion question followed by a prompt to find the supporting evidence from the text.
3. Provide corrective feedback if students misunderstand the material.

After reading, there are two more steps:

Letter From M. Goodstein to His Aunt in Poland

(1)

San Bernardino, California
November 28, 1890

This past November 4, it was exactly 1 year since I left home. On December 4, I arrived in New York, and on the 12th, I reached San Bernadino. I can tell you for sure that I should have left home 15 years earlier. It would have been much better for me, a thousand times better. I am not able even to describe it to you how I looked at first and how different I look now. I do not want to write about it because if I start, I may never finish with it. I would like to ask the people at home just this one question: Why is it forbidden for a young man to take a walk with a girl, to talk to her, and to get to know her? I do not consider it a sin, and I did not find it in the Gemora (part of the Jewish holy book) to be a sin either. Only you, the Polish people, are so backward. And as a result, when this type of young man arrives here, he is called a "greener," and in Germany, "Polish" or "Russian pig." This is the truth.

Is the author eager to assimilate? Underline the sections in the text that support your answer.

(2)

I do not mean to insult you, but it is especially true that in your small towns, within a half hour everything is known all over and becomes gossip. And so when a young man from there arrives here, what kind of an impression does he make? First, he cannot open his mouth because he does not know the language. Then, when he gets together with people, he does not know how to behave and how to have a good time. So people make fun of him. I can understand it because first, he is not able to talk, and then, he is not able to eat because he is not used to this kind of food. He also does not know how to hold a knife or a fork or a table napkin. And he does not know how to sing or raise a toast in company. At home, we only used to say, "Lehayim" (a Hebrew toast to someone's good health). At home, we only sang zmires (Jewish songs). And he does not know how to dance because I have never seen anyone dance or play at home because people would open their mouths in wonder. They would not go to the theater because this, too, was considered a sin. And as far as dress at home—one used to put on a shirt and a scarf around one's neck and this was all. Here, however, one has to have different clothes for the summer and for the winter. The same is true for women.

(continued)

FIGURE 7.9. Sample reading passage divided into sections for use in the Critical Reading instructional practice. Copyright © 2015 The Meadows Center for Preventing Educational Risk, The University of Texas at Austin. The PACT and PACT Plus research teams from The University of Texas at Austin, Florida State University, and Texas A&M University developed these materials with funding from the Institute of Education Sciences (No. R305F100013) and Office of Special Education Programs (No. H326M150016).

"Letter From M. Goodstein" • 2 of 2 Embracing Heritage • Lesson 2

How does the author's heritage affect him in his new life in America?

(3)

In our store, we also sell women's dresses and even underwear. And it may happen that a young man has to sell to some young girl some such things or whatever. We also sell, here, undershirts, shirts, collars, fine ties, pocket watches, top hats, and overcoats. All this the young man had never seen at home. So here he is shown everything like a small child. And people laugh at him. I am not telling this, God forbid, about myself. When I arrived here, I was already different. The only thing was that I could not speak English, but now, this is all already behind me.

Why does the author say, "I am not telling this, God forbid, about myself"?

Adapted from Thomas, W. I., & Znaniecki, F. (1918). *The Polish peasant in Europe and America: Monograph of an immigrant group*. Boston, MA: Gorham Press.

FIGURE 7.9. *(continued)*

4. Facilitate student note-taking in response to the final questions.
5. Have students write connections to any essential words in their notes.

If our struggling seventh-grade reader, Caroline, receives the type of instruction described above in her science, social studies, and ELA classes, a very solid foundation has been built. These practices can now be intensified for the intervention setting to provide Caroline and other students like her with a better chance of closing the gap between their skills and those of their grade-level peers.

INTENSIFYING EVIDENCE-BASED CONTENT-AREA LITERACY PRACTICES

Intensifying PACT

Intensifying instructional practices used in content-area classrooms can be of great benefit to students who struggle with reading. Not only should it increase their reading skills, but also their participation in grade-level classes and access to grade-level curriculum. Fuchs and colleagues wrote recently about six indicators in the taxonomy of intervention effectiveness (Fuchs, Fuchs, & Malone, 2017): (1) strength, (2) dosage, (3) alignment, (4) attention to transfer, (5) comprehensiveness, and (5) behavioral support. We encourage teachers to consider each of these indicators when intensifying instruction for middle school students who struggle substantially with reading. Figure 7.10 lists each indicator, offers a short description, and explains the ways in which PACT may be intensified according to the indicators.

What we propose here is using PACT instructional practices in Tier 1 science, social studies, and ELA classes and intensifying the PACT practices for use in Tier 2 or Tier 3 classes. Recently, we conducted a study where we aligned the literacy practices delivered during Tier 1 social studies and Tier 2 intervention (Stevens, Vaughn, & Swanson, 2020). Early findings from the study indicate that aligning Tier 1 instruction and Tier 2 intervention was beneficial to the readers who struggled the most and positively impacted content knowledge and reading comprehension outcomes.

Students who struggle with reading require more practice with instructional

Indicator	Description of Indicator	PACT Considerations
Strength	How well the program works for students. This can be reflected in the effect sizes published in scientific research.	For middle school students with disabilities and struggling readers, effect sizes for PACT range from 0.26 to 0.65. These are medium in size and compare favorably to other interventions provided to struggling middle school readers.
Dosage	The number of opportunities a student has to respond and engage actively in instruction.	PACT provides many opportunities for student engagement. When used in a Tier 2 or Tier 3 setting with smaller groups of students, the opportunities increase.
Alignment	How well the program addresses skill deficits and does not waste time on skills already mastered. It also provides a meaningful focus on grade-level curriculum.	PACT focuses on vocabulary and reading comprehension development and uses grade-appropriate text to build content-area understanding.
Attention to transfer	The extent to which the intervention helps students transfer skills to other contexts.	The intensifications we suggest complement PACT instructional practices, and we offer some goal-setting activities to increase generalizability.
Comprehensiveness	The use of explicit instruction.	PACT instructional practices can and should be taught using explicit instruction.
Behavioral support	The extent that students are taught self-regulation, with the program encompassing practices that minimize disruptive behavior.	The PACT instructional practices are highly interactive and interesting. When a teacher uses the variety of interactive methods, student misbehavior is lessened. The added goal-setting activities support self-regulation.

FIGURE 7.10. Potential methods to intensify PACT.

routines, more exposure to key vocabulary, and repeated exposure to content in order to experience success (Harmon, Hendrick, & Wood, 2005; Swanson et al., 2017; Wanzek & Vaughn, 2008). Implementing evidence-based practices at the Tier 1 level combined with intensified intervention at the Tier 2 or Tier 3 level provides this extra exposure that struggling readers need. In 2019, we published an article in the journal *Teaching Exceptional Children* (Swanson, Stevens, & Wexler, 2019). In it, we offer ideas for intensifying instruction to support students who struggle with text-based discussion in the content areas. A copy of the article, "Engaging Students with Disabilities in Text-Based Discussions," is available on this book's companion website (see the box at the end of the table of contents).

Goal-Setting Practices to Increase Transfer

One way to encourage generalization of skills learned in the intensive intervention environment is to add a series of goal-setting activities at the end of each lesson. Introducing the idea of goal setting is straightforward and simple. The teacher might say something like this:

> "A goal is something that we want to achieve. For example, I may set the goal that I want to read one new book a week. Or I might want to exercise every day by going for a walk. What are some goals that you set for yourself? [Students answer.] We can also set goals to do better in school and to become better readers. Each time we meet, we will set a goal about how you will take what you've learned in this class and share that learning in science, social studies, and English language arts."

Then, students should be asked to write a goal for applying in other classes what they learned in this one. Goals can be very simple, such as "I will raise my hand to read aloud to the class." It can be more content-focused, such as "I will tell the class what heritage means," or "I will give a classmate an example of an artifact." The goal might be something related to classroom discussions, such as "I will raise my hand to answer a question that starts with 'What' or 'Where.'" At the end of every class, the teacher should ask students if they achieved their goal, invite students to share their successes, and celebrate those accomplishments. This very simple procedure has led to some important reflections from general education teachers once their students return from intervention classes (Stevens et al., 2020):

- "When [my students] came back to class, they were eager to share what they had learned. Oh, yes! All three of their hands went up immediately when I asked for discussion during social studies that week."
- "They had more confidence in their ability when it came to answering questions. They weren't afraid to look for the answers!"
- "It builds their confidence. Whereas in the past I noticed that he would never answer. He would tell me, 'I'm dumb, teacher.' Now, I see a huge difference in him. He's the first one to raise his hand. Basically, he has confidence now."

Multisyllabic Word Reading

If a student's main area of deficit lies in reading comprehension, an intensified version of PACT alone might be appropriate. However, there is evidence that many struggling middle school readers also experience word-level deficiencies (Vaughn, Cirino, et al., 2010) that require multisyllabic word study and **reading fluency** instruction. These components are not included in PACT and should be added to the intensive intervention class for middle school learners with those deficits. What follows are some ideas for providing multisyllabic word study and fluency instruction to struggling middle school readers.

When it comes to planning for **foundational reading skills** and multisyllabic word study, many teachers wonder what skills to teach beyond the 44 phonemes in the English language. Once students enter the middle school years, the texts they use in content-area classrooms become substantially more difficult and require the ability to decode multisyllabic words. Teachers of struggling middle school readers must learn how to teach students to recognize different syllable patterns paired with a strategy for reading multisyllable words (Denton, Bryan, Wexler, Reed, & Vaughn, 2007).

A reliable strategy for reading multisyllabic words is to look for parts you already know and to then sound out the rest. Many readers learn to do this with relatively little instruction, but others require explicit, intensive instruction to become proficient at decoding multisyllabic words. In order to use the strategy of identifying word parts within a longer word, students must learn five related skills:

1. That long words are made up of parts called *syllables*;
2. That each syllable contains one vowel sound;
3. How to recognize prefixes, suffixes, and root words;
4. How to divide the word into syllables, read each syllable, and then combine them to read the word; and
5. How to make adjustments when a word has a syllable that is irregular.

Learning about different syllable types can help students divide a word into syllables, read each syllable, and combine them to read the word. The six syllable types are listed and described in Figure 7.11 (Denton et al., 2007).

Each of the syllable types should be taught using carefully designed lessons that employ explicit instruction adhering to the following sequence (Denton et al., 2007, p. 238):

1. Introduce closed syllables. Review short vowel sounds. Practice reading closed syllables. Practice reading words made up of only closed syllables.
2. Introduce open syllables. Review long vowel sounds. Practice reading open syllables. Practice reading open syllables mixed with closed syllables. Practice reading words made up of open syllables and closed syllables.
3. Introduce silent-*e* syllables. Practice reading silent-*e* syllables. Practice reading silent-*e* syllables mixed with open and closed syllables, Practice reading words made up of open syllables, closed syllables, and silent-*e* syllables.
4. Continue this pattern of practicing the new syllable type. Practice it mixed with

Syllable Type	Description	Examples
Closed	One vowel sound that is "closed in" by a consonant or consonant digraph. The vowel makes its short sound.	VC: *at, in* CVC: *dig, mat* CCVC: *plot, slug* CVCC: *nest, mint*
Open	One vowel sound at the end of the syllable. It is not closed in by a consonant; instead, it is "open." The vowel makes its long sound.	CV: *no, hi, fly*
Silent *e*	One vowel sound in addition to an *e* at the end. It may begin with a vowel or consonant. The vowel that precedes the *e* makes its long sound.	VC*e: ate, pine, rope, shake, smile*
Vowel team	The vowel sound in these syllables is made with a vowel pair.	*rain, boat, snow, boot, play*
Vowel *r*	The vowel is followed by the letter *r*. The pronunciation of the vowel sound changes when it is followed by the letter *r*.	*park, herd, sir, for, fur*
Consonant *-le*	These are usually found at the end of the word. They contain a consonant followed by *-le*.	*bottle, cable, maple, puddle*

FIGURE 7.11. Descriptions and examples of various syllable types.

previously learned syllable types. Practice reading words with all the syllable types learned so far.

Fluency Instruction

According to the theory of automatic word processing, when reading fluency is achieved, it allows students to focus on meaning (LaBerge & Samuels, 1974; Logan, 1988). Fluent reading is hallmarked by speed, accuracy, and expression (National Reading Panel, 2000). Many students with reading difficulties struggle with fluency. In 2016, Wexler wrote a research brief, *Targeting the 2 Percent* (available on this book's companion website [see the box at the end of the table of contents]), that details the most recent fluency research and provides sample routines for repeated reading and wide reading. The routines themselves are very similar, but the reading materials used differ. For repeated reading, the teacher selects one independent-level text. Partners use it to read and then reread the same text, improving fluency each time. For wide reading, teachers choose a series of texts (in the example within Wexler's brief, a series of five texts). During each fluency-building session, students read new passages.

Recently, Reed and colleagues (2018) studied the effects of a fluency program that controlled student practice passages by varying them systematically. With Varied Practice Reading, students read three different passages, one time each. However, these passages were carefully written, so 85% of the unique words from passage one appeared in passage two or three. The authors refer to this as *word overlap*. Students in the study engaged in fluency practice for 20 minutes per session, and they practiced 3 to 4 times per week. After an average of 26 sessions, all students made substantial gains in words read correct per minute. However, students who engaged in the Varied Practice Reading outperformed, to a **statistically significant level**, their peers assigned to the repeated reading condition. The Iowa Reading Research Center has posted 30 sets of Varied Practice passages at *https://iowareadingresearch.org/file/variedpracticepassagesetspdf-0*. While the currently posted passages are designed for fourth graders, new sets are planned for additional grade levels.

In Figure 7.12, we provide a guide that teachers can use to implement partner reading in the classroom. This partner-reading routine combines both repeated reading with some questions designed to check for understanding. For more information, you can find a detailed guide to partner reading (Swanson, Wexler, Shelton, Kurz, & Vaughn, 2018) on this book's companion website (see the box at the end of the table of contents).

REVIEW AND PREVIEW

In this chapter, we presented PACT instructional practices that teachers can use in science, social studies, and English language arts classes. We also explained how to intensify these practices for students with substantial reading comprehension needs. In addition, we briefly discussed multisyllabic word reading and fluency for students who also have these instructional needs. In the next chapter, we will explore the role of instructional fidelity in improving outcomes for students who struggle with reading.

Terms to Know

Foundational reading skills: Phonics, word reading, and fluency skills that are considered the foundation of reading and necessary for comprehending written text.

Reading comprehension: A reader's ability to gather meaning from a text and integrate that meaning with what the reader already knows.

Reading fluency: The ability to read text with prosody (smoothness), speed, and expression.

Statistically significant: Statistical significance is determined through statistical analysis and is a measure of the likelihood that differences between groups are due to chance. The statistical significance threshold is usually set at .05. In other words, analysts are testing to make sure there is a 5% or less probability that the differences are due to chance. If an effect size, for example, is statistically significant at the .05 level, this means there is a 95% chance that the group differences are due to the intervention itself and only a 5% probability that the difference is due to chance.

Partner Reading Routine

The partner reading routine consists of three basic steps. First, the reader reads aloud while the listener follows along, checking for errors. Second, the listener provides feedback focused on accuracy of reading, and the partners go over any missed words together. Third, after the partners have established a complete understanding of the words in the passage, they check the reader's comprehension of the passage. The students then switch roles and repeat the three-step process.

Materials

- Text, one for each student
- Highlighters or pens for marking errors
- Cue card, one per pair (provided later in this document)

Step 1: Read Aloud

The reader reads aloud the designated section of text at an appropriate rate.

The listener follows along, underlining or highlighting errors.

Step 2: Feedback

The listener uses the cue card script to provide feedback for each error: "Here is a word that I underlined. The word is _______. Let's read the sentence together."

The partners correctly read aloud the sentence together. This process is repeated for each sentence with an error.

Step 3: Check for Understanding

The listener checks the reader's understanding by using the question on the cue card: "How well did you understand the section?"

The reader responds with the choices listed on the cue card and the partners take any necessary corrective action:

- "Not at all": Repeat steps 1 and 2.
- "Some of it": Be ready to ask your partner for help answering the critical reading question.
- "All of it": You are ready to answer the critical reading question with your partner.

Switch Roles and Repeat

The students then switch roles. There are two options for the second round of reading aloud, repeated or continued reading. In repeated reading, the new reader rereads the same section of text. In continued reading, the new reader moves on to the next section of text.

FIGURE 7.12. Sample lesson on the silent-*e* syllable type. Copyright © 2018 The University of Texas at Austin/The Meadows Center for Preventing Educational Risk *Partner Reading: Teacher's Guide* licensed under Creative Commons BY-NC-ND 4.0 International.

Reflection Questions

1. Evidence is clear that once students reach middle school, reading difficulties are exceedingly difficult to remediate. Why might that be the case, and what can teachers in middle schools do about it?
2. How do you define *academic rigor*?
3. What are the benefits of aligning regular classroom instruction and intensive intervention?
4. Can you describe one type of instructional practice that increases generalizability?
5. What are the benefits of using the turn-and-talk practice in the classroom?

CHAPTER 8

Fidelity of Implementation

Teachers hear professional development leaders mention the importance of implementing lessons "with fidelity." It leaves some teachers wondering, "Does fidelity mean I need to follow the lesson plans? I would like to change these lessons. Am I allowed? If I don't get through all of the material, will my students benefit from the curriculum?" It is important that you as an instructional coach understand the concept of fidelity thoroughly so that when teachers' questions arise, your answers are well informed. This chapter provides instructional coaches with (1) a thorough definition of the term *fidelity,* (2) a summary of research evidence supporting the importance of fidelity, (3) details on how to monitor fidelity data, (4) ideas for presenting the concept of fidelity to teachers, and (5) an explanation of some actions you may take to encourage high levels of fidelity.

FIDELITY DEFINED

Federal law requires that schools adopt evidence-based practices (Every Student Succeeds Act [ESSA], 2015). Evidence-based practices are practices that were subject to at least one **efficacy trial** and resulted in positive effects (ESSA, 2015). The effects detected during an efficacy trial are tied directly to the way the instructional practices were delivered. When researchers publish the results, they report key information about the essential elements of the instructional practices and how they were implemented. They also discuss the dosage, or the number of lessons that were delivered and how long the lessons lasted (e.g., 30 minutes daily over 6 weeks). If school leaders and coaches want to replicate the effects of the instructional practices in their schools, incorporating the same elements of the practices with the same dosage is of critical importance. (See Chapter 2 for a more thorough review of the idea of evidence-based practices.)

School leaders often adopt evidence-based practices with the expectation that the practices will improve student outcomes the same way they did when studied by researchers. However, when the teachers implement the practices in their classrooms, this does not always happen. Although many factors may contribute to these less-than-ideal results, one of the keys to replicating the effects found during research is to implement the instructional practices as they were designed. The extent to which instructional practices are delivered as intended (or designed) is referred to as **fidelity**. Dr. Doug Fuchs, a professor of special education and of pediatrics at Vanderbilt University, had this to say about the importance of implementing instructional practices as they were designed:

> Teachers and ancillary personnel should be using . . . research validated instruction . . . that was developed through a . . . very carefully conceptualized and operationalized process of instruction to determine its effects on student performance. . . . The researchers then share these instructional programs with practitioners and they should be saying . . . "Look, this is how we developed the program. . . . If you deliver the program the way we have detailed it, it's a good bet that you will get results as we did." (Reading Rockets, 2021)

RESEARCH EVIDENCE SUPPORTING THE IMPORTANCE OF FIDELITY

Intuitively, it makes sense that if we expect the same results achieved during research, teachers will need to implement the same set of instructional practices the same way it was implemented during the research study. This makes sense to any of us who have ever adopted a diet to manage a health condition or lose weight. An evidence-based guide (Raynor & Champagne, 2016) suggests that 1,500 calories or fewer can lead to weight loss. The 1,500 daily calorie intake becomes our *program* or *intervention* and weight loss is our *goal*. Now, if we want the same outcome mentioned in the study (i.e., weight loss), we will most likely achieve it by following the exact same program—the 1,500 daily calorie intake. If we are lax on Tuesday and say, "Oh, this brownie and ice cream won't hurt" and consume 800 extra calories, we might still be okay in the long run. But, what if we cheat regularly and eat a 500-calorie cookie every day? A month later, we wonder, "Why didn't I lose weight?" The answer is, "Because we did not implement the program with fidelity." Without fidelity to a proven set of practices, we may not attain our desired outcome.

Within the field of education, recent research has examined the role of fidelity in student outcomes. Findings from many studies converge to show that when interventions are delivered with higher levels of fidelity, students perform better on reading outcomes. This is true for struggling elementary school readers' performance on early reading outcomes (Vadasy & Sanders, 2009; Vadasy, Sanders, & Nelson, 2015; Wolgemuth et al., 2014). It is also true for secondary students' performance on measures of reading comprehension (Cantrell, Almasi, Carter, & Rintamaa, 2013; Fogarty et al., 2014; Vaughn, Swanson, et al., 2013; Vaughn, Roberts, Wexler, et al., 2015) and, in particular, the performance of students who receive the PACT intervention, as described in detail in the previous chapter (Vaughn, Roberts, Wexler, et al., 2015). In other words, when secondary teachers implement reading instructional practices as designed, their students benefit to a greater extent.

MONITORING FIDELITY

Your primary role as an instructional coach is to improve classroom instruction to impact students' reading outcomes. Therefore, you should spend time monitoring teachers' fidelity of implementation of adopted schoolwide literacy practices. By monitoring fidelity, you will have data to guide your instructional support. In this section, you will learn how to monitor fidelity in teachers' classrooms.

Monitoring fidelity will probably be achieved through classroom observations. What are some important things to look for when assessing fidelity? When examining how teachers implement the key elements of instructional practices, you might ask questions like these:

- To what extent do teachers adhere to the curriculum scope and sequence?
- Is the curriculum implemented with sufficient **frequency**?
- Do teachers focus on the goals identified in the lesson plans?
- Do teachers use the recommended teaching practices?
- Do teachers use the recommended materials?
- To what extent do teachers follow the steps in the lessons?
- Do teachers make adaptations? If so, what adaptations, and do these adaptations align with the "active ingredients" of the adopted set of instructional practices (see below for an explanation of making appropriate adaptations)?

In Chapter 7, we introduced you to PACT, the set of evidence-based practices used in various examples throughout this book. Appendix 8.1 at the end of this chapter presents the PACT Implementation Fidelity Checklist, designed for instructional coaches to use during classroom observations. At the top, there are spaces to fill in identifying information (i.e., teacher name, date, class period, etc.). Skip down to the section on the fidelity checklist called "Comprehension Canopy." You will see all of the elements that are contained within the Comprehension Canopy. While the coach is observing a teacher, she can check off all of the elements she observes. You'll also notice a fidelity rating section under Comprehension Canopy. In this section, you may rate the observed instruction on a scale of 1 (low alignment) to 4 (high alignment). Refer to the table at the top (under Procedural Fidelity) for guidance on how to assign a fidelity rating. At the extreme ends for Comprehension Canopy, if one or none of the elements was observed, the lesson fidelity is rated as 1. If all elements are observed, the lesson fidelity is rated as 4. Finally, there is a place to take notes for each instructional practice.

Some publishers of curricula, instructional practices, or programs include fidelity checklists or observation protocols. Others do not. You may use the PACT

Implementation Fidelity Checklist as a model for recording the extent to which a set of instructional practices was delivered as intended. To create your own, take these steps:

1. List each of the instructional practices or strategies.
2. Focus on one instructional practice or strategy at a time, and list each of the elements contained within each.
3. Assign decision rules to each of the fidelity ratings. Follow these general guidelines for assigning rules: 1 = no or almost no elements observed; 2 = few elements observed; 3 = most of the elements observed; 4 = all of the elements observed.

PRESENTING THE IDEA OF FIDELITY TO TEACHERS

Whether you use the PACT Implementation Fidelity Checklist or create a new one to monitor fidelity, you will need to plan how to explain fidelity to teachers so that they know you will be monitoring their implementation, with the goal of supporting them when necessary. We want to emphasize that monitoring fidelity should not be done to catch teachers doing something wrong (Reed et al., 2012). Gathering information about fidelity should not be presented to teachers as a "gotcha" activity. Instead, present fidelity monitoring as a way for coaches to identify what support teachers and students need while using the adopted set of instructional practices.

Before collecting any fidelity data, teachers should be informed about how the data will be used. Many teachers are hesitant to allow instructional coaches into their classroom for fear of criticism, being reported to the principal, or plain old "stage fright" when others are observing them. If one of your jobs as an instructional coach is to build a teacher–coach alliance, then trust is the cornerstone that must be laid again and again. Presenting the idea of fidelity to teachers is a perfect opportunity. We believe teachers want to know a few things about fidelity data collection and use. They may have the following questions:

- "What is fidelity?"
- "Why is it important?"
- "Are you visiting my classroom?"
- "What are you looking for?"
- "What form will you use?"
- "How will the information be used?"
- "Who will see the information?"

It is with these items in mind that we have created a series of presentation slides and accompanying notes that align with the above questions. These materials, which you may replicate or revise to fit your needs, are available on the companion website (see the box at the end of the table of contents). You can use the slides to introduce the concept of fidelity to your teachers.

Let's focus on an eighth-grade team to learn how to collect fidelity data to identify teachers' instructional needs. This eighth-grade team is made up of two teachers in each core subject area—English language arts, social studies, science, and math. During a 9-week period, teachers focused on learning and implementing the Essential Words PACT instructional practice (see Chapter 7). During week 1, teachers attended a 1.5-hour professional development session the instructional coach delivered. The principal supported the implementation of Essential Words by funding substitute teachers to cover for teachers' classrooms while they attended the session. The instructional coach began the session by introducing and modeling the instructional practice. Afterward, she explained why it was important that teachers implement the routine with *fidelity* and that she would be observing their implementation on a weekly basis to support their fidelity. Next, the instructional coach gave teachers time to practice the routine. Also, the instructional coach remembered that a barrier teachers often cited for why they didn't take up new practices was that they "don't have enough teaching resources ready to use." Therefore, the coach built into the professional development session time to create Essential Words documents. Here is the schedule:

11:30–12:00	The instructional coach provides evidence supporting the Essential Words routine and models the instructional practice. Teachers hear from a sixth-grade science teacher about how it works in his classroom.
12:00–12:30	Introduce fidelity. Practice the Essential Words routine and discuss what teachers need to be able to implement it.
12:30–1:00	In same-subject groups, teachers identify a set of 10 terms that they will teach over the next 5 weeks using the Essential Words routine. They split the terms among them (three to four terms each) and begin creating the Essential Words guides needed for instruction.

During the next 3 weeks, teachers implemented the Essential Words routine with their students. Each week, the instructional coach and an assistant principal made appointments to visit teachers' classrooms to observe their implementation of Essential Words. They used the PACT Implementation Fidelity Checklist to record elements that they observed and make notes about areas of need. See Figure 8.1 for an example from the Essential Words section of the checklist.

ENCOURAGING HIGH LEVELS OF FIDELITY

We have established that fidelity matters—when teachers implement reading interventions with fidelity, their students perform better on reading outcomes. Now is the time for you to think more deeply about your role as an instructional coach and how you can encourage fidelity. Research reveals that instructional coaches can encourage high levels

Mr. Barnes, Science Teacher

Essential Words Introductory Routine				
Check all elements that were observed:				
The teacher provides an Essential Word guide containing the following: ☑ Student-friendly definition ☑ Visual representation ☑ Related words ☑ Example usage ☑ Example and non-example ☑ Prompt for students to write important information about the word ☐ "Turn-and-talk" activity				
Fidelity Rating:	1 ☐	2 ☐	3 ☐	4 ☐
Notes: *A lot of teacher talk. Very little student talk. Teacher said that turn and talk disrupts his classroom.*				

FIGURE 8.1. Sample Essential Words section of the PACT Implementation Fidelity Checklist.

of fidelity. Allison Kretlow and Christina Bartholomew (2010) conducted a review of 13 studies to determine the impact of coaching interventions on teachers' fidelity of implementation of evidence-based practices. They found that all the coaching interventions they reviewed yielded positive effects on teachers' fidelity. The features of these interventions included engaging group training sessions, follow-up observations, and specific individual feedback. Thus, we can infer that, in order to encourage high fidelity among teachers, instructional coaches should deliver interactive professional development sessions, monitor teachers' implementation, and provide teachers with feedback based on fidelity data. Therefore, fidelity observations should guide your coaching activities. In Part III of this book, we will present a model that relies heavily on professional development and coaching as a way to encourage high levels of fidelity among teachers when implementing evidence-based practices as part of a schoolwide model.

ADDITIONAL CONSIDERATIONS

Without fidelity, we cannot expect evidence-based practices to have the same positive outcomes they did in studies that researchers conduct. However, we would be remiss if we did not acknowledge that fidelity is not the only factor that influences the effects of instructional practices on student outcomes. There may be important differences between a teacher's school or class context and the particular context of a study (e.g., study setting or student sample). These differences may result in varying effects. For example, instructional practices that work for proficient readers may not be sufficient for students with intensive reading needs *despite* teachers' implementation of these practices with fidelity. That is why it is important to adopt and implement evidence-based practices to provide across Tiers 1, 2, *and* 3 in a schoolwide model.

Additionally, as the instructional coach, you can help teachers make acceptable adaptations to help improve student outcomes. These adaptations should not alter the active ingredients or essential elements of an instructional practice—these are the non-negotiables. Instead, adaptations should give teachers the opportunity to *add* to the active ingredients without overloading students. For Essential Words, this could look like asking students to write down explanations of the example and non-example of the target word so that students can demonstrate their understanding and the teacher can provide students with individual feedback. Thus, it is essential that evidence-based practices meet students' specific needs *and* are implemented with high fidelity.

REVIEW AND PREVIEW

In this chapter, we provided (1) a thorough definition of the term *fidelity,* (2) a summary of research evidence supporting the importance of fidelity, (3) guidance on collecting fidelity data, (4) guidance on how to inform teachers about the importance of monitoring their fidelity of implementation, (5) an explanation of some actions you may take to encourage high levels of fidelity among teachers implementing a schoolwide literacy mode, and (6) the importance of coaches considering other factors that might influence fidelity and how to make acceptable adaptations to an instructional practice that does not alter its "active ingredients."

We also provided presentation slides on the book's companion website that you may use with teachers when describing the fidelity process (see the box at the end of the table of contents).

Part II (Chapters 4–8) was designed to provide instructional coaches with background knowledge on a variety of topics related to implementing a schoolwide literacy model within a multi-tiered system of supports. In Part III, we will provide instructions for a coaching model that leverages a multi-tiered system of supports to provide targeted coaching to teachers based on need.

Terms to Know

Efficacy trial: A study designed to measure the effects of an intervention.

Fidelity: The extent to which instructional practices are delivered as intended (or designed).

Frequency: How often instructional practices should be delivered (daily, once per week, etc.).

Reflection Questions

1. Can you explain the definition of *fidelity* to a colleague?
2. How is fidelity related to student outcomes?
3. What are the two main goals for monitoring fidelity?
4. What is one common tool you can use to monitor fidelity?
5. What are some questions you might ask yourself when assessing fidelity data collected on a fidelity observation checklist?
6. What are the steps to take to create your own fidelity checklist?
7. Besides fidelity, what are some other factors that might influence the effect of instructional practices on student outcomes?
8. Can you think of an acceptable adaptation to an instructional practice that wouldn't alter the active ingredient(s) of that practice?
9. Can you list two or three ways in which you will use fidelity data?

APPENDIX 8.1

PACT+ Implementation Fidelity Checklist

Teacher: ______________________________ Date: ________ Grade: ______ Average Fidelity:______

Subject: _______________________________ Period: ______ Instructional Leader: _______________

Procedural Fidelity

Rate the teacher's fidelity of implementation for the following three components on a 4-point scale as outlined in the table below.

Rating	**Comprehension Canopy** *(5 total elements)*	**Essential Words Introductory Routine** *(7 total elements)*	**Critical Reading of Text** *(8 total elements)*
4	5 elements	7 elements	8 elements
3	3–4 elements	5–6 elements	5–7 elements
2	2 elements	2–4 elements	2–4 elements
1	0–1 elements	0–1 elements	0–1 elements

Comprehension Canopy				
Check all elements that were observed:				
The teacher does the following: ☐ Introduces the unit and accesses students' prior knowledge ☐ Introduces the purpose of Springboard ☐ Presents a Springboard video or visual ☐ Prompts students to do a "turn-and-talk" activity ☐ Presents a comprehension question				
Fidelity Rating:	1 ☐	2 ☐	3 ☐	4 ☐
Notes:				

(continued)

This form was adapted from the Collaborative Strategic Reading IVC (Vaughn et al., 2011). Some items were also adapted from the English-Language Learner Classroom Observation Instrument (Haager, Gersten, Baker, & Graves, 2003), the Classroom Observation Checklist (Stanovich & Jordan, 1998), and Features of Effective Reading Instruction in Special Education (Klingner, Urbach, Golos, Brownell, & Menon, 2010).

© 2019 The University of Texas at Austin/The Meadows Center for Preventing Educational Risk. *PACT Plus Fidelity Form* licensed under Creative Commons BY-NC-ND 4.0 International. Reprinted in *Literacy Coaching in the Secondary Grades: Helping Teachers Meet the Needs of All Students* by Jade Wexler, Elizabeth Swanson, and Alexandra Shelton (The Guilford Press, 2021). Permission to photocopy this material is granted to purchasers of this book for personal use or use with students (see copyright page for details). Purchasers can download enlarged versions of this material (see the box at the end of the table of contents).

Essential Words Introductory Routine				
Check all elements that were observed:				
The teacher provides an Essential Word guide containing the following: ☐ Student-friendly definition ☐ Visual representation ☐ Related words ☐ Example usage ☐ Example and non-example ☐ Prompt for students to write important information about the word ☐ "Turn-and-talk" activity				
Fidelity Rating:	1 ☐	2 ☐	3 ☐	4 ☐
Notes:				

Critical Reading of Text				
Check all elements that were observed:				
The teacher does the following: ☐ Previews text for students ☐ Sets the purpose for reading ☐ Reads the first section of the text ☐ Prompts students to do partner reading ☐ Asks key questions ☐ Asks follow-up questions ☐ Engages students in text-based discussion ☐ Clarifies vocabulary and/or points out connections to essential words when applicable				
Fidelity Rating:	1 ☐	2 ☐	3 ☐	4 ☐
Notes:				

PART III

AN ADAPTIVE COACHING MODEL TO IMPROVE LITERACY INSTRUCTION FOR ALL STUDENTS

CHAPTER 9

An Adaptive Approach to Literacy Instructional Coaching

Enhancing Intensive Instruction in a Schoolwide Literacy Model

By now, you have some idea about the state of adolescent literacy for students at the secondary level. In sum, many students continue to struggle with reading and comprehending text. Because of this, it is essential that we implement schoolwide adolescent literacy models to provide (1) instruction in evidence-based literacy practices across the content areas and (2) evidence-based literacy practices to support students in need of intensive intervention. You also learned from Chapter 3 that many teachers are missing key opportunities when it comes to implementing these practices. Put simply, many schools do not have an effective schoolwide adolescent literacy model in place that is essential for students to make gains.

It is clear that school reform is necessary in many secondary settings, but how do school administrators effectively set up a schoolwide adolescent literacy model? This kind of schoolwide reform is not easy, but administrators can rely on help from instructional coaches (Bryk, Sebring, Allensworth, Luppescu, & Easton, 2010). Effective instructional leadership has been linked to positive student outcomes (Robinson, Lloyd, & Rowe, 2008; Waters, Marzano, & McNulty, 2003) and is essential for facilitating implementation of a schoolwide adolescent literacy model. This means that an instructional coach is a critical member of a school's leadership team. To help teachers implement evidence-based practices with fidelity, an instructional coach can systematically promote practices that are essential to implement in a schoolwide adolescent literacy model through ongoing professional development and instructional coaching support. We reviewed the specific literacy practices that are essential for an instructional coach to know and teach teachers at the secondary level in Part II of this book. In Part III, we will provide a systematic **adaptive intervention** model used by instructional coaches to support teachers' implementation of these practices. We provide step-by-step guidance on how to offer support in the form of modeling and performance feedback to teachers coupled with strategies that can help extend generalization of practices teachers learn during professional development. By providing this support, instructional coaches can help teachers improve implementation fidelity and sustainability of practices (Brock & Carter, 2017; Reddy & Dudek, 2014).

First, let's pause and clarify who exactly we mean when we say "instructional coach." As mentioned in the prologue of this book, we consider an instructional coach to be a literacy coach, a specialist (e.g., reading specialist or special education teacher), or an assistant principal who can provide professional development and ongoing coaching support to teachers. It is likely that a school has only one instructional coach dedicated to leading the design and implementation of a schoolwide literacy plan. Despite the expertise this person has, supporting a large group of teachers can seem like a daunting task. This person might have a full 40 hours per week to dedicate to the instructional coaching role, or this person might have other duties, leaving him roughly 20–30 hours per week to dedicate to literacy instructional coaching activities. Naturally, questions might come to mind about how just one instructional coach can possibly help all teachers in a school implement these practices with fidelity. When will the instructional coach provide professional development to all the teachers who need it? After teachers participate in professional development, how will this one instructional coach give ongoing support to all teachers? Will all the teachers in a school be motivated to learn, and will they attempt to implement the practices with the same conviction? How will the instructional coach tailor her support to teachers' various needs in a systematic manner that is adaptive based on teachers' needs?

We begin this chapter by taking a step back to consider why current typical professional development support provided by instructional coaches on secondary campuses is not necessarily aligned with best practice. By understanding how we "miss the mark" when it comes to providing professional development and support, you will gain a better understanding of the kinds of support instructional coaches *do* need to offer teachers. After presenting some of this essential background information, we will introduce an instructional coaching model: Adaptive Intervention Model (AIM) Coaching. We use AIM Coaching as a model to provide guidance as instructional coaches adapt the type and dosage of support they give to teachers in a secondary setting. Using AIM Coaching, instructional coaches can support all teachers as they build and implement a schoolwide adolescent literacy model collectively.

PROFESSIONAL DEVELOPMENT ON SECONDARY CAMPUSES IS NOT ALIGNED WITH BEST PRACTICES

As noted above, implementing evidence-based adolescent literacy practices with fidelity requires instructional coaches to provide systematic and ongoing professional development and support for teachers. Unfortunately, just as students do not consistently receive the support they need from their teachers, instructional coaches do not consistently provide ongoing professional development opportunities that include the right type and amount of support for teachers (Darling-Hammond, Wei, Andree, Richardson, & Orphanos, 2009; Wexler et al., 2017). This results in teachers' inconsistent implementation of evidence-based adolescent literacy practices. For example, Wexler and colleagues (2017) interviewed high school science teachers about their perceptions of their role in implementing literacy instruction. When asked about the increasing pressure to meet the CCSS (NGACBP & CCSSO, 2010a) that require *all* teachers to meet literacy objectives, several teachers acknowledged they had participated in professional development that provided an overview of the standards, but "they had not received guidance on *how* to address these standards" (p. 12). If we expect teachers to implement evidence-based adolescent literacy practices, it is essential that we provide professional development and ongoing support to these teachers.

Several guidance documents (e.g., Desimone, 2009) and syntheses (e.g., Desimone & Garet, 2015; Yoon, Duncan, Lee, Scarloss, & Shapley, 2007) summarize professional development literature, providing the field with guidance on how best to support teachers as they learn new teaching techniques. Reports converge on five characteristics that are critical to increasing teacher knowledge, improving teacher **skill** (i.e., implementing evidence-based practices with fidelity) and practice, and impacting student outcomes (Desimone, 2009; Garet, Heppen, Walters, Smith, & Yang, 2016): (1) focus on content that is rated highly applicable and feasible by teachers; (2) include **active learning opportunities** (e.g., observing expert teachers, reviewing student work); (3) establish coherence between evidence-based practices and teacher knowledge, teacher beliefs, and school policy and initiatives; (4) provide at least one semester and 20–100 hours of contact time; and (5) encourage **collective participation** where all teachers in a grade level or school learn together.

Evidence suggests that most teachers in the United States do not have access to professional development that meets these criteria (Garet et al., 2016). According to the 2003–2004 Schools and Staffing Survey, most professional development offered to teachers was in the form of short-term workshops (Darling-Hammond et al., 2009), and recent large-scale randomized controlled trials funded by the USDOE Institute of Education Sciences indicate that teachers received an average of 12 hours of professional development across the academic year (Garet et al., 2008; Garet et al., 2010; Garet et al., 2016). A lack of time in training opportunities is not the only problem preventing effective professional development. For example, in their meta-analysis of group-design studies examining the efficacy of training to improve implementation of interventions for students with disabilities, Brock and Carter (2017) suggest that increasing time alone does little to change teachers' behaviors. They emphasize that *how* we train teachers is more important than the number of hours they spend in training. However, when considering quality of training, many secondary teachers receive professional development on literacy instruction (Rotermund, DeRoche, & Ottem, 2017) that is rated as being of "not much value" (Darling-Hammond et al., 2009). In addition, it seems that even when teachers work together to learn new teaching techniques, the collaboration tends to be "weak" and "not focused on strengthening teaching and learning" (Darling-Hammond et al., 2009, p. 5). See Figure 9.1 for a summary of the ways in which current professional development practices do *not* typically align with best practice.

Even when instructional coaches *do* provide professional development that meets the criteria outlined above, the outcome is not always ideal. Garet and colleagues (2008, 2010, 2016) implemented a professional development program that met many of Desimone's (2009) criteria, and impacting student outcomes remained difficult. In these studies, teachers attended summer institutes to learn evidence-based practices and received follow-up professional development and instructional coaching over the course of the year. Combined professional development activities totaled 68–110 hours. Across all three studies, teacher knowledge improved, and instructional practices changed to statistically significant levels, but none of the studies impacted student outcomes. This is concerning when the primary reason for providing professional development is to impact student outcomes! *We might conclude that some ingredient of the coaching component from the instructional coaches was not potent enough in these studies to effect student-level gains.*

Is it also possible that the secondary setting poses unique challenges that impact the efforts of instructional coaches who provide professional development and follow-up instructional coaching support? Instructional coaches on secondary campuses face a sizable teacher constituency. In 33 U.S. states, the average middle school size exceeds 500 students (Parsad, Lewis, & Farris, 2001). These schools employ upward of 40+ teachers, with the national average somewhere around 24 teachers. Along with a large population of teachers comes a variety of teacher needs. For example, some teachers will exhibit high levels of skill, while others may struggle and exhibit only average or even low levels of skill. When examining the reasons for average or low levels of skill, instructional coaches might wonder if teachers' ability has to do with their **will**. In

- Teachers might be provided with professional development opportunities, but ongoing follow-up support that includes modeling and feedback is rare.
- Most teachers are receiving professional development opportunities (i.e., short-term workshops) that do not meet recommendations outlined in several seminal guidance documents and syntheses (e.g., Desimone & Garet, 2015; Yoon et al., 2007).
- The provision of literacy professional development at the secondary level is sparse (Rotermund et al., 2017) and the professional development that does occur is rated as being of "not much value" (Darling-Hammond et al., 2009).
- The secondary setting is complex (e.g., a plethora of teachers with varying needs who require different types of professional development and ongoing support).
- Instructional coaches have many roles that leave them with limited hours to provide professional development and ongoing support.
- Many instructional coaches do not receive the training needed to know how to implement high-quality professional development and ongoing support systematically (Blazar & Kraft, 2015).

FIGURE 9.1. Reasons why current professional development practices are not aligned with best practice.

other words, are they not capable of implementing evidence-based practices with fidelity or, put bluntly, do they just not want to do it? And if they do not want to implement these practices, what might be the reason? Perhaps they feel that it is not feasible to implement the practice because they lack access to text that they need. Perhaps they do not believe the intervention aligns with the curriculum their administration expects them to cover. How does an instructional coach know the source of a teacher's low skill or will, and how do they intervene based on these deficits? It is essential that instructional coaches are able to diagnose the various skill and will levels of teachers, as well as potential reasons that explain teachers' skill and will levels. This will help instructional coaches provide the right amount and type of support to promote teachers' implementation of evidence-based literacy practices. We will discuss the idea of skill and will in more depth in Chapters 10–12.

Compounding the challenges presented above is the often dual role (i.e., literacy coaching and other administrative duties) instructional coaches face on secondary campuses as previously described. This means that some instructional coaches have relatively little time to spend in direct contact with teachers engaged in ongoing professional development activities that support implementation of evidence-based adolescent literacy practices. In addition, even when instructional coaches do have time to support teachers, this support is often unsystematic and not based on data (e.g., teacher fidelity to the evidence-based practices; Kraft, Blazar, & Hogan, 2018). This is likely a result of the fact that instructional coaches typically receive little training themselves in how to support teachers as they learn to implement new instructional practices (Blazar & Kraft, 2015).

AN INTRODUCTION TO AIM COACHING

In Part I, we described several potential challenges that contribute to the difficulties of implementing schoolwide adolescent literacy models and the overall poor outcomes of secondary students. The challenges we presented include the fact that an excessive number of students are struggling and need support, and many teachers are missing key opportunities to implement evidence-based adolescent literacy practices, indicating that there are many teachers who lack the knowledge and skills needed to provide support to students. Many teachers require professional development and instructional coaching to enhance their implementation of evidence-based adolescent literacy practices. In this chapter, we added another level to our challenges: Professional development opportunities for teachers are not aligned with current best practices, indicating that even though many teachers need support to improve their knowledge and skills, they are not getting the support required. A final challenge is that the learning opportunities for instructional coaches—the people who support teachers' implementation of evidence-based adolescent literacy practices—are lacking. Therefore, we can attribute the dismal state of adolescent literacy, at least in part, to a *trickle-down effect*. By a trickle-down effect, we mean that many instructional coaches lack guidance about how to support teachers,

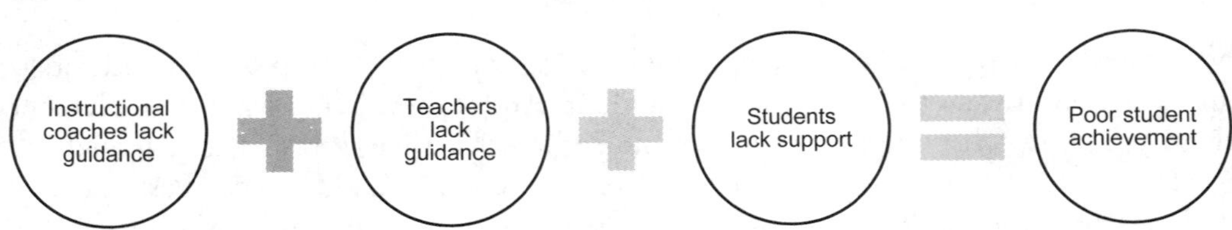

FIGURE 9.2. The trickle-down effect of instructional coaches' lack of guidance on student achievement.

many teachers lack guidance for how to support students, and, therefore, many students do not receive the support they need for success (see Figure 9.2). Thus, student achievement suffers when instructional coaches do not receive the support they need.

We know that providing professional development and instructional support to teachers is associated with improved teacher implementation of evidence-based literacy practices (Becker, Bradshaw, Domitrovich, & Ialongo, 2013; Brock & Carter, 2017) and an essential component for facilitating teachers' translation of research to practice (Joyce & Showers, 2002). For these reasons, it is troublesome that we are not adequately building a corps of instructional coaches who provide support that aligns with Desimone's (2009) five components of high-quality professional development (Blazar & Kraft, 2015). This is a gap that must be addressed.

To fill this gap, we next introduce a model for guiding instructional coaches as they support secondary teachers in a schoolwide adolescent literacy model. It is called AIM Coaching, an adaptive intervention model designed to positively impact both teacher and student outcomes. AIM Coaching not only aligns with Desimone's components of high-quality professional development (see Figure 9.3), but it also capitalizes on the strength of adaptive interventions, allowing instructional coaches to tailor professional development support to teachers' varying needs (i.e., skill and will levels).

Desimone	**AIM Coaching**
Content focus—activities focusing on subject matter content and how students learn	Evidence-based adolescent literacy practices (e.g., PACT Plus)
Active learning—opportunities to engage in active learning (e.g., observing or being observed, interactive feedback and discussion)	Plan–monitor–reflect sessions + check-ins
Coherence—extent to which teacher learning is consistent with teachers' knowledge and beliefs	Determining teacher skill (i.e., fidelity) and will level (e.g., Implementation Survey)
Duration—sufficient duration (time span + number of hours)	Entire school year; 9-week cycles
Collective participation—participation of teachers from same school	Schoolwide

FIGURE 9.3. Alignment between the components of high-quality professional development (Desimone, 2009) and AIM Coaching.

Before we get to the in-depth guide for using AIM Coaching (see Chapters 10–12), let's explore some underlying assumptions foundational to understanding adaptive intervention models.

WHAT ARE THE ASSUMPTIONS BEHIND ADAPTIVE INTERVENTION MODELS?

The key assumption underlying adaptive intervention models is that individuals (e.g., students and teachers) differ in their response to interventions, and in order to optimize outcomes, interventions should be individualized and adapted based on individual progress (e.g., Bierman, Nix, Maples, & Murphy, 2006; Marlowe et al., 2008; McKay, 2005; Nahum-Shani et al., 2012). Two key characteristics describe adaptive intervention models: (1) The type or **dosage of intervention** offered to participants is individualized based on participants' characteristics, and (2) the intervention is repeatedly adjusted over time in response to ongoing performance. Adaptive interventions that include these key characteristics are multistage in nature and include a sequence of decision rules that recommend when and how the intervention should be modified to sustain long-term impact.

Adaptive interventions are not new. They have been used with increasing frequency in the mental health field to improve outcomes such as mood disorders (e.g., Kilbourne et al., 2013), problem school behaviors (e.g., Connell, Dishion, Yasui, & Kavanagh, 2007), and addiction (e.g., McKay, 2005). Educational game developers are even capitalizing on adaptive interventions to increase learning online (e.g., Kickmeier-Rust et al., 2007). They are also becoming common in the field of special education.

Recall that in Part I of this book, we introduced a study by Vaughn, Wexler, and colleagues (2012). This study provides an example of an adaptive intervention. In this study funded by the Eunice Kennedy Shriver National Institute of Child Health and Human Development (NICHD), researchers experimented with an adaptive intervention provided to middle school students with or at risk for disabilities who received differing doses of literacy instruction based on their initial scores on standardized reading measures. Biweekly, students were re-assessed by the teacher, and differing doses of literacy component instruction were provided based on student need (see Figure 9.4).

Results from this randomized controlled trial indicated that students who received the adaptive intervention outperformed the comparison business-as-usual students (i.e., students with or at risk for disabilities who received business-as-usual reading instruction) to a statistically significant level on measures of decoding, fluency, and comprehension. Fidelity to the adaptive intervention delivery was very high, providing evidence that adaptive interventions are effective and also feasible to implement.

One area left relatively untouched by adaptive intervention is instructional coaching for teachers. For example, in a meta-analysis of coaching interventions, Kraft and colleagues (2018) reviewed 60 coaching studies. None employed adaptive intervention design. This makes AIM Coaching a unique way for instructional coaches to provide support for teachers and ultimately impact students' reading achievement.

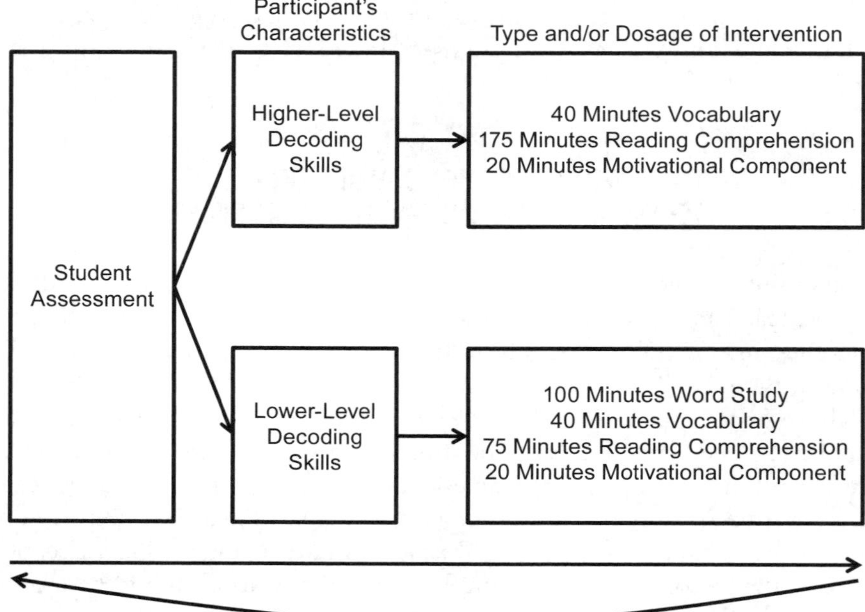

FIGURE 9.4. Example of an adaptive intervention.

THE THEORY BEHIND AIM COACHING

It is important to consider the theory behind AIM Coaching as well. As described above and in previous sections of this book, AIM Coaching incorporates assumptions about adaptive interventions and research on professional development, instructional coaching, and adolescent literacy. It is also driven by Adult Learning Theory (Edwards, Hanson, & Thorpe, 2013; Knowles, 1984, 1989). See Figure 9.5 for a visual explaining the research and theory underlying AIM Coaching.

While there are multiple theories of learning that apply to adults, AIM Coaching is rooted in the theory of andragogy (Knowles, 1980), which includes a set of assumptions: Adult learners are self-motivated, want to apply new knowledge immediately, and move from dependency to increasing self-directedness as their knowledge increases. Using these assumptions, Knowles suggests several practical implications for adult educators. For instance, adult educators (e.g., instructional coaches) should assess adult learners' (e.g., teachers) specific needs, establish learning objectives based on their findings, and work with learners collaboratively to increase their learning experience, knowledge, and, ultimately, their skills (e.g., implementing literacy interventions).

Aligned with the theory of andragogy, AIM Coaching requires instructional coaches to (1) assess teachers' skill and will levels with regard to implementing evidence-based adolescent literacy practices and (2) determine how to target teachers' individual needs. Instructional coaches then work collaboratively with teachers, as suggested by Knowles (1984, 1989), to improve implementation of evidence-based adolescent literacy practices. Specifically, instructional coaches address teachers' needs using performance feedback (Pierce, 2014), which includes direct observation of a teacher implementing a specific practice in a classroom setting, followed by feedback on the practice (Stormont & Reinke, 2014). Providing immediate feedback to teachers is critical to ensure high levels of fidelity and sustainability in implementation, particularly in the early stages of learning a new teaching practice (Kretlow & Bartholomew, 2010; Scheeler, Ruhl, & McAfee, 2004). Knowles (1984) suggests that adult learners are problem-centered and motivated to learn by internal factors. Thus, during reflect sessions, instructional coaches and teachers consider the performance feedback and collaboratively set goals that will enhance future implementation. Adult Learning Theory also incorporates the assumption that adults must know why they need to learn something, and effective adult educators explain their reasons for teaching specific skills (Knowles, Holton, & Swanson, 2012).

To summarize, Adult Learning Theory combined with the research base behind adaptive interventions, professional development and instructional coaching, and adolescent literacy (described throughout this book) drive AIM Coaching. Instructional

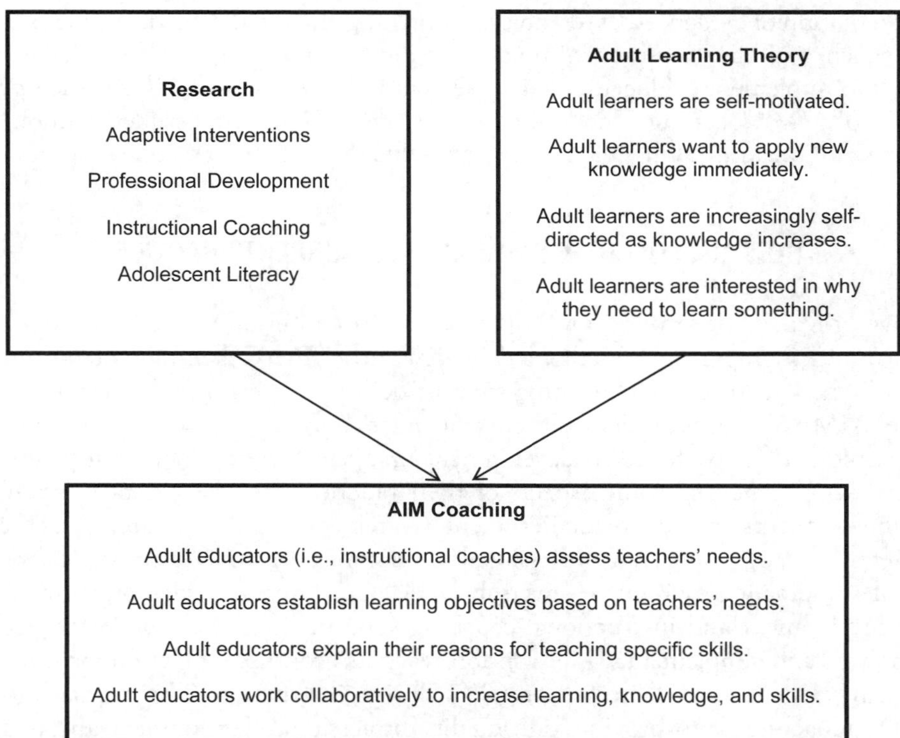

FIGURE 9.5. Research and theory underlying AIM Coaching.

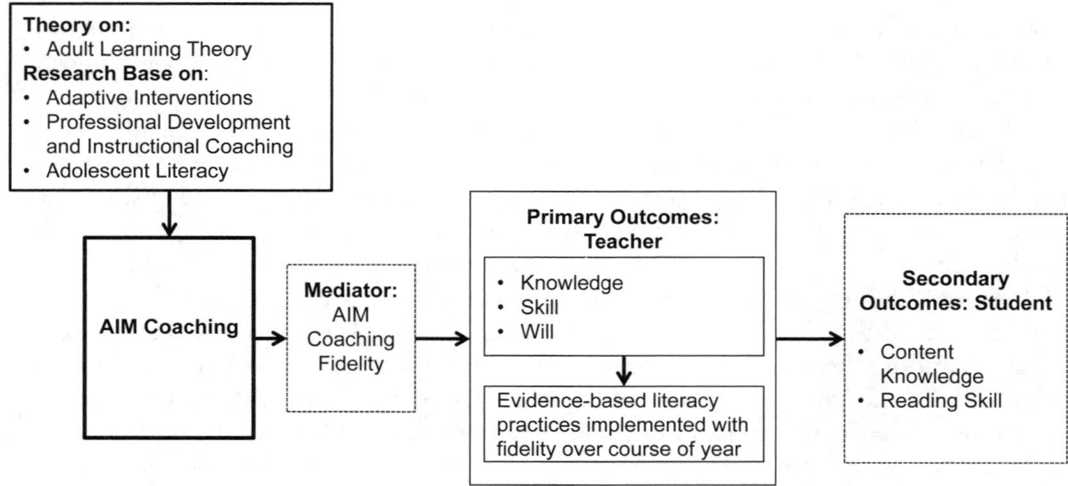

FIGURE 9.6. AIM Coaching theory of change.

coaches implement AIM Coaching, an adaptive intervention, to improve teachers' implementation of evidence-based adolescent literacy practices. The idea is that instructional coaches will impact teacher implementation by improving their knowledge, skill, and will to implement evidence-based adolescent literacy practices. This is the primary outcome of AIM Coaching. The secondary outcome is to improve students' knowledge of content and reading skills. Figure 9.6 represents this theory of change.

HOW AIM COACHING DIFFERS FROM CURRENT PRACTICE

We have provided background on AIM Coaching in addition to rationale about why such a model is important. Finally, let's review how AIM Coaching differs from the current literacy instructional coaching support delivered in schools and what makes it unique. AIM Coaching differs from current practice in five key ways. First and foremost, while current professional development practices have the potential to improve teachers' knowledge and some aspects of their practice, the effect does not translate into improvements in student achievement (Garet et al., 2008; Garet et al., 2010; Garet et al., 2016). "One-shot professional development" characterizes typical professional development provision. Conversely, AIM Coaching provides ongoing professional development and instructional coaching support throughout the year. Second, content-area and supplemental intervention teachers are missing key opportunities to implement evidence-based literacy practices during instruction. The primary goal of the AIM Coaching is to provide high-quality professional development and ongoing support for all teachers to improve implementation of evidence-based literacy practices to build a schoolwide model. Third, building a cadre of capable instructional coaches is currently a challenge (Blazar & Kraft, 2015). AIM Coaching provides fully developed systematic guidance needed to produce more capable instructional coaches, and it will help instructional coaches implement a comprehensive, well-thought-out plan of ongoing professional development and teacher support. Fourth, the key components of AIM Coaching draw from research on adaptive interventions, professional development and instructional coaching, and adolescent literacy as well as Adult Learning Theory.

REVIEW AND PREVIEW

In this chapter, we reviewed some of the challenges related to the implementation of a schoolwide adolescent literacy model. One of these challenges is that current professional development practices on secondary campuses are not aligned with best practice. We next introduced a solution to address these challenges—AIM Coaching—an adaptive intervention for instructional coaches to support teachers. Assumptions behind AIM Coaching are that individuals (e.g., students *and* teachers) differ in their response to intervention, and it is therefore essential that we are able to adapt the type and dosage of an intervention over time. AIM Coaching draws from research on adaptive interventions, professional development and instructional coaching, and adolescent literacy. It also integrates principles of Adult Learning Theory. In Chapter 10, we will provide a detailed overview of AIM Coaching. We also begin explaining how to implement AIM Coaching with a guide to implementing Stage 1 Intervention.

Terms to Know

Active learning opportunities: Experiences that give teachers the opportunity to engage with newly learned material in order to increase their understanding and skill in a particular area.

Adaptive intervention: A model in which intervention support is differentiated and adapted according to a teacher's level of responsiveness to the original support provided.

Collective participation: Occurs when teachers receive professional development with a group of other teachers (e.g., all teachers within a school).

Dosage of intervention: The amount of support a teacher receives from a particular intervention.

Skill: Teachers' ability to implement evidence-based practices with fidelity.

Will: Teachers' willingness to implement evidence-based practices with fidelity.

Reflection Questions

1. How can an instructional coach support a schoolwide adolescent literacy model?
2. What are some of the challenges instructional coaches face when trying to implement schoolwide adolescent literacy practices?
3. In what ways does current professional development *not* align with best practice?
4. What are the five characteristics critical to professional development designed to increase teacher knowledge and skill, improving teacher practice, and impacting student outcomes?
5. How might typical characteristics of the secondary setting impact the efforts of an instructional coach?
6. How might teacher skill and will impact teachers' fidelity of implementation, and what are the implications for instructional coaches?
7. What are some assumptions behind adaptive interventions?
8. Can you list any examples of adaptive interventions?
9. Can you explain how AIM Coaching incorporates some of the principles of the theory of andragogy?

CHAPTER 10

A Introduction to AIM Coaching

In Chapter 9, we introduced the idea of adaptive interventions. As a reminder, key assumptions behind adaptive interventions are that (1) individuals (e.g., teachers) differ in their response to intervention, and (2) the type and dosage of intervention should be adapted over time to meet each individual's need. In this chapter, we will begin to provide step-by-step guidance on how to implement AIM Coaching, an adaptive intervention for instructional coaches to use to improve teachers' implementation of evidence-based adolescent literacy practices in a schoolwide adolescent literacy model.

HOW AIM COACHING REFLECTS AN ADAPTIVE INTERVENTION AND ESSENTIAL TERMS

Before we provide more detail about how to implement AIM Coaching, let's consider how AIM Coaching fits the definition of an adaptive intervention (Nahum-Shani et al., 2012), as described in Chapter 9. In essence, AIM Coaching is a multistage process that provides a framework to support teachers as they teach evidence-based practices. AIM Coaching includes objective **decision rules** that the instructional coach can use to identify when and how intervention should be adapted to address teacher need. We designed AIM Coaching to impact high-quality teacher implementation of evidence-based adolescent literacy practices that we believe "trickles down" to the secondary outcome of improving student achievement. AIM Coaching includes a set of (1) **decision points**, (2) **tailoring variables**, (3) decision rules, and (4) **intervention options** (Lei, Nahum-Shani, Lynch, Oslin, & Murphy, 2012). These terms, critical to understanding adaptive intervention, are described below in relation to AIM Coaching.

Decision points are times during which the instructional coach reflects on data and considers options for intervening with teachers. In AIM Coaching, decision points last

1 week. During this time, the instructional coach takes into account tailoring variables and applies decision rules to determine the type and dosage of support each teacher needs (all described below).

Tailoring variables are characteristics that we hypothesize to stand between an intervention and target outcomes. For example, in thinking about teachers' implementation of an evidence-based adolescent literacy practice, we believe there are two characteristics that stand between teachers' implementation and student achievement, as mentioned in Chapter 9: teacher skill (e.g., fidelity to the evidence-based practice; Vaughn, Roberts, Swanson, et al., 2015) and teacher will (e.g., Abrami, Poulsen, & Chambers, 2004; Dijkstra, Walraven, Mooij, & Kirschner, 2017). These are the two tailoring variables in AIM Coaching. The instructional coach can determine the skill and will for each teacher to help tailor (or adapt) the intervention to meet teacher need, thus called "tailoring variables." We discuss skill and will—the tailoring variables—in more detail below and in the subsequent chapters.

Decision rules are rules that the instructional coach uses to guide the amount and type of support she gives to the teachers. We describe the decision rules the instructional coach uses during AIM Coaching below.

Intervention options are options for varying the type and dosage of support that the instructional coach can use when supporting teachers. We will describe intervention options in Chapter 12.

HOW TO IMPLEMENT AIM COACHING: AN OVERVIEW

Before we provide more detail about AIM Coaching, it is important to note that we designed AIM Coaching to be practice- and program-agnostic. What does this mean? It means that instructional coaches can use this instructional coaching model to support teachers' implementation of *any* evidence-based practice. For example, instructional coaches can use AIM Coaching to support teachers in their implementation of other literacy practices or even math practices. This makes AIM Coaching a universal model for all instructional coaches! For the purposes of this book, we provide you with a set of evidence-based adolescent literacy practices called PACT. These practices were detailed in Chapter 7 and will be used as examples throughout the remainder of this book.

It might help you digest the details of AIM Coaching if we first provide an overview. Take a look at Figure 10.1. This illustration depicts the AIM.

We designed AIM Coaching for the instructional coach to implement on a 9-week basis. Since there are typically four 9-week quarters in a school year, the instructional coach can engage teachers in four AIM cycles per year. In this way, if the school has adopted a set of instructional practices, each 9-week period can be focused on one or two practices. By the end of the year, all practices have been introduced to teachers. Providing professional development using this additive approach has been successful for many teachers who report that it prevented them from feeling overwhelmed and allowed them to perfect each practice in their classroom before adding another (Vaughn, Swanson, Wexler, & Roberts, 2015–2019; Swanson, Vaughn, & Roberts, 2015).

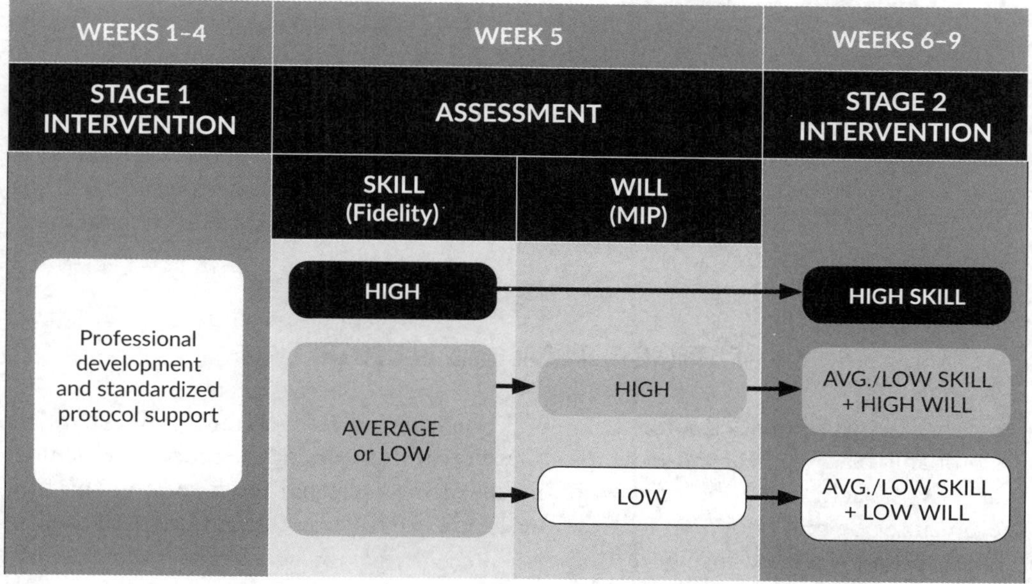

FIGURE 10.1. Adaptive Intervention Model (AIM) Coaching.

The instructional coach begins by providing **Stage 1 Intervention** for all teachers in weeks 1–4 of AIM cycle 1. This includes providing professional development in week 1 on the first instructional practice that teachers will be responsible for implementing, followed by **standardized protocol support** (i.e., the same type and dosage of support for every teacher) during weeks 2–4. You can see Stage 1 Intervention in the left-hand column of the AIM in Figure 10.1.

Next is the AIM Assessment Stage (i.e., a decision point) that occurs in week 5. The Assessment Stage involves assessing teachers' skill and will (i.e., tailoring variables).

The instructional coach determines skill by reflecting on teachers' fidelity scores from Stage 1 Intervention. You probably recall reading about the importance of fidelity in Chapter 8. We can use fidelity to gauge a teacher's skill level, which we will explain in detail below. Once the instructional coach knows each teacher's skill level, she will also want to know the will level of *some* teachers (i.e., those with average or low skill). The instructional coach can use two primary pieces of information to determine a teacher's will level:

1. Teacher scores from the Implementation Survey. These items provide the instructional coach with teachers' self-reported perceptions of their level of motivation, investment, and persistence (i.e., MIP) related to implementation.
2. Collaborative effort ratings the instructional coach assigns each teacher weekly during Stage 1 Intervention. This reflects the level of collaboration or cooperation each teacher exhibits.

We will describe these tools in more detail in Chapter 11.

Once the instructional coach has skill and will data on a teacher, she is ready to apply decision rules and then provide **Stage 2 Intervention** during weeks 6–9. You can see Stage 2 Intervention in the right-hand column of the AIM in Figure 10.1. We will describe intervention options for Stage 2 Intervention in Chapter 12. Once Stage 2 Intervention is complete, teachers are ready to add the next instructional practice. To facilitate this, the instructional coach returns to Stage 1 and delivers professional development on the next instructional practice, while continuing to build on the practice(s) from the previous AIM cycle(s).

PUTTING AIM COACHING IN CONTEXT

Now that we have provided information on key terms and an overview of the AIM, you are probably ready to hear more details about how to implement the model. Remember that AIM Coaching can be used with any set of instructional practices and that, for the purposes of this book, we will use the PACT instructional practices described in Chapter 7 and reviewed in Figure 10.2.

Part of the instructional coach's job may be to help identify student needs and instructional practices that can be implemented schoolwide to improve student outcomes. AIM Coaching is designed for a scaffolded approach that focuses stepwise on one instructional practice at a time so that by the end of the school year, all target instructional practices are infused into every content-area classroom. For a review on how to select evidence-based practices, see Chapter 2 in this book. Next, we describe Stage 1 Intervention.

PACT Instructional Practice	Description
Comprehension Canopy	Introduced at the beginning of a unit to build background knowledge and motivate students to learn new content, students watch a brief, engaging video that introduces the topic. Teachers then introduce an overarching question to guide students' learning throughout the unit.
Essential Words	Teachers introduce and review a few high-utility words or concepts that are essential to comprehending unit content. Words are introduced using an explicit instruction routine and then reviewed using daily warm-up activities. Students continue to receive exposure to the word in text.
Critical Reading of Text	Students read and discuss information from high-quality primary and secondary texts. At various stopping points within a text, teachers and peers facilitate discourse and annotation of text related to the overarching question, essential words, and previously learned material.

FIGURE 10.2. An overview of three PACT instructional practices.

STAGE 1 INTERVENTION

The first step in an AIM cycle is to engage all teachers in Stage 1 Intervention for 4 weeks. As mentioned in our overview of the AIM, Stage 1 Intervention comprises both professional development and standardized protocol support. In Figure 10.3, Stage 1 is at the far left.

During week 1, the instructional coach delivers initial professional development on a chosen evidence-based practice. In most middle schools, leaders adopt a set or series of evidence-based practices. When this is the case, we suggest that the instructional coach repeat the AIM cycle every 9 weeks, each time focusing on only one practice. We have learned that this approach increases buy-in (i.e., we avoid the "it's too much" complaint) and fidelity because teachers have ample time to improve their implementation of one instructional practice at a time until all instructional practices are used in all content-area classes and in intensive intervention settings. See Figure 10.4 for an example of the AIM cycle schedule for PACT.

During weeks 2–4 of Stage 1 Intervention, the instructional coach provides standardized protocol support to all teachers, meaning that every teacher receives the same type and dosage of instructional coaching support as an extension of professional development (Joyce & Showers, 2002). The standardized protocol includes three types of support whereby the instructional coach (1) "plans" with teachers on a by-request basis; (2) "monitors" classroom implementation through observation, support, and/or modeling at least once a week; and then (3) "reflects" with teachers after each monitor session to provide performance feedback and set goals to guide future implementation. The

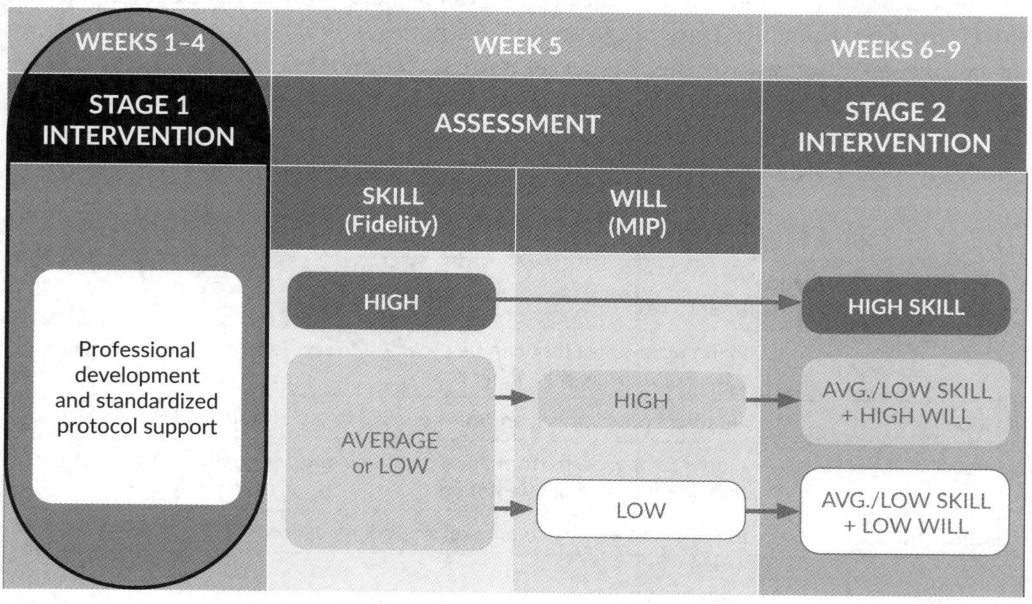

FIGURE 10.3. Stage 1 Intervention of the AIM.

<table>
<tr><th>AIM CYCLE 1</th><th>AIM CYCLE 2</th><th>AIM CYCLE 3</th><th>AIM CYCLE 4</th></tr>
<tr><td>Introduce Comprehension Canopy</td><td colspan="3">Continue Comprehension Canopy</td></tr>
<tr><td></td><td>Introduce Essential Words</td><td colspan="2">Continue Essential Words</td></tr>
<tr><td></td><td></td><td>Introduce Critical Reading</td><td>Continue Critical Reading</td></tr>
</table>

FIGURE 10.4. AIM cycle schedule for PACT.

instructional coach also provides at least one weekly "check-in" to identify and address teachers' immediate needs. We refer to this as the *plan–monitor–reflect–check-in sequence*. See Figure 10.5 for dosage guidelines for Stage 1 Intervention.

To facilitate Stage 1 support, refer to the Stage 1 Log in Appendix 10.1. The instructional coach should make enough copies of the Stage 1 Log to assign one log per teacher. The instructional coach will use the log to track teacher progress and keep a record of the types of support she provides to each teacher. We will use this log as a guide to explain Stage 1 Intervention in further detail, beginning with plan, monitor, and reflect sessions as well as check-ins. Let's start with a plan session.

Plan Session

The goal of a plan session is to provide support to teachers as they prepare to implement the instructional practice in their classroom. Activities will vary during a plan session depending on the needs of the teacher. We list recommended activities on the Stage 1 Log in the Plan column under weeks 2–4 (also see Figure 10.6). The instructional coach can use the checkboxes to record which activities were completed, so she has maintained a record of the type of planning support she provided to each teacher.

Type of Standardized Protocol Support	Description	Dose
Plan	Planning support that can be provided to one teacher at a time or a group of teachers	By request
Monitor	Observation, support, and/or modeling in the classroom	Once a week
Reflect	A time to provide performance feedback and set goals to guide future implementation	Once a week
Check in	Identify and address teachers' immediate needs	Once a week

FIGURE 10.5. Dosage guidelines for Stage 1 Intervention.

Plan (by request)
☐ Review goals
☐ Review student data
☐ Choose materials
☐ Fill out lesson template
☐ Review fidelity form
☐ Discuss and practice
☐ Discuss coach role
Notes:

FIGURE 10.6. Recommended intervention guidelines for plan sessions.

The instructional coach can choose the suggested activities based on teacher need. The following sections list the activities, offering a short description of each.

Review Goals

At the end of each professional development session, ask teachers to establish one or two goals for the coming weeks. You may consider asking the teacher to share his goals with you and discuss how you can help as he moves toward achieving each goal. There may also be times when the goal needs to be revised based on student need or teacher proficiency with the instructional practices.

Review Student Data

Student data can be a powerful tool for convincing teachers to take up new instructional practices. You may review screening or progress monitoring data. You may also conduct an observation of the classroom and collect behavioral data on students, particularly because a common issue in middle schools is student engagement. You may present data indicating that one student was disengaged for 20 minutes during class. Then, ask the teacher why he believes the student was disengaged and what he might do to get the student involved in the lesson. A powerful method for using student data to provide instructional coaching support is detailed in Hasbrouk and Denton's (2005) book featuring the idea of student-focused coaching.

Choose Materials

During PACT implementation, teachers frequently need reading passages, essential words' instructional guides, and warm-up activities. These are things that you can provide (e.g., text library); you can also facilitate development across a team of teachers by, for instance, identifying essential words and preparing materials.

Lesson Template

During the early stages of implementation of new instructional practices, teachers may need to script or semi-script their lessons. This can be done using a lesson template.

Review Fidelity

Sometimes, it helps to review what is expected in the classroom. One way to do this is to review why fidelity is important and what are considered to be high levels of fidelity to the instructional practice as it was designed. You might consider the fidelity checklist to be too complex to share with teachers. In this case, you can transfer the fidelity information onto a teacher-friendly version of the fidelity checklist, known as a Criteria for Success sheet. You can share a Criteria for Success sheet during initial professional development as a means of helping teachers understand their expectations. You can then revisit the Criteria for Success sheet during plan sessions. See Appendix 10.2 for an example of a Criteria for Success sheet.

Discuss/Practice

It might help teachers to discuss and even practice certain parts of a lesson prior to the teacher's implementation. For example, a teacher might want to practice how he will provide background knowledge about a text during Critical Reading.

Discuss Instructional Coach's Role

Based on teacher need, you may choose from several different roles while supporting instruction in the classroom. You may model the instructional practice and ask the teacher to observe. Alternatively, you may observe the teacher and provide feedback. It is helpful to discuss these roles and make a decision with teachers so that they know what to expect and what types of support they may request.

You are probably wondering how many plan sessions the instructional coach should implement with each teacher. This is an important question for the instructional coach who is trying to use her time wisely. You may be thinking, "Some teachers will need a lot of my support, but I bet some teachers won't need any of my support. Some teachers might not even *want* my support, regardless of whether they need it or not." During Stage 1 Intervention, we do not require teachers to plan with the instructional coach; instead, we leave this as an option for support. This is why the dosage is listed as "by request" on the Stage 1 Log. Just as you suspected, the idea is that some teachers might not need planning support; therefore, there is no reason to spend precious time supporting these teachers with a plan session. Some teachers might *want* the support even if they do not technically need it, and some teachers might *need* the support but then not request it. By keeping the plan session optional during Stage 1 Intervention, it is likely that a natural distribution will occur, with some teachers requesting plan sessions and some teachers preferring to try out planning a lesson on their own. Holding plan sessions with some teachers and not all teachers is one way to reduce the burden on the instructional coach. However, as we mentioned, some teachers might actually benefit from planning support but won't request it without prompting. When we reach Stage 2 Intervention (Chapter 12), you'll see how to adapt the plan activities according to teacher need, but for Stage 1 plan sessions, spend your time with those who request such sessions.

Monitor Session

Regardless of whether teachers plan a lesson on their own or with the support of the instructional coach, AIM Coaching requires the instructional coach to schedule a monitor session with each teacher at least one time per week during weeks 2–4. The idea behind a monitor session is for the instructional coach to have a chance to observe, support, and/or model implementation of the evidence-based practice. You will see these activities listed on the Stage 1 Log under the Monitor column in weeks 2–4 as well as the expected dosage (i.e., 1 per week). We also display these activities in Figure 10.7.

While we suggest engaging in three different activities, the instructional coach may add activities based on her own knowledge of instructional coaching techniques.

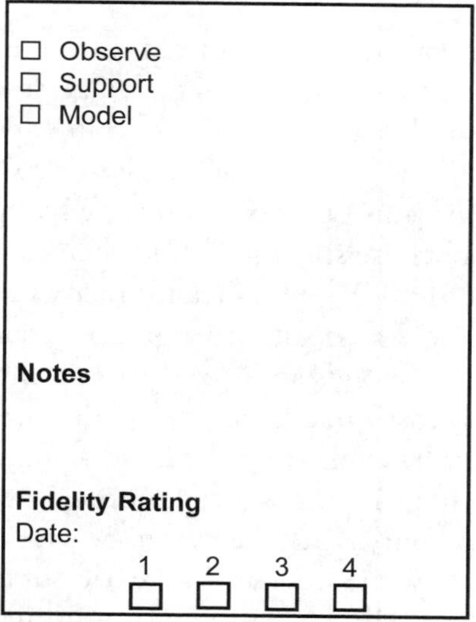

FIGURE 10.7. Recommended intervention guidelines for monitor sessions.

The key here is to engage in a monitor session at least a few times over weeks 2–4 to provide support to that teacher and observe the teacher's implementation at least once in order to ultimately determine each teacher's skill (i.e., fidelity to the evidence-based practice). Short descriptions of each of the activities we suggest follow.

Observe

Depending on the needs of a teacher, you might simply *observe* the teacher implementing the lesson. We encourage you to avoid sitting idly in the back of the classroom taking notes. This can be stressful to a teacher and his students. Instead, use these observations as an opportunity to learn more about teacher skill *and* build rapport by helping the teacher while you are there. For example, you may monitor students as they work and use proximity control to assist with behavior (e.g., stand close to a student who is off task). You may hand out materials or circulate the room to assist students who are struggling. The goal here is to collect information on a teacher's skill level (i.e., fidelity), but this can be done while being of service to your teachers.

Support

Another option is to *support* a teacher's implementation of all or part of the lesson. A wonderful way to support teachers is to co-teach with them. This requires setting the stage before the co-teaching session. Such messages are not always clear through an email. Therefore, we find that this is best done during a face-to-face conversation (e.g., during a plan session) and *not* by email. During the conversation, you want to make it clear that you're there to support the teacher and improve outcomes for his students.

In one such scenario, you may have noticed during a prior observation that the teacher didn't use very many techniques to encourage student response and engagement. Instead of focusing on his actions, you can frame it based on student behavior. You might tell the teacher, "I noticed that about five or six students in the back of the room never answered any of your questions and were really passive during the lesson. What can you tell me about those students?" And then carefully listen to the teacher's response. Next, you might say, "I have an idea for increasing student engagement, and I'd love to try it out with those students. It's a group response method that uses hand signals so that every student responds at once to your prompts. May I join you the next time you teach Essential Words?" You can even explain further what method you'll use during the lesson, "I'll start by explaining the hand signals. I'll also tell students that you'll be teaching the lesson, but I might jump in to have them use their hand signals. Does that sound okay with you?" After the lesson, be sure to debrief during the reflect session and ask the teacher how the students in the back of the room performed. Did he notice if they were more engaged? Also, prompt him to repeat the lesson components he saw you implement in a future lesson.

Model

The final option is to *model* a portion of the lesson or the whole lesson for the teacher. Modeling during monitor sessions should be purposeful and planned ahead of time. Let's imagine that a teacher approaches you and says, "Essential Words does not work with my kids. They are super-bored." After you observe a lesson, you realize that the teacher does all of the talking with no participation from his students. You might say to the teacher, "I noticed what you are talking about. The students were very passive during the lesson. May I teach a lesson and try some things to get them more involved?" When you enter the classroom and before you model the lesson, quickly brief the teacher and give him a purpose for watching that day. In this case, you might say, "While I teach, keep an eye on Andrew, Lailani, and Oliver. See if they are more engaged than usual. Then, think about what is happening in the lesson to encourage their engagement."

Once the monitor session is complete, you can mark the checkbox in the Monitor column about what type(s) of support occurred. After all, it is always possible that whatever you and the teacher plan to happen can change during a lesson! For example, the two of you may have decided that you will observe the teacher, but you might have also agreed that if the teacher seems to be struggling at any point during the lesson, you can "jump in" and *support* or *model* a portion of the lesson. The goal is to provide the teachers with the type and amount of support they need to eventually implement the practices independently and with fidelity, so it's okay if the plan changes. However, regardless of the plan and what actually happens, it is important to record data about the type and dosage of support each week on the Stage 1 Log so that you can make data-based decisions in the future.

Fidelity Rating

During each monitor session that the teacher is leading instruction (and the instructional coach is serving in the "observer" role) on the evidence-based literacy practice(s), you should use a fidelity checklist to record the appropriate ratings to indicate the teacher's adherence to the practice(s). Note that we use a 1–4 rating scale on the Stage 1 Log, based on PACT fidelity as explained in Chapter 8. However, you can adapt this rating scale if the fidelity ratings you use are different.

Once teachers have learned more than one evidence-based practice (e.g., in AIM cycle 2), you can observe more than one practice in a lesson (e.g., Comprehension Canopy *and* Essential Words). If you observe a teacher's implementation of more than one practice, you should record fidelity information on the fidelity checklist for each practice observed and then record the average of those ratings on the Stage 1 Log under the Monitor column.

You will use fidelity data to determine each teacher's skill level at week 5. Therefore, AIM Coaching *requires* during weeks 2–4 that each teacher implement at least one lesson on his own that incorporates the pre-selected evidence-based practice(s) with no support or modeling from you. This will allow you to collect fidelity data from at least

Reflect (once a week)
☐ Teacher reflect
☐ Provide feedback
☐ Review student data
☐ Problem-solve
☐ Set goals
Notes:

FIGURE 10.8. Recommended intervention guidelines for reflect sessions.

one lesson where the teacher takes the lead implementing the evidence-based literacy practice(s).

Reflect Session

After each monitor session, the instructional coach and teacher participate in a reflect session together. Reflect sessions provide opportunities for the instructional coach and teacher to reflect on the success of the monitor activities (i.e., observations, support, and modeling), review student data, and establish plans for moving forward. In practice, reflect sessions are closely tied to the monitor activities. Therefore, the reflect session dosage mirrors the same once per week dose. Depending on teacher need, reflect sessions can be relatively short (e.g., 5 minutes between classes), or they can occur during a longer period of time (e.g., during a planning period). Reflect sessions can occur immediately following a monitor session or at another convenient time shortly after the monitor session. It is even possible to conduct reflect sessions virtually (e.g., Skype). See Figure 10.8, where we list recommended reflect session activities.

Teacher Reflect

At the beginning of each reflect session, you should give the teacher a chance to reflect on his implementation. There are many questions that you can ask to elicit different responses. In Figure 10.9 below, see some question types and accompanying examples.

Provide Feedback

It is important to provide teachers with as much immediate, corrective feedback as possible, just as we do for students. In their book about explicit instruction, Archer and Hughes (2011) explain that the goal of feedback for students is to "close the gap between the student's current response and the desired response" (p. 175). This also

Type of Question	Example
Identifying the teaching action that caused a change	• At what point in the lesson did you notice that the students really understood the meaning of *liberty*? • Describe what happened when you increased the pacing of your lesson.
Brainstorming solutions to classroom problems	How many students struggled reading the passage today? Why do you think they struggled? What can we do to help those students?
Planning for future lessons	If you had the opportunity to teach the lesson again to the same group of students, what would you do differently? Why? How can you apply this to your next PACT lesson?

FIGURE 10.9. Types of questions to ask during reflect sessions.

applies to teachers: The goal of feedback is to close the gap between the teacher's current implementation and the desired implementation.

One type of feedback that can be especially important for teachers is behavior-specific praise. Praise can enhance learning and shape future actions (Archer & Hughes, 2011). For example, dropping by a teacher's classroom and thanking the teacher for helping another teacher with lower fidelity, or thanking a teacher for valuable input provided during a professional development session, are examples of praise. Of course, you can also provide additional praise about his performance during a monitor session. For example, you might email a teacher and say, "I really think that the way you paired students for partner reading was effective. All of the students were engaged in the task."

Feedback can be a powerful ingredient for change. However, some teachers do not receive frequent feedback and some instructional coaches might have very little experience providing feedback to adults. Therefore, we believe that you and the teachers you're working with should agree on some norms for providing feedback. Feldman (2016) suggests the following norms:

- *Humility:* No one knows it all, and everyone can improve. Open-mindedness is valued.
- *Curiosity:* We all have an interest in learning, changing, growing, wondering, and becoming more effective as teachers. This can be done by inquiring together as colleagues.
- *Kindness/respect:* Care will be taken to make sure all conversations are grounded in kindness and respect.

Review Student Data

There are many types of data that might be considered at this point, including samples of student work, notes from an observation, scores from a screening measure, or scores from a practice version of a high-stakes test. Sometimes, reviews of student data are sources for celebration. Be sure to always connect the teacher's actions directly to student outcomes, saying things like "You've been engaging your students in text reading 3 to 4 times per week. I notice that their grades are really improving on the district benchmarks. What else do you think contributed to the increased scores?"

Problem-Solve

Sometimes, student data expose problems. It is during student-data reviews that problem-solving can begin. Keep the discussion focused on the students and ask plenty of "wondering" questions such as "I noticed that half of the students struggled with the questions related to informational text. I wonder what could happen in the classroom to improve the outcomes." Or, "I noticed that many students were off task during the turn-and-talk routine. I wonder what you could do tomorrow to help them stay on task."

Set Goals

After discussing student progress and how it is tied to teacher instruction, setting new goals might be appropriate. Goals should include an action that can be measured. For example, "I will use more group response methods to increase student participation in class" is measurable. When you observe the teacher, you can look for both the teacher's behavior and the students' response.

Check-Ins

In addition to plan, monitor, and reflect sessions, the instructional coach should implement check-ins with teachers. Check-ins are designed to require a minimal amount of time and effort from the instructional coach and teachers, typically delivered by the instructional coach via email or a brief in-person encounter. The purpose of a check-in is to provide a "lighter" form of support to teachers between plan, monitor, and reflect sessions. Check-ins can serve as subtle reminders for teachers that the instructional coach is an ally in their corner. Check-ins typically fall into four different categories: feedback, questions with support, content resources, and process resources. See Figure 10.10 for a list of possible types of check-ins and the dosage of check-ins (i.e., once a week). Just like the plan, monitor, and reflect activities, there is a column on the Stage 1 Log that includes a list of these types of check-ins so that the instructional coach can record the number and type of check-ins that she provides to each teacher during weeks 2–4. When the instructional coach is supporting many teachers in a building, it will be important for the instructional coach to fill out the Stage 1 Log on an ongoing basis so that she does not forget any support that she provided to any teacher. Knowing the type and dosage of support for each teacher will be helpful for making data-based decisions, which is essential during the week 5 Assessment Stage. Below we describe each type of check-in.

Check In (once a week)
☐ Feedback ☐ Question with support ☐ Content resources ☐ Process resources
Notes:
Collaborative Effort 1 ☐ 2 ☐ 3 ☐ 4 ☐

FIGURE 10.10. Recommended intervention activities for check-ins.

Feedback

It is important you provide feedback that is immediate and corrective and helps close the gap between the current response and desired one. For example, you might say something like this to the teacher: "You did a great job pairing students strategically for partner reading in our plan session. All students were engaged. I'm looking forward to seeing how it goes during our monitor session in third period on Tuesday!"

Question

You can also provide a question with an offer of support. For example, you might ask, "How did the students in fifth period do with the text we picked? Do you need me to help you locate a new text for your next topic?"

Content Resource

Another form of check-in is when you provide the teacher with a resource that enhances his knowledge of intervention components or related content. For example, you might provide a link to the videos of PACT implementation on the University of Texas at Austin MCPER website. The video of Essential Words can be found at *www.meadowscenter.org/projects/detail/promoting-adolescents-comprehension-of-text-pact.*

Process Resource

Another type of resource that you can provide to the teacher as a form of check-in is a process resource, something that enhances his knowledge of pedagogical or management processes. For example, you might provide the teacher with a copy of the document on how to intensify instruction available at *www.centeroninstruction.org/intensive-interventions-for-students-struggling-in-reading-and-mathematics.*

Instructional coaches can use the Adolescent Literacy Resource Menu: A Guide for Instructional Leaders (see *www.meadowscenter.org/library/resource/adolescent-literacy-resource-menu-a-guide-for-instructional-leaders*) during check-ins (or even plan or reflect sessions). It is appropriate for use by instructional coaches who are trying to support teachers as they build a schoolwide adolescent literacy model. You will see that the Resource Menu contains a list of commonly experienced challenges that could affect a teacher's ability to implement evidence-based adolescent literacy practices with fidelity. The Resource Menu provides a short explanation of each challenge as well as resources from established sources, organizations, and research centers that the instructional coach can use to address such challenges. The Resource Menu also provides information about the cost and time requirements associated with each resource, since these are important factors that the instructional coach and teacher need to consider before choosing to use one. Once the instructional coach finds a resource, she can determine how to use it: Is it something that is appropriate for use by the instructional coach alone, or is it a resource appropriate to share with the teacher directly so the teacher can work through it independently? The instructional coach can continue to add to the Resource Menu as various needs unfold. After all, there might be some needs that are specific to her setting.

Collaborative Effort

Finally, turn your attention back to the Stage 1 Log. You will notice that a collaborative effort rating section appears at the bottom of the Check-In column for each week. At the end of each week during weeks 2–4, the instructional coach should rate a teacher's level of collaborative effort. What do we mean by collaborative effort? In order for a schoolwide adolescent literacy model to be successful, all teachers need to implement the chosen evidence-based adolescent literacy practices. After all, we developed AIM Coaching to support teachers in this endeavor. However, building a schoolwide adolescent literacy model can only be successful to the extent that teachers are willing, collaborative participants. Some examples of teachers who display a high level of collaborative effort are those who:

- are punctual for and attend entire professional development, plan, and reflect sessions.
- are actively engaged (e.g., limiting their cell phone use or other distractions) during professional development, plan, and reflect sessions.
- respond to email communication and/or requests from the instructional coach in a timely, professional manner.
- actively pursue scheduling of instructional coaching sessions (i.e., plan, monitor, reflect).

- acknowledge receipt of emails or resources from the instructional coach and request more when needed.
- allow the instructional coach to model or support lessons during monitor sessions, when appropriate.
- attempt to implement the evidence-based adolescent literacy practices from the professional development as intended.
- incorporate adaptations drawn from the reflect sessions.

For a rubric that corresponds to these examples of collaborative teachers using a 1–4 rating, see the AIM Coaching Manual in Appendix 10.3. We expect that some teachers will be very collaborative, while others may not for a variety of reasons. Also, the collaborative effort of each teacher might ebb and flow from week to week. In the next chapter, you will learn how to use the collaborative effort ratings during the Assessment Stage in week 5.

A NOTE ABOUT LOGISTICS

Implementing all the activities in AIM Coaching requires a lot of coordination and scheduling between the instructional coach and the teacher. For example, you have learned that in Stage 1 Intervention, the instructional coach needs to schedule plan, monitor, and reflect sessions with many teachers. This can become a lot to manage! For this reason, we recommend that the instructional coach set up a scheduling system. For example, she might create a Google spreadsheet with dates and times for teachers to fill out to sign up for a session. Even a simple sign-up sheet will serve the same purpose. These are details that the instructional coach can determine based on what is most convenient for her and the teachers she supports. The goal is to maintain some type of organized system so that the instructional coach is able to implement AIM Coaching with fidelity. This also applies to staying on top of Stage 1 logs. The instructional coach will need to develop a system to keep track of all of this paperwork. Some instructional coaches might choose to set up a notebook with dividers for each teacher and his or her Stage 1 logs. Others may choose to collect information electronically and then transfer it to the Stage 1 logs.

REVIEW AND PREVIEW

In this chapter, we reviewed adaptive interventions in general and how the principles align with AIM Coaching. We then provided a step-by-step guide on how to begin implementing AIM Coaching with Stage 1 Intervention, using PACT as an example. In Chapter 11, we will provide an overview of the week 5 Assessment Stage.

Terms to Know

Decision points: Times during an intervention when an instructional leader reviews each teacher's data to determine how intervention support should be differentiated and adapted to meet the teacher's needs and optimize teaching outcomes.

Decision rules: The guidelines an instructional leader follows to determine how to adapt the type and dosage of support each teacher receives on the basis of the teacher's tailoring variable data at a decision point.

Intervention options: Options the instructional leader has for varying the type and dosage of intervention for each teacher.

Stage 1 Intervention: The intervention period in which an instructional leader provides all teachers with initial professional development to introduce a new practice as well as standardized protocol support.

Stage 2 Intervention: The intervention period in which an instructional leader provides each teacher with adapted support on the basis of the teacher's tailoring variable data at a decision point.

Standardized protocol support: The type and dosage of intervention support a coach gives after providing initial professional development. Standardized protocol support is the same for all teachers.

Tailoring variables: The specific characteristics or types of data (e.g., teacher fidelity) that influence a teacher's target outcomes and that an instructional leader reviews at a decision point.

Reflection Questions

1. Can you describe how AIM Coaching represents the essential elements of an adaptive intervention?
2. How many weeks are in one AIM cycle?
3. How many stages are in the AIM?
4. What log does the instructional coach use to record weekly AIM Coaching data? Why is it important that the instructional coach record these data?
5. What does the instructional coach do during week 1 of Stage 1 Intervention?
6. What type of support does the instructional coach provide to teachers during weeks 2–4 of Stage 1 Intervention?
7. Describe the recommended intervention activities of a plan session. What is the expected weekly dosage?
8. Describe the recommended intervention activities of a monitor session. What is the expected weekly dosage?

9. Describe the recommended intervention activities of a reflect session. What is the expected weekly dosage?
10. What is the purpose of a weekly check-in? What are some types of check-ins that the instructional coach can provide?
11. What is a resource the instructional coach can refer to if she needs to recommend resources for teachers?
12. How often and when does the instructional coach record fidelity data? Where does the instructional coach put this rating on the Stage 1 Log?
13. What is the purpose of a collaborative effort rating? When does the instructional coach assign this rating for a teacher? Where does the instructional coach record this information on the Stage 1 Log? Can you list some example traits of a teacher who would receive a high score on the collaborative effort rating? Where can you find a rubric that corresponds to the collaborative effort rating?

APPENDIX 10.1

Stage 1 Log

Teacher Name: ____________________

Last Cycle Notes:

STAGE 1 EBP: ____________________

Week 2

Plan (by request)	**Monitor** (1/week)	**Reflect** (1/week)	**Check In** (1/week)
☐ Review goals ☐ Review st. data ☐ Choose materials ☐ Lesson template ☐ Review fidelity ☐ Discuss/practice ☐ Discuss coach role	☐ Observe ☐ Support ☐ Model	☐ Teacher reflect ☐ Provide feedback ☐ Review st. data ☐ Problem solve ☐ Set goals	☐ Feedback ☐ Question w/ support ☐ Content resources ☐ Process resources
Notes:	**Notes:** **Fidelity Rating** Date: ______ 1 ☐ 2 ☐ 3 ☐ 4 ☐	**Notes:**	**Notes:** **Collaborative Effort** 1 ☐ 2 ☐ 3 ☐ 4 ☐

(continued)

© 2019 The University of Texas at Austin/The Meadows Center for Preventing Educational Risk. *PACT Plus Coaching Form* licensed under Creative Commons BY-NC-ND 4.0 International. Reprinted in *Literacy Coaching in the Secondary Grades: Helping Teachers Meet the Needs of All Students* by Jade Wexler, Elizabeth Swanson, and Alexandra Shelton (The Guilford Press, 2021). Permission to photocopy this material is granted to purchasers of this book for personal use or use with students (see copyright page for details). Purchasers can download enlarged versions of this material (see the box at the end of the table of contents).

APPENDIX 10.1 *(continued)*

Week 3

Plan (by request)	**Monitor** (1/week)	**Reflect** (1/week)	**Check In** (1/week)
☐ Review goals ☐ Review st. data ☐ Choose materials ☐ Lesson template ☐ Review fidelity ☐ Discuss/practice ☐ Discuss coach role **Notes:**	☐ Observe ☐ Support ☐ Model **Notes:** **Fidelity Rating** Date: ______ 1 ☐ 2 ☐ 3 ☐ 4 ☐	☐ Teacher reflect ☐ Provide feedback ☐ Review st. data ☐ Problem solve ☐ Set goals **Notes:**	☐ Feedback ☐ Question w/ support ☐ Content resources ☐ Process resources **Notes:** **Collaborative Effort** 1 ☐ 2 ☐ 3 ☐ 4 ☐

(continued)

APPENDIX 10.1 *(continued)*

Week 4

Plan (by request)	**Monitor** (1/week)	**Reflect** (1/week)	**Check In** (1/week)
☐ Review goals ☐ Review st. data ☐ Choose materials ☐ Lesson template ☐ Review fidelity ☐ Discuss/practice ☐ Discuss coach role **Notes:**	☐ Observe ☐ Support ☐ Model **Notes:** **Fidelity Rating** Date: ______ 1 ☐ 2 ☐ 3 ☐ 4 ☐	☐ Teacher reflect ☐ Provide feedback ☐ Review st. data ☐ Problem solve ☐ Set goals **Notes:**	☐ Feedback ☐ Question w/ support ☐ Content resources ☐ Process resources **Notes:** **Collaborative Effort** 1 ☐ 2 ☐ 3 ☐ 4 ☐

(continued)

APPENDIX 10.1 *(continued)*

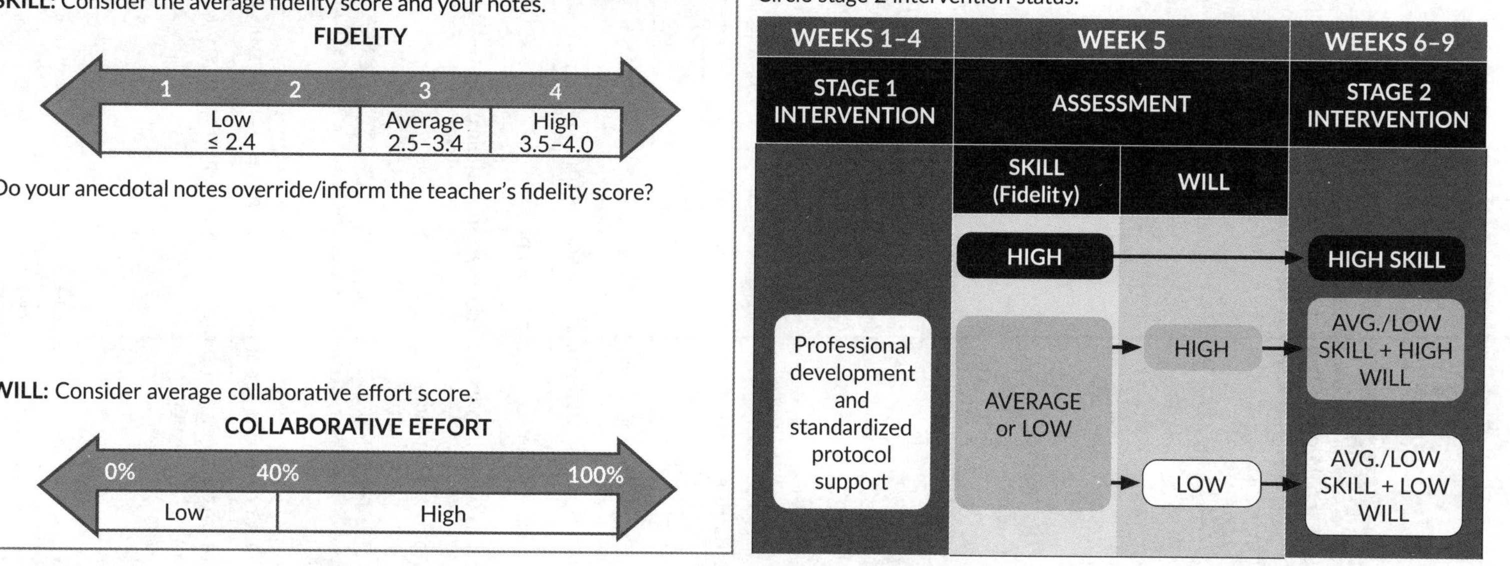

Week 5: Assessment Stage

SKILL: Consider the average fidelity score and your notes.

FIDELITY

1	2	3	4
Low ≤ 2.4		Average 2.5–3.4	High 3.5–4.0

Do your anecdotal notes override/inform the teacher's fidelity score?

WILL: Consider average collaborative effort score.

COLLABORATIVE EFFORT

0%	40%	100%
Low	High	

STAGE 2

Circle stage 2 intervention status.

WEEKS 1–4	WEEK 5		WEEKS 6–9
STAGE 1 INTERVENTION	ASSESSMENT		STAGE 2 INTERVENTION
	SKILL (Fidelity)	WILL	
	HIGH	→	HIGH SKILL
Professional development and standardized protocol support	AVERAGE or LOW	HIGH	AVG./LOW SKILL + HIGH WILL
		LOW	AVG./LOW SKILL + LOW WILL

APPENDIX 10.2

Teacher Criteria for Success: Essential Words

Criteria for Planning: The Teacher...	Y	N

Completed the Essential Words Planning Guide and does the following:
• Brainstorms or lists all words to teach for the unit (from required word lists, high-utility words necessary for content understanding, or words frequently encountered in the unit)
• Looks for connections to meet the goal of understanding overarching concepts
• Chooses essential words based on connections to overarching concepts
• Creates an essential word guide for each essential word
• Includes the following in each essential word guide:
  • Student-friendly definition
  • Image
  • Related words (from list of words)
  • Example of word in a sentence (example usage)
  • Examples and nonexamples
  • Turn-and-talk activity
	☐	☐

Criteria for Implementation: The Teacher...	Y	N
Teaches a minimum of two essential words per week, using an essential word guide for each word	☐	☐
Pronounces words and has students repeat words	☐	☐
Presents and discusses student-friendly definitions	☐	☐
Facilitates discussion of the visual representations	☐	☐
Presents and discusses related words	☐	☐
Provides an example of essential words in a sentence	☐	☐
Presents and discusses examples and nonexamples	☐	☐
Prompts students to write important information in their essential words log	☐	☐
Conducts a turn-and-talk activity	☐	☐

Quality Indicators: The Teacher...	Y	N
Provides modeling	☐	☐
Provides immediate corrective feedback and reteaches as necessary	☐	☐
Promotes student engagement with multiple opportunities for students to practice and respond through the following: • Group responses • Think-pair-share • Turn and talk	☐	☐

© 2019 The University of Texas at Austin/The Meadows Center for Preventing Educational Risk. Licensed under Creative Commons BY-NC-ND 4.0 International. Reprinted in *Literacy Coaching in the Secondary Grades: Helping Teachers Meet the Needs of All Students* by Jade Wexler, Elizabeth Swanson, and Alexandra Shelton (The Guilford Press, 2021). Permission to photocopy this material is granted to purchasers of this book for personal use or use with students (see copyright page for details). Purchasers can download enlarged versions of this material (see the box at the end of the table of contents).

APPENDIX 10.3

AIM Coaching Manual

This document summarizes the steps instructional coaches take to implement Adaptive Intervention Model (AIM) Coaching.

Stage 1 Intervention

1. **Week 1:** Deliver professional development on a single evidence-based practice.
2. **Weeks 2–4:** Follow the guidelines below to provide each teacher with standardized protocol support.

Stage 1 Support

	Plan	Monitor	Reflect	Check In
Standardized Protocol Support	By request	1/week	1/week	1/week

3. On each teacher's Stage 1 Log, record information about the plan, monitor, and reflect session activities, and check-ins.
4. Monitor each teacher's implementation using the fidelity checklist at least once a week.
5. Record each teacher's fidelity rating in the Monitor column of the Stage 1 Log.
6. On the Stage 1 Log, record any relevant notes that can inform future decisions about the teacher's skill and will.
7. At the end of each week during Stage 1 Intervention, record a collaborative effort rating on each teacher's Stage 1 Log using the rubric and description below.

Rubric

Rating	Collaborative Effort (8 Total Elements)
4	8 elements
3	5–7 elements
2	2–4 elements
1	0–1 elements

(continued)

© 2019 The University of Texas at Austin/The Meadows Center for Preventing Educational Risk. *Adaptive Intervention Model Manual* licensed under Creative Commons BY-NC-ND 4.0 International. Reprinted in *Literacy Coaching in the Secondary Grades: Helping Teachers Meet the Needs of All Students* by Jade Wexler, Elizabeth Swanson, and Alexandra Shelton (The Guilford Press, 2021). Permission to photocopy this material is granted to purchasers of this book for personal use or use with students (see copyright page for details). Purchasers can download enlarged versions of this material (see the box at the end of the table of contents).

Description

- ☐ Attend and be punctual for entire professional development, plan, and reflect sessions.
- ☐ Be actively engaged (e.g., limited use of cell phone) during professional development, plan, and reflect sessions.
- ☐ Respond to e-mail communication and/or requests from the coach in a timely, professional manner.
- ☐ Actively schedule coaching essions (i.e., plan, monitor, reflect).
- ☐ Acknowledge receipt of e-mails or resources from instructional coaches and request more when needed.
- ☐ Allow the instructional coach to model or support lessons during monitor sessions, when appropriate.
- ☐ Attempt to implement the literacy evidence-based practices from the professional development as intended.
- ☐ Incorporate adaptations drawn from the reflect sessions.

Assessment Stage

1. **Week 5:** Calculate the average of each teacher's fidelity ratings recorded during Stage 1 Intervention.
2. Record the average fidelity score on the Stage 1 Log fidelity scale.
3. Use any relevant notes to answer the following question: *Do your anecdotal notes override or inform the teacher's fidelity score?*
4. Administer the MIP scale to teachers with **average** or **low** skill (as measured by an average of all fidelity ratings recorded during Stage 1 Intervention).
5. Calculate the average Stage 1 Intervention collaborative effort score for each teacher with average or low skill.
6. Record the average collaborative effort score and use it to answer the following question: *Does collaborative effort override or inform the teacher's MIP score?*
7. Follow the decision rules below to determine the level of support each teacher needs during Stage 2 Intervention.
8. Record each teacher's Stage 2 Intervention level of support on the Stage 2 Log.

(continued)

Decision Rules

Average Fidelity Score	Skill Level	MIP Score	Will Level	Support
3.5–4.0	High Skill	N/A	N/A	High Skill
2.5–3.4	Average Skill	≥ 40%	High Will	Average or Low Skill + High Will
2.5–3.4	Average Skill	< 40%	Low Will	Average or Low Skill + Low Will
≤ 2.4	Low Skill	≥ 40%	High Will	Average or Low Skill + High Will
≤ 2.4	Low Skill	< 40%	Low Will	Average or Low Skill + Low Will

Stage 2 Intervention

1. **Weeks 6–9:** Follow the guidelines below to provide each teacher with differentiated support.

Stage 2 Support

	Plan	Monitor	Reflect	Check In
High Skill	By request	By request	By request	1/week
Average or Low Skill + High Will	1/week	1/week	1/week	2/week
Average or Low Skill + Low Will	Low Will Support			

2. On each teacher's Stage 2 Log, record information about plan, monitor, and reflect session activities, and check-ins.
3. Monitor each teacher's implementation using the fidelity checklist at least once a week.
4. Record each teacher's fidelity rating in the Monitor column of the Stage 2 Log.
5. For teachers with low will, use the Low Will Guide to identify interventions to use in place of or alongside the plan-monitor-reflect-check-in sequence.
6. On the Stage 2 Log, record any relevant notes that can inform future decisions about the teacher's skill and will.
7. At the end of each week during Stage 2 Intervention, record a collaborative effort rating on each teacher's Stage 1 Log using the same rubric and description shown in the Stage 1 directions above.

(continued)

End of Stage 2 Intervention

1. Calclulate the average of each teacher's fidelity ratings recorded during Stage 2 Intervention.
2. Use any relevant notes to answer the following qustion: *Do your anecdotal notes override or inform the teacher's fidelity score?*
3. Record the MIP score of teachers with **average** or **low** fidelity ratings from Stage 1 Intervention.
4. Calculate the average Stage 2 Intervention collaborative effort score for each teacher with average or low skill.
5. Record the average collaborative effort score and use it to answer the following question: *Does collaborative effort override or inform the teacher's MIP score?*

Future AIM Cycles

Use the same set of instructions to facilitate future AIM cycles, with the following additions.

1. Request that teachers implement more than one evidence-based practice (i.e., evidence-based practices from previous and current AIM cycles) during monitor sessions.
2. Monitor teachers' implementation of each evidence-based practice using the fidelity checklist.
3. Calculate each teacher's average fidelity rating across evdence-based practices and record it in the Monitor column of the Stage 1 and 2 Logs weekly.
4. List the evdence-based practices that the teacher implemented with low fidelity in the notes section of the Monitor column weekly.
5. During the Assessment Stage, readminister the MIP scale to teachers with **average** or **low** skill.
6. Individualize Stage 2 Intervention support based on the evidence-based practice areas of need identified during Stage 1 Intervention monitor sessions.

CHAPTER 11

Determining Teachers' Skill and Will Levels

In Chapter 10, we provided an overview of AIM Coaching, and we described Stage 1 Intervention in detail. You learned that in week 1, the instructional coach provides professional development on an evidence-based adolescent literacy practice. You also learned that during weeks 2–4, the instructional coach provides standardized protocol support to teachers, meaning that all get the same level of support through the plan–monitor–reflect–check-in sequence. Record-keeping is simple using the Stage 1 Log (see Appendix 10.1):

- Record the fidelity score during the monitor session(s); and
- Assign every teacher a weekly collaborative effort rating at the end of each week.

All of these data are important for making data-based decisions during the Assessment Stage, week 5 of the AIM cycle.

ASSESSMENT STAGE

At week 5 comes a decision point—a point during the AIM when the instructional coach uses data on a teacher's *skill* and *will* to help determine what level of support a teacher needs during Stage 2 Intervention (Yoshino et al., 2009). See that we have circled the Assessment Stage in Figure 11.1.

This is the point when the instructional coach really needs to think about the idea of change. In order to build a schoolwide adolescent literacy model, we are asking teachers to change their practice. This will be easy and quick for some teachers. In fact,

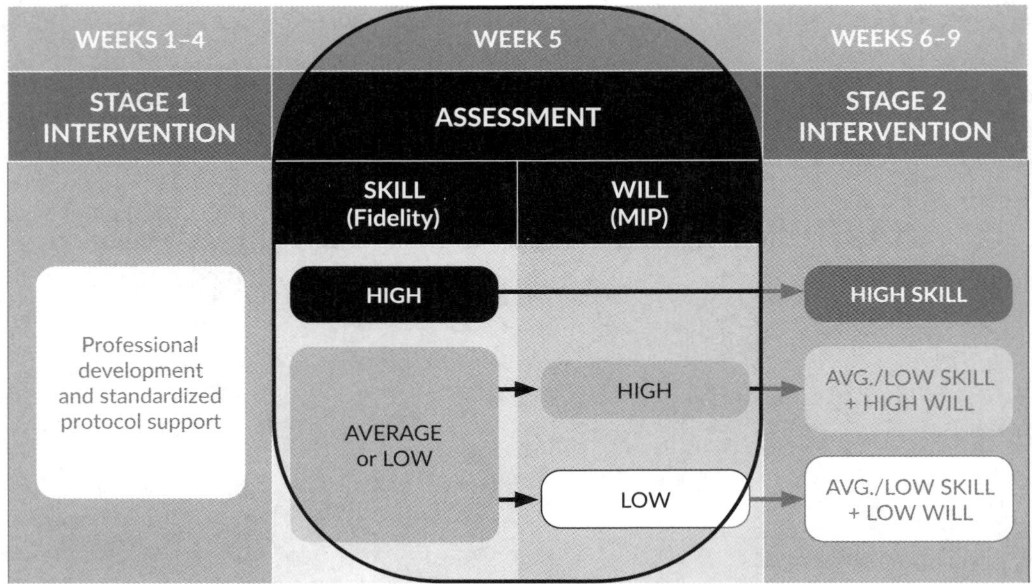

FIGURE 11.1. Assessment Stage of AIM Coaching.

some might have already changed their practice (i.e., adopted and implemented the chosen evidence-based practice with fidelity) during Stage 1 Intervention. Others will need a lot of support. They might be willing but not yet have the skills to translate their willingness into action. Others might have the skills but be resistant and unwilling to change. Some might lack both skill and will.

SKILL AND WILL

Skill

The first set of data to consider is teacher skill level. We equate skill level with average fidelity of implementation, so we ask, "How well does the teacher implement the evidence-based practice(s)?" Instructional coaches use fidelity checklists to monitor a teacher's adherence to implementation of the evidence-based practice. When measuring fidelity, we're looking for the extent to which a teacher implements the practice as intended coupled with the quality with which she implements the practice.

Will

What might be contributing to teachers' low or average skill level, as demonstrated by their fidelity score(s)? It may be, at least in part, a result of low *will* (e.g., Abrami et al., 2004; Baker, Chard, Ketterlin-Geller, Apichatabutra, & Doabler, 2009; Dijkstra et al., 2017; Duckworth, 2009; Robertson-Kraft & Duckworth, 2014). Thus, knowing a teacher's will level can help the instructional coach provide the appropriate support for that teacher. We believe that by capitalizing on the teacher's will during Stage 2 intervention, instructional coaches can improve fidelity of implementation, or skill level, of the evidence-based practice(s). For example, Thoonen, Sleegers, Oort, Peetsma, and Geijsel (2001) demonstrated that teacher motivational factors, such as will, influence teachers' engagement in professional learning activities and ultimately their practices. So, what "represents" a teacher's will level? We consider a teacher's will level to be a representation of how much motivation, investment, and persistence (i.e., MIP) she has when it comes to implementing an evidence-based practice.

You can likely define motivation, investment, and persistence, but to make sure we are all on the same page, we will explain what we mean by MIP in the context of instructional coaching. We conceptualize *motivation* as interest in completing a task (i.e., Do I *want* to do this task?). It is likely that people will be motivated to implement evidence-based practices if they have a robust interest to do so. For example, a teacher might be very interested in helping her struggling readers be successful. Thus, she is motivated. To exhibit a high will level, an individual also needs to see the task as a worthy *investment* (i.e., be convinced of a task's value; Maehr, 1991). For example, a teacher might be motivated to (i.e., want to) help her struggling readers but not believe the task is valuable because she thinks, "This is just another fad. It will pass." In this case, the teacher is not convinced that implementing a particular practice is of value, or a good investment. Being motivated and/or seeing great value in completing a task does not necessarily mean teachers will "get it done." Another important piece of a high will level, therefore, is *persistence* (e.g., Duckworth, 2009), or the willingness to work hard to accomplish a task (e.g., implementing an instructional practice). In other words, being motivated in a task and/or convinced of the task's value will not necessarily result in improved student achievement if the teacher is not willing to stick with implementing the practice, even when it becomes challenging. We bet you can think of many reasons why a teacher might not be persistent. Does she lack confidence in her ability to implement the task? Is she unwilling to work hard at the task because she isn't motivated in the task and/or perceives the task as having low value? Does she have other priorities?

This brings us to Figure 11.2. In this illustration, we provide profiles of teachers who exhibit different combinations of motivation (M), investment (I), and persistence (P) when implementing an evidence-based practice. As you review Figure 11.2, note several things:

- These profiles are not comprehensive and may not apply to all teachers, but they are a starting point to provide instructional coaches with potential explanations about different teacher profiles.
- Thinking about these different teacher profiles can help us understand the challenges instructional coaches face: supporting teachers with different levels of will.

Is this a teacher who . . . (M) wants to implement the practice? (I) is convinced the practice is helping, or will help, her students become more proficient in reading? (P) is willing to work hard to implement the practice?				
Teacher	**M**	**I**	**P**	**Teacher Profiles**
A	✓	✓	✓	*It is likely that this teacher will be a champion of the practice in her school. She will work hard to implement the practice with fidelity. She will likely work collaboratively with the instructional coach.*
B	✓	O	✓	*Teacher B wants to implement the practice and is willing to work hard to do so. Despite his willingness to work hard, he does not particularly value the practice. This may seem counterintuitive at first. How can he be willing to work hard at implementing a practice but not value it? Perhaps his willingness to implement the practice is due to compliance rather than believing in the practice's value. This teacher will likely work collaboratively with the instructional coach because he is expected to do so. However, he will not go out of his way to be a champion of the practice. Simultaneously, he might push his administration to adopt other practices.*
C	✓	✓	O	*This teacher is a teacher who is motivated to implement the practice and thinks it is a worthy investment. She wants to implement the practice, perhaps due to the fact that she values it. She feels that her students will benefit from the practice. However, she is not willing to work hard to implement it. This also sounds counterintuitive. You would think that if a teacher is motivated and invested in a practice and believes it's a worthy investment, she would also be persistent. Some people might just not be willing to work hard at implementing a practice. Perhaps she has other priorities that she is also working on implementing that are consuming all of her effort. Perhaps she is getting ready to retire or change jobs and is unwilling to change her routine at this point in order to actually translate the practice(s) into action.*
D	✓	O	O	*This is a teacher who wants to implement the practice, perhaps due to compliance or because he thinks his students need something to help improve their achievement. He does not, however, see the value in this particular practice. Maybe he sees value in a different practice or set of practices. To this end, he is not willing to work hard to implement the practices. However, he might work collaboratively with the instructional coach for compliance reasons.*
E	O	✓	✓	*This is an example of a teacher who does not necessarily want to change her current routine. She does not want to implement the practice. She does, however, see value in the practice, and feels that she is willing to work hard to do so if she has to. Perhaps her lack of motivation reflects a lack of confidence when it comes to changing her current routine. Perhaps she is anticipating behavior problems in her class if she implements this practice. There is something standing in the way of her motivation; nevertheless, she is willing to work hard to implement the practice. She might work with the instructional coach to the extent that she is required to.*

(continued)

FIGURE 11.2. Teacher MIP profiles.

Teacher	M	I	P	Teacher Profiles
F	O	✓	O	*This is a teacher who believes that his students would benefit from the practice, which he sees as valuable. However, he does not want to implement the practice and is unwilling to do so. Why? Perhaps he does not want to implement the practice because he believes he does not know what steps to take to implement it. Thus, he is not willing to work hard to implement the practice either. Perhaps he has other priorities he is working on. Because he values the practice, he might work with the instructional coach collaboratively.*
G	O	O	✓	*This is a teacher who does not want to implement the practice and does not value it. Why, then, is she willing to persist at the task? This is likely a teacher who is compliant. Despite her lack of motivation and perception of whether or not it is a good investment, she will attempt to implement the practice, at least according to the minimum requirements. She will not go above and beyond that. She will work with the instructional coach to the extent that it is required.*
H	O	O	O	*This teacher does not want to implement the practice. She does not value the practice. She is also not willing to work hard to implement the practice. She will likely not work collaboratively with the instructional coach.*

FIGURE 11.2. *(continued)*

- Do not assume there is a causal linkage among the components. This means that having a sufficient amount of one component does not necessarily cause a teacher to have a sufficient amount of another component. For example, a teacher's motivation and investment do not necessarily cause her to be persistent.
- Some teacher profiles are more conducive to instructional coaching activities. In Chapter 12, we will provide suggestions on how instructional coaches can use these teacher profiles to help them choose interventions to target teachers' needs.

DETERMINING SKILL AND WILL LEVELS

Now that you know a little more about the concepts of skill and will, we need to consider how to measure and keep a record of teachers' skill and will levels.

Determining Skill

For any monitor session where the teacher is leading at least a portion of the lesson with her students, the instructional coach records fidelity data. Because AIM Coaching requires that each teacher lead implementation of the evidence-based practice in at least one lesson during weeks 2–4, the instructional coach should be able to collect fidelity information from that one lesson (if not more). During the week 5 Assessment Stage, the instructional coach uses the rating from the single teacher-led lesson or an average fidelity score based on as many fidelity checklists that the instructional coach completed during weeks 2–4 to help determine skill. Instructional coaches can determine cut points, based on the average fidelity scores, and divide skill level into three categories: high skill, average skill, or low skill. For example, when using PACT with the accompanying 4-point scale for determining average fidelity (see Appendix 8.1 for the PACT fidelity checklist), high skill = 3.5 or more, average skill = 2.5 to 3.4, and low skill = 2.4 or less.

This is a lot of information to process. Perhaps an example related to PACT implementation will help. In AIM cycle 1, the instructional coach might support a teacher by co-teaching a Comprehension Canopy lesson during weeks 2 and 3. The teacher is not implementing the lesson on her own in this situation, and, thus, determining the teacher's fidelity ratings in these sessions is difficult. Because there is only one more monitor session (week 4) before the week 5 Assessment Stage, it is necessary that this teacher lead the week 4 Comprehension Canopy lesson, so the instructional coach has a chance to observe the teacher leading the lesson and, therefore, is able to record a fidelity rating. For illustration's sake, let's say that this teacher did an average job implementing Comprehension Canopy and received a fidelity rating of 3. The instructional coach can record the single fidelity rating on the week 5 Assessment Stage section of the Stage 1 Log with an X (see Figure 11.3).

Another teacher might have led more than 1 week of lessons, giving the instructional coach multiple opportunities to record fidelity information. In this case, the instructional coach should average multiple fidelity ratings and then record where the average score falls on the fidelity arrow on the Stage 1 Log. For example, if the instructional coach recorded the following fidelity ratings: week 3 fidelity rating = 2 and week

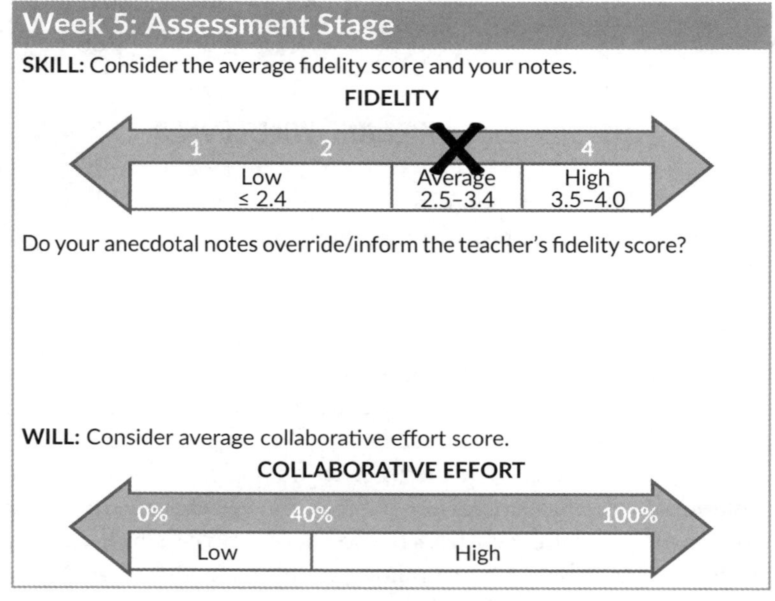

FIGURE 11.3. Sample fidelity arrow on the Stage 1 Log.

4 fidelity rating = 3, the instructional coach can average those ratings (average fidelity score = 2 + 3/2 = 2.5) and record the average score in the correct location on the arrow.

Before we explain how this equates to a skill level, let's consider one other situation you might be wondering about. What if we are in AIM cycle 2, and teachers are now implementing two evidence-based literacy practices, such as Comprehension Canopy (learned in AIM cycle 1) *and* Essential Words (learned in AIM cycle 2)? Well, guess what? The same rules apply! In this situation, the instructional coach should average all fidelity ratings *across all the practices implemented during weeks 2–4* and record the average fidelity score on the fidelity arrow of the Stage 1 Log. In other words, it doesn't matter what practices the teachers are implementing; we want to know their overall skill level for the practices they *do* implement.

What if a teacher's average fidelity score results from high ratings on Comprehension Canopy (i.e., the evidence-based practice from AIM cycle 1) and low ratings on Essential Words (i.e., the evidence-based practice from AIM cycle 2)? First, nice job! It is critical that you use data to drive your decisions, and this is an important pattern drawn from the data that you will want to consider. It also happens to be a pattern that makes sense. The teacher has had more time to practice implementing Comprehension Canopy, and Essential Words may still be relatively new to her. In this case, the instructional coach still records the average fidelity score.

Finally, you will see that there is a question below the arrow. It says: Do your anecdotal notes override/inform the teacher's fidelity score? For example, in the situation above that described the teacher who earned high fidelity ratings on Comprehension Canopy and low fidelity ratings on Essential Words, it would be helpful for the instructional coach to have a space on the log where he can make notes about this. See Figure 11.4 for how the coach did this. These notes will help him remember that the teacher needs the most support with Essential Words due to her low fidelity ratings. Therefore, the instructional coach can use this information to individualize future support during Stage 2 Intervention as much as possible. This question is also necessary because it gives the instructional coach the ability to "override" the average fidelity score if he has a reason to believe that the average fidelity score was not indicative of the teacher's true level of skill during Stage 1 Intervention. After all, the instructional coach should ideally have had several interactions with each teacher by this point and might have collected information that contradicts the teacher's average score. We don't anticipate this happening a lot, but it is possible! As a reminder, the instructional coach should make decisions based on data, even if the data are informal in nature, so having a record of notes from the previous weeks on the Stage 1 Log may be very helpful. Can you think of an example of when this might occur?

How about if there is a fire drill in the middle of a week 4 monitor session when you are collecting fidelity data? This is the instructional coach's last chance to assign a fidelity rating before the week 5 Assessment Stage. However, what if the fire drill uses up 15 minutes of class time? By the time the teacher and students return to the classroom, the teacher decides to skip key elements of the first practice (i.e., Comprehension Canopy) to move on to the next practice (i.e., Essential Words). Technically, the teacher's data will indicate low fidelity, bringing her average fidelity score into the

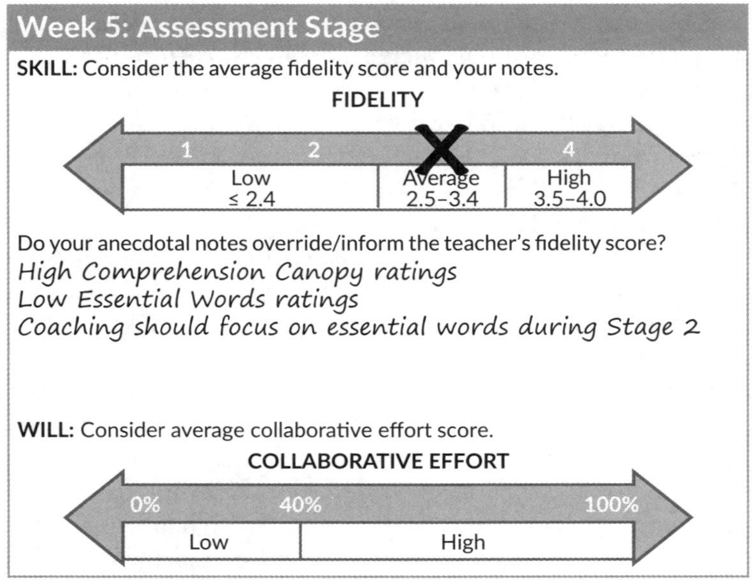

FIGURE 11.4. Sample anecdotal notes on the Stage 1 Log.

low-skill range. However, based on monitor sessions when the instructional coach was supporting the teacher during the AIM cycle 1, the instructional coach feels that if it weren't for the fire drill, the teacher would have implemented more elements of the first evidence-based practice and earned at least an average fidelity rating. What can the instructional coach do about this? He can override the teacher's fidelity score. Again, we don't expect this to happen a lot, but we do believe it is important that the instructional coach be able to make decisions based on "real-life" situations. *After all, while we designed AIM Coaching to be systematic, we do not intend for the systematic nature of the model to override the ability of the instructional coach to make good decisions.*

INTRODUCING MR. RYAN: A CASE STUDY

Let's consider a real-life case study illustrating the process of determining a teacher's skill. In Chapter 3 of this book, we introduced the example of a school that had participated in an adolescent literacy model demonstration project (i.e., PACT Plus). One of the teachers in this project was Mr. Ryan, a seventh-grade science teacher. In weeks 1–4 of AIM cycle 3, Mr. Ryan's instructional coach provided Stage 1 Intervention just as she had done during AIM cycles 1 and 2. In AIM cycle 1, Mr. Ryan demonstrated high skill when implementing Comprehension Canopy. In AIM cycle 2, Mr. Ryan demonstrated high skill when implementing Comprehension Canopy *and* Essential Words. In AIM cycle 3, Mr. Ryan attended the professional development session on

Critical Reading. During weeks 2–4 of AIM cycle 3 Stage 1 Intervention, he did not request any plan sessions, as he had done during weeks 2–4 in the previous AIM cycles. However, he did respond to his instructional coach's requests to schedule and conduct monitor sessions each week. He participated in one reflect session via phone, but said he was too busy for the other two reflect sessions. He also responded to her check-in emails cordially. Because he did not request any plan sessions, her role during the monitor sessions was simply to observe Mr. Ryan.

Because he was not as engaged during AIM cycle 3 Stage 1 Intervention as he was during AIM cycles 1 and 2, the instructional coach was curious how Mr. Ryan's implementation of Critical Reading would compare to his previously implemented Comprehension Canopy and Essential Words lessons. During week 5 of AIM cycle 3, Mr. Ryan's instructional coach was able to calculate an average fidelity score for weeks 2–4 lessons. Mr. Ryan earned a 2.4, which equated to low skill (see Figure 11.5). While this score was on the high end of the low skill range, it was still considered low skill. Mr. Ryan's instructional coach was concerned since this contrasted with his previous performance. She reviewed the anecdotal notes that she had recorded on the Stage 1 Log and determined that there was nothing out of the ordinary that would contrast with this low skill score.

What was impacting Mr. Ryan's skill level? Was there something about Critical Reading that was causing confusion? Before determining the best course of action to support Mr. Ryan during Stage 2 Intervention, his instructional coach needed more information about his will level. See the following for an explanation on how to do this.

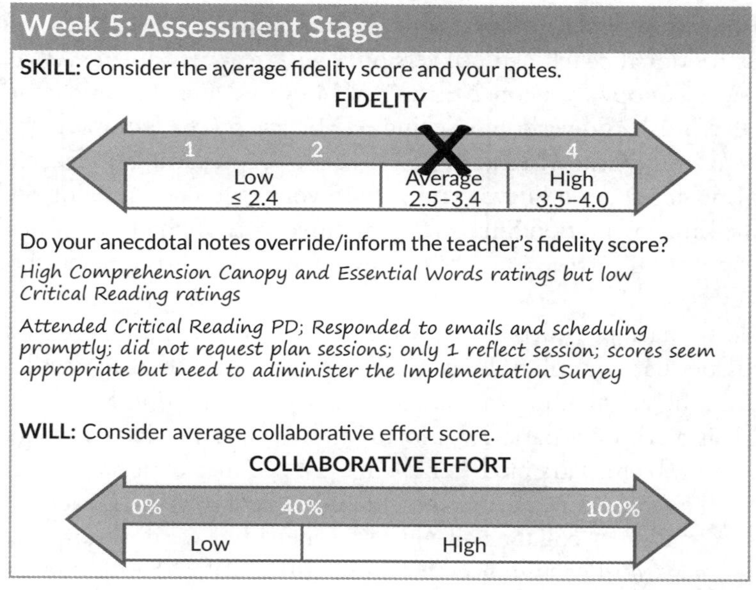

FIGURE 11.5. Mr. Ryan's skill data on the Stage 1 Log.

Determining Will

For teachers who have average or low skill, it is important to determine their will. AIM Coaching includes two pieces of information to inform the instructional coach's assessment of a teacher's will level: (1) the teacher's collaborative effort ratings from weeks 2–4 recorded on the Stage 1 Log, and (2) the teacher's self-reported information related to her MIP from an Implementation Survey. The Implementation Survey contains two parts. In Part I, we focus on measuring MIP. In Part II below, we focus more on diagnosing the reasons behind the MIP score (Part II will be further discussed in Chapter 12).

Implementation Survey: Part I

Part I of the Implementation Survey requires teachers to self-report information about their level of motivation, perceptions of investment, and level of persistence based on three statements linked to each PACT instructional practice. The first statement targets motivation (i.e., I want to implement Comprehension Canopy in my classroom). The second statement targets investment (i.e., I think Comprehension Canopy is helping, or will help, my students become more proficient in reading). The third statement targets persistence (i.e., I am willing to work hard to implement Comprehension Canopy). For each item, teachers indicate their level of agreement on a 7-point scale (1 = do not agree at all; 7 = completely agree).

As you add instructional practices over time, it is important to assess MIP on every instructional practice. After all, teachers may be motivated in Essential Words and believe it's a worthy investment, but not think the same about Critical Reading. For this reason, we provide three versions of the Implementation Survey in Appendix 11.1. The instructional coach can use version 1 with teachers during AIM cycle 1 (i.e., Comprehension Canopy), version 2 during AIM cycle 2 (i.e., Comprehension Canopy and Essential Words), and version 3 during AIM cycle 3 (i.e., Comprehension Canopy, Essential Words, and Critical Reading). These are only examples; feel free to take the ideas in our Implementation Survey and plug in your own chosen set of evidence-based practices. The Implementation Survey can be universally applied to any evidence-based practice to support all instructional coaches who are trying to build a schoolwide adolescent literacy model.

Now that we have provided an overview of the Implementation Survey, we want to address one issue that you might be considering. If a teacher has low will, it is possible that she will not be very willing to complete the Implementation Survey! We acknowledge that this is a tricky situation. Unfortunately, we do not have a magic solution if this becomes a problem. Part of the challenge for the instructional coach is finding a way to encourage teachers to participate collaboratively in AIM Coaching, and, thus, this becomes a matter of collaborative effort. One thing we do know is that without knowing a teacher's skill or will level, it will be difficult for the instructional coach to tailor her support in Stage 2 Intervention, making the goal of building a schoolwide adolescent literacy model even more difficult.

Therefore, we recommend that the instructional coach explain the importance of teachers' participation in AIM Coaching and set expectations about AIM Coaching when she provides an overview of AIM Coaching during the first professional development session (or soon thereafter) in AIM cycle 1. Note that we provide additional guidelines about how to do this in the AIM Coaching FAQs available on this book's companion website (see the box at the end of the table of contents). Also, note that the instructional coach can administer the Implementation Survey in a number of ways. The instructional coach can administer it individually or with multiple teachers at once. The instructional coach can also turn the Implementation Survey into an online survey if that would help facilitate administration. In other words, there is flexibility in how and in what setting the instructional coach administers the Implementation Survey, but it is up to the instructional coach to get this information from all teachers with average or low skill, to the extent possible.

SCORING PART I: AN EXAMPLE FROM MR. RYAN

To illustrate scoring, let's revisit Mr. Ryan, the seventh-grade science teacher. Mr. Ryan demonstrated low skill in AIM cycle 3, so his instructional coach asked him to complete the Implementation Survey to learn more about his MIP. See Figure 11.6 for an example of Part I of Mr. Ryan's completed Implementation Survey from AIM cycle 3. Once Mr. Ryan completes the survey, the instructional coach calculates the MIP score by simply adding the ratings the teacher reported in Part I and dividing his total by 63 (the highest possible score during AIM cycle 3). At the bottom of Figure 11.6, you can see the resulting overall MIP score.

Mr. Ryan's MIP score in Figure 11.6 is 81%, but what does that mean? Using the MIP data from the statements in Part I of the Implementation Survey, the instructional coach can sort teachers into the high or low will category. Can we consider Mr. Ryan

Part I		1	2	3	4	5	6	7
I want to implement the practice in my classroom.	**Comprehension Canopy**	☐	☐	☐	☐	☐	☒	☐
	Essential Words	☐	☐	☐	☐	☐	☐	☒
	Critical Reading	☐	☐	☒	☐	☐	☐	☐
I think that the practice is helping, or will help, my students become more proficient in reading.	**Comprehension Canopy**	☐	☐	☐	☐	☐	☒	☐
	Essential Words	☐	☐	☐	☐	☐	☐	☒
	Critical Reading	☐	☐	☐	☒	☐	☐	☐
I am willing to work hard to implement the practice.	**Comprehension Canopy**	☐	☐	☐	☐	☐	☐	☒
	Essential Words	☐	☐	☐	☐	☐	☐	☒
	Critical Reading	☐	☐	☐	☒	☐	☐	☐
	Total: 51 /63 = 81 %							

FIGURE 11.6. Part I of Mr. Ryan's Implementation Survey.

to have high or low will? There are no specific rules that exist on what percentage to use to determine high or low will. After all, we are recommending that instructional coaches base their decisions on the Implementation Survey, and the Implementation Survey is not a standardized measure that has psychometric data (i.e., reliability and validity information). Still, it can be useful as a decision-making tool for the instructional coach to draw conclusions related to MIP. Therefore, we do want to provide *some* guidance for instructional coaches about how to use teachers' scores to divide teachers into different categories: high and low will. To do this, we based our chosen cut scores on prior research that used similar decision-making tools (see the Self-Empowerment Index; Wilson, 1993).

Naturally, some teachers will have higher MIP scores, while other teachers will have lower MIP scores. We are particularly interested in teachers who fall into the low will category. Therefore, we don't consider a teacher's MIP score to be low until it reaches below 40%. In other words, instructional coaches should identify teachers who score less than 40% on Part I of the Implementation Survey as *low will* teachers. This low cut point assures that teachers assigned to the low will status are teachers whose low will is likely negatively affecting their ability to implement the evidence-based practice with fidelity. Once the instructional coach has a MIP score for a teacher, she can record it in the Stage 1 Log on the week 5 Assessment Stage will arrow. We recorded Mr. Ryan's MIP score of 81% from Figure 11.6 on the will arrow in Figure 11.7. You can see that Mr. Ryan's 81% equates to a high will level.

Similar to using anecdotal notes to override/inform the teacher's fidelity score when determining a teacher's skill level, the instructional coach also has the opportunity to

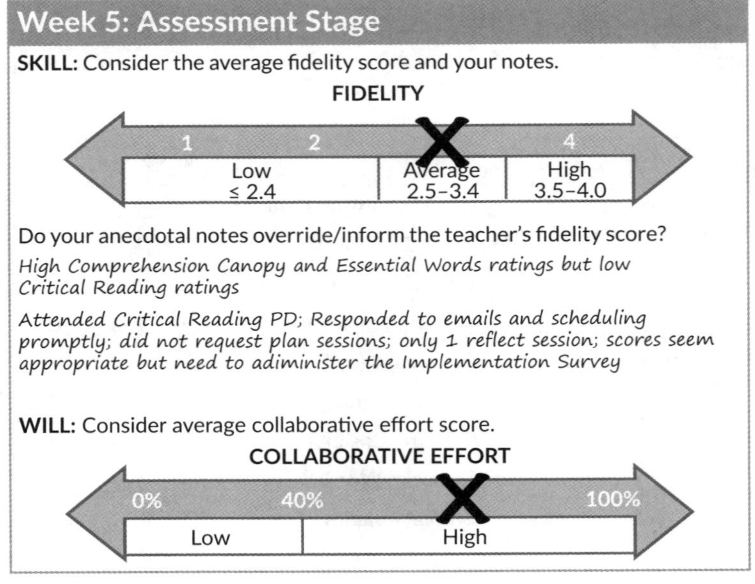

FIGURE 11.7. Mr. Ryan's will data on the Stage 1 Log.

use additional information to override/inform a teacher's MIP score. We recommend that the instructional coach use the average collaborative effort score from Stage 1 Intervention to override/inform a teacher's MIP score. As discussed in Chapter 10, a teacher's level of collaborative effort is a useful indicator of how willing she is to participate in the schoolwide adolescent literacy model. The instructional coach can simply calculate the average collaborative effort score, based on the weekly collaborative effort ratings, and use the score to override a teacher's MIP score when there is misalignment between a teacher's MIP score and her average collaborative effort score. We do not propose a specific cut score for this process; the instructional coach can simply use her judgment.

We can think of a few examples when this might occur. For instance, once in a while, a teacher may have an unusually difficult day. The teacher's lessons did not go according to plan, there were multiple interruptions throughout the day, and students' behaviors seemed impossible to manage in each class. Sound familiar? If this is the day that the instructional coach asks the teacher, who also has average skill, to complete the Implementation Survey, her responses may reflect the many setbacks she faced that day. The teacher's score on Part I of the Implementation Survey (i.e., the MIP items) might suggest that the teacher has low will, but when the instructional coach refers to her Stage 1 Log for this particular teacher, she sees that the teacher has consistently demonstrated high levels of collaborative effort. In fact, when she averages the weekly ratings, the teacher has a 3.7 average collaborative effort score (out of 4). Based on these data, the instructional coach may conclude that the teacher's average skill is not the result of low will. Therefore, she can decide to override the teacher's low MIP score. The instructional coach can use this information to inform her decisions about the teacher's will level and, ultimately, tailor Stage 2 Intervention support for this teacher.

Let's circle back to Mr. Ryan. Mr. Ryan's instructional coach determined that he had low skill during AIM cycle 3 but high will according to his MIP score (i.e., 81%). Before she considered his high will status to be final, she calculated an average collaborative effort score from the weekly ratings she had recorded on the Stage 1 Log during AIM cycle 3. Mr. Ryan's instructional coach assigned him a rating of 3 (out of 4) during each week for weeks 2–4. Therefore, his average collaborative effort score was 75%. Mr. Ryan attended the professional development session on Critical Reading, but, after reflecting on the session, his instructional coach remembered that he had made several comments to his colleague sitting next to him and left for a short amount of time to take a call. She was unsure about the nature of his comments. He did not request any plan sessions, but he responded promptly to schedule monitor sessions and even to check-in emails. He did only participate in one short reflect session, but Mr. Ryan's instructional coach was impressed that he emailed her during week 3, asking if she had any texts on ecosystems—the topic he wanted to cover during a Critical Reading lesson. Therefore, he met most of the indicators on the Collaborative Effort Rubric included on the AIM Coaching Manual in Appendix 10.3. Mr. Ryan's average collaborative effort score was aligned with his MIP score. In this case, the instructional coach decided that the average collaborative effort score only reinforced Mr. Ryan's high will status. While he was seemingly somewhat disengaged during the professional development session and did not request any plan sessions, for the most part, he demonstrated effort to implement

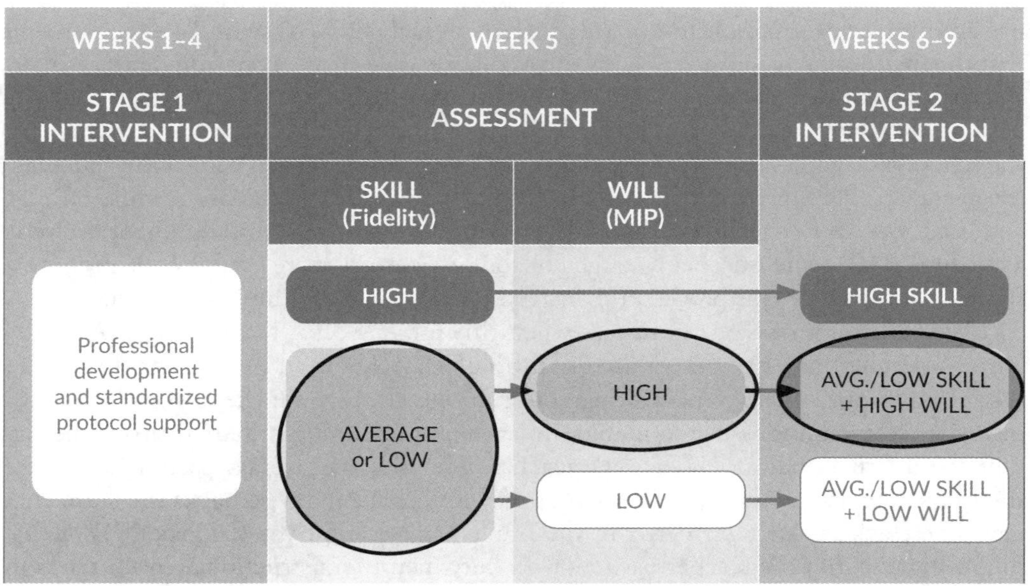

FIGURE 11.8. Stage 2 Intervention decision for Mr. Ryan.

Critical Reading (and Comprehension Canopy and Essential Words) and showed collaborative effort when working with his instructional coach.

TIME TO MAKE A DECISION

Once the instructional coach has determined the skill level of each teacher and the will level of each average or low skill teacher, she can make a decision about each teacher's Stage 2 Intervention status. See Figure 11.8, which is also included at the bottom of the Stage 1 Log. For Mr. Ryan, we circled his skill and will levels and followed the arrow over to determine the Stage 2 Intervention most appropriate for him in the coming weeks. During this decision-making process, you will begin to notice that teachers across the middle school setting fall into different categories. In Chapter 12, we will show you how to provide intervention for teachers in all categories.

REVIEW AND PREVIEW

In this chapter, we provided a step-by-step guide on how to implement the Assessment Stage of the AIM. First, we explained how we define skill and will, and how we determine what a teacher's skill and will levels are. Specifically, we explained how the instructional coach can use a teacher's fidelity ratings, informed by anecdotal information, from the Stage 1 Log to determine skill level. For teachers who have average or low skill, the instructional coach can assess their will level. To assess a teacher's will level, the instructional coach can administer the Implementation Survey. The instructional coach can then use the MIP items in Part I of the Implementation Survey to determine a teacher's MIP score. To inform the MIP score, the instructional coach can use the teacher's average collaborative effort score. In Chapter 12, we will describe how to use Part II of the Implementation Survey, which yields teachers' self-reported information about the **perceived feasibility** of the PACT instructional practice(s). We will also present ideas for using all the data gathered from the Implementation Survey data **diagnostically** to provide individualized Stage 2 Intervention support for all teachers.

Terms to Know

Diagnostically: The way information is used to identify specific areas of need that impact a teacher's skill or will.

Perceived feasibility: A teacher's perception of his ability to implement an intervention with ease.

Reflection Questions

1. What is the purpose of the Assessment Stage?
2. What does the instructional coach use to determine a teacher's skill level?
3. Explain what happens if a teacher has more than 1 week of monitor sessions during Stage 1 Intervention. Does the instructional coach use the fidelity ratings for each week to calculate a skill score? How does this work?
4. Explain what happens if a teacher is implementing more than one practice during a monitor session. Does the instructional coach record fidelity data for each observed practice? How are fidelity scores calculated and transferred to the Stage 1 Log?
5. What information can override/inform a teacher's fidelity score?
6. How would you describe the construct of will?
7. Can you explain how the instructional coach uses the Implementation Survey to determine a teacher's will level?
8. What information can override/inform a teacher's MIP score?

APPENDIX 11.1

Implementation Survey

AIM Cycle 1

Please rate your level of agreement with the following statements about the PACT instructional practice **Comprehension Canopy** in Cycle 1. The scale ranges from 1 (strongly disagree) to 7 (strongly agree). A rating of 4 would indicate that you are neutral about a statement.

Part I	1	2	3	4	5	6	7
I want to implement **Comprehension Canopy** in my classroom.	☐	☐	☐	☐	☐	☐	☐
I think that **Comprehension Canopy** is helping, or will help, my students become more proficient in reading.	☐	☐	☐	☐	☐	☐	☐
I am willing to work hard to implement **Comprehension Canopy.**	☐	☐	☐	☐	☐	☐	☐
	Total: _____ / 21 =_____%						

Part II	1	2	3	4	5	6	7
I have enough materials to implement **Comprehension Canopy** weekly in my classroom.	☐	☐	☐	☐	☐	☐	☐
The time preparing to implement **Comprehension Canopy** weekly in my classroom is manageable.	☐	☐	☐	☐	☐	☐	☐
The time to implement **Comprehension Canopy** weekly in my classroom is manageable.	☐	☐	☐	☐	☐	☐	☐
My students' behavior is good enough for me to implement **Comprehension Canopy** weekly in my classroom.	☐	☐	☐	☐	☐	☐	☐
I have the support I need to implement **Comprehension Canopy** weekly in my classroom.	☐	☐	☐	☐	☐	☐	☐

(continued)

© 2019 The University of Texas at Austin/The Meadows Center for Preventing Educational Risk. *PACT Plus Implementation Survey* licensed under Creative Commons BY-NC-ND 4.0 International. Reprinted in *Literacy Coaching in the Secondary Grades: Helping Teachers Meet the Needs of All Students* by Jade Wexler, Elizabeth Swanson, and Alexandra Shelton (The Guilford Press, 2021). Permission to photocopy this material is granted to purchasers of this book for personal use or use with students (see copyright page for details). Purchasers can download enlarged versions of this material (see the box at the end of the table of contents).

AIM Cycle 2

Please rate your level of agreement with the following statements about the PACT instructional practices **Comprehension Canopy** and **Essential Words** in Cycles 1 and 2. The scale ranges from 1 (strongly disagree) to 7 (strongly agree). A rating of 4 would indicate that you are neutral about a statement.

Part I		1	2	3	4	5	6	7
I want to implement the practice in my classroom.	**Comprehension Canopy**	☐	☐	☐	☐	☐	☐	☐
	Essential Words	☐	☐	☐	☐	☐	☐	☐
I think that the practice is helping, or will help, my students become more proficient in reading.	**Comprehension Canopy**	☐	☐	☐	☐	☐	☐	☐
	Essential Words	☐	☐	☐	☐	☐	☐	☐
I am willing to work hard to implement the practice.	**Comprehension Canopy**	☐	☐	☐	☐	☐	☐	☐
	Essential Words	☐	☐	☐	☐	☐	☐	☐
		Total: ______ /42 = ______ %						

Part II		1	2	3	4	5	6	7
I have enough materials to implement the practice weekly in my classroom.	**Comprehension Canopy**	☐	☐	☐	☐	☐	☐	☐
	Essential Words	☐	☐	☐	☐	☐	☐	☐
The time preparing to implement the practice weekly in my classroom is manageable.	**Comprehension Canopy**	☐	☐	☐	☐	☐	☐	☐
	Essential Words	☐	☐	☐	☐	☐	☐	☐
The time to implement the practice weekly in my classroom is manageable.	**Comprehension Canopy**	☐	☐	☐	☐	☐	☐	☐
	Essential Words	☐	☐	☐	☐	☐	☐	☐
My students' behavior is good enough for me to implement the practice weekly in my classroom.	**Comprehension Canopy**	☐	☐	☐	☐	☐	☐	☐
	Essential Words	☐	☐	☐	☐	☐	☐	☐
I have the support I need to implement the practice weekly in my classroom.	**Comprehension Canopy**	☐	☐	☐	☐	☐	☐	☐
	Essential Words	☐	☐	☐	☐	☐	☐	☐

(continued)

AIM Cycle 3

Please rate your level of agreement with the following statements about the PACT instructional practices **Comprehension Canopy**, **Essential Words**, and **Critical Reading** in Cycles 1–3. The scale ranges from 1 (strongly disagree) to 7 (strongly agree). A rating of 4 would indicate that you are neutral about a statement.

Part I		1	2	3	4	5	6	7
I want to implement the practice in my classroom.	**Comprehension Canopy**	☐	☐	☐	☐	☐	☐	☐
	Essential Words	☐	☐	☐	☐	☐	☐	☐
	Critical Reading	☐	☐	☐	☐	☐	☐	☐
I think that the practice is helping, or will help, my students become more proficient in reading.	**Comprehension Canopy**	☐	☐	☐	☐	☐	☐	☐
	Essential Words	☐	☐	☐	☐	☐	☐	☐
	Critical Reading	☐	☐	☐	☐	☐	☐	☐
I am willing to work hard to implement the practice.	**Comprehension Canopy**	☐	☐	☐	☐	☐	☐	☐
	Essential Words	☐	☐	☐	☐	☐	☐	☐
	Critical Reading	☐	☐	☐	☐	☐	☐	☐
	Total: ______ /63 = ______ %							

Part II		1	2	3	4	5	6	7
I have enough materials to implement the practice weekly in my classroom.	**Comprehension Canopy**	☐	☐	☐	☐	☐	☐	☐
	Essential Words	☐	☐	☐	☐	☐	☐	☐
	Critical Reading	☐	☐	☐	☐	☐	☐	☐
The time preparing to implement the practice weekly in my classroom is manageable.	**Comprehension Canopy**	☐	☐	☐	☐	☐	☐	☐
	Essential Words	☐	☐	☐	☐	☐	☐	☐
	Critical Reading	☐	☐	☐	☐	☐	☐	☐
The time to implement the practice weekly in my classroom is manageable.	**Comprehension Canopy**	☐	☐	☐	☐	☐	☐	☐
	Essential Words	☐	☐	☐	☐	☐	☐	☐
	Critical Reading	☐	☐	☐	☐	☐	☐	☐
My students' behavior is good enough for me to implement the practice weekly in my classroom.	**Comprehension Canopy**	☐	☐	☐	☐	☐	☐	☐
	Essential Words	☐	☐	☐	☐	☐	☐	☐
	Critical Reading	☐	☐	☐	☐	☐	☐	☐
I have the support I need to implement the practice weekly in my classroom.	**Comprehension Canopy**	☐	☐	☐	☐	☐	☐	☐
	Essential Words	☐	☐	☐	☐	☐	☐	☐
	Critical Reading	☐	☐	☐	☐	☐	☐	☐

CHAPTER 12

Tailoring Support to Meet Teachers' Needs

In Chapter 11, we provided an overview of the Assessment Stage in the AIM. During this stage, the instructional coach uses fidelity ratings, collected during Stage 1 Intervention and recorded on the Stage 1 Log, to determine a skill level for each teacher. For teachers whom the instructional coach identifies as having average or low skill, the instructional coach administers an Implementation Survey. The purpose of this survey is twofold. First, it provides a teacher's self-reported MIP score for the instructional coach to use to determine a teacher's will level (which is informed by collaborative effort ratings from Stage 1 Intervention). Second, the instructional coach can use the MIP score as well as the feasibility items on the Implementation Survey in Part II diagnostically to determine how to individualize the Stage 2 Intervention.

In this chapter, we first revisit the concept of teacher change in relation to how the instructional coach can tailor his support for each teacher. Next, we explain how to use the Implementation Survey data from Parts I and II diagnostically, and then we provide an overview of Stage 2 Intervention for teachers in all categories. During Stage 2 Intervention, the instructional coach adapts the dosage of the plan–monitor–reflect–check-in sequence for high skill teachers. He also adapts the dosage of the plan–monitor–reflect–check-in sequence for average or low skill + high will teachers and individualizes his support based on information from the Implementation Survey, as well as other data collected during Stage 1 Intervention. For low will teachers, the instructional coach examines data diagnostically to determine which alternate intervention(s) he might use to target their will.

TAILORING SUPPORT BASED ON TEACHERS' WILLINGNESS TO CHANGE

In Chapter 11, we brought up the concept of teacher change in relation to the Assessment Stage. In order to implement new evidence-based practices with fidelity, teachers must change their behavior. The Assessment Stage allows the instructional coach to examine data related to the extent to which teachers have or have not changed their behavior (i.e., demonstrated high skill by implementing evidence-based practices with fidelity) and the reasons behind their change or lack of change (e.g., high or low will). Did a teacher already change her practice in Stage 1 Intervention? Did she not change her practice but is willing to do so? Did she not change her practice, and is she not willing to do so? The instructional coach will likely find that teachers' readiness to change their behavior (i.e., implementation of a practice[s]) falls on a continuum of change with some being very willing, ready, and able to change, while others find it difficult to change for a multitude of reasons.

Thinking about a teacher's readiness for change can help the instructional coach tailor his support for each teacher. To help us think about change, we turn to a model of behavior change (Norcross, Krebs, & Prochaska, 2011). Researchers and practitioners have applied this model to many fields, including smoking cessation, bullying, and depression. The model helps us understand people's stages of change and helps interventionists provide support based on those stages. Therefore, this model of behavior change might also be of interest to instructional coaches. Figure 12.1 depicts the six stages of change, possible characteristics of teachers in each stage, and a connection to teachers' skill and will levels, which can help the instructional coach operationalize these stages of change. Note that there is no scientific way to determine where teachers fall on the stages of change, but the instructional coach can use the data to which he has access and make a judgment call.

Implementation Survey: Part II

In Chapter 11, we reviewed how to use the MIP items in Part I of the Implementation Survey to determine if a teacher with average or low skill has low or high will. These teachers will likely be in the precontemplation, contemplation, preparation, or action stage of change. It will be important for the instructional coach to "dig deeper" into the reason for these teachers' low or high will status by examining additional data. The purpose of Part II of the Implementation Survey is to determine the reasons behind a teacher's will level and subsequently target the most appropriate type and amount of intervention for teachers. What are some possible reasons behind teachers' differing amounts of will? In reality, there are a multitude of reasons explaining will levels, and these will levels are dynamic, too. They change from year to year, month to month, and even sometimes day to day. There are personal reasons for a teacher's will level changing (e.g., distracted with a problem with her own children) and many professional reasons for differing amounts of will. For example, a common barrier of implementing

Stage of Change	Description	Characteristics of Teachers in This Stage	AIM Skill and Will Level Connection
Precontemplation	No intention to take action.	They are either uninformed or underinformed about the consequences of poor instruction, or they may have tried new things in the past that did not work for them. They tend to avoid reading, talking, or thinking critically about their current practices. They are characterized as resistant or unmotivated.	Low skill + low will
Contemplation	Recognizes there is a problem and is thinking about taking action.	These teachers will probably change their practices over the next 6 months. They are more aware of the pros of learning new instructional practices, but also may be fixated on the cons. This can produce ambivalence and keep people stuck in this stage for a long time. Such teachers are not ready for action-oriented instructional coaching that expects them to take action immediately.	Average/low skill + low will
Preparation	Intends to take action and has made plans to make a change.	These teachers intend to take action soon. They're probably attentive at the professional development sessions and are ready to develop (or already have) a plan of action. These are the teachers who are ready to change action-oriented activities or improve instructional procedures.	Average/low skill + high will
Action	Taking action toward change, but he or she is early in the process.	They have made specific, overt modifications to the instructional practices used in their classroom. Action is observable, and teachers tend to show enthusiasm for using the practices. There may still be a need to fine-tune or improve fidelity to the instructional practices, but these teachers are open to improvement.	Average/low skill + high will
Maintenance	Has taken action toward more change; onboard with the plan and has enacted it for a long time.	These teachers have made changes to their instructional practices and are actively working to prevent interruptions or interference with their developing skills. They are less tempted to use former or contrary instructional practices and are increasingly more confident in their teaching.	High skill
Termination	Change has taken place! Behaviors have changed and he or she has completely bought into the new program.	These teachers are considered 100% self-efficacious. They need very little support and have mastered the instructional practices in their classrooms. The adaptations they make to the practices are reasonable and do not interfere with the core principles of the instructional practices. The practices have become "automatic" in a sense and, therefore, teachers may use the practices across subject areas. It should be noted that this is relatively rare, and you should expect 20% or fewer of your teachers to reach this stage.	High skill

FIGURE 12.1. Six stages of change for teachers.

an intervention is the perceived feasibility of the intervention. Does a teacher feel she does not have the materials she needs to implement the intervention? Does she not feel supported by administrators? Does she feel that it will take too much time to implement? There is no doubt that perceived feasibility barriers can influence a teacher's will level. Barron and Hulleman (2015) refer to barriers as "cost." On the other hand, there are facilitating factors that can influence will in a positive way. For example, an administrator might highlight the work of a teacher in a weekly newsletter by revealing the improved achievement of his students. This reinforcement might impact the teacher's level of will in a positive way by encouraging him to want to implement the practice more (i.e., motivation), improving his perceptions of the practice as an investment, and encouraging his persistence.

Part II of the Implementation Survey includes five items designed for teachers to self-report their perceptions of the feasibility of implementing the PACT instructional practice. The perceived feasibility of an intervention is an important factor that can influence a teacher's will level. While the purpose of the feasibility items is not to inform the instructional coach's decision about a teacher's will level (the purpose of Part I of the survey), the instructional coach can use these items to inform the *reason* for a teacher's MIP score. Additionally, this information will help the instructional coach make diagnostic decisions about how to intervene with teachers. Next, we will describe how exactly the instructional coach can use the Implementation Survey diagnostically.

HOW TO USE THE IMPLEMENTATION SURVEY DIAGNOSTICALLY

In Chapter 11, we introduced Mr. Ryan. Mr. Ryan scored in the low skill range when the instructional coach conducted monitor sessions during Stage 1 Intervention in AIM cycle 3. The instructional coach asked Mr. Ryan to complete the Implementation Survey so she could determine his MIP score and would have more data to inform how she might support him moving forward. Mr. Ryan's instructional coach considered how she might ask Mr. Ryan to fill out the Implementation Survey before she gave it to him. She was worried that he would be hesitant to do so if he considered it to be an evaluative task. Therefore, she told Mr. Ryan that this was "simply a survey to gather more information about facilitators and barriers to implementation. It will help me provide you with the support you need in the next few weeks." Mr. Ryan's instructional coach felt fortunate that Mr. Ryan was willing to complete the Implementation Survey, unlike many teachers she had worked with who were not as willing to comply. She was not too surprised that he completed it, however, as he had exhibited mostly average to high levels of collaborative effort during Stage 1 Intervention. Mr. Ryan scored above 40% on the MIP items (see Figure 11.6), which was reinforced by the average score on his collaborative effort ratings. Therefore, the instructional coach determined that he had a high will level. She circled average/low skill + high will on the Stage 1 Log. See Figure 12.2 where she noted this.

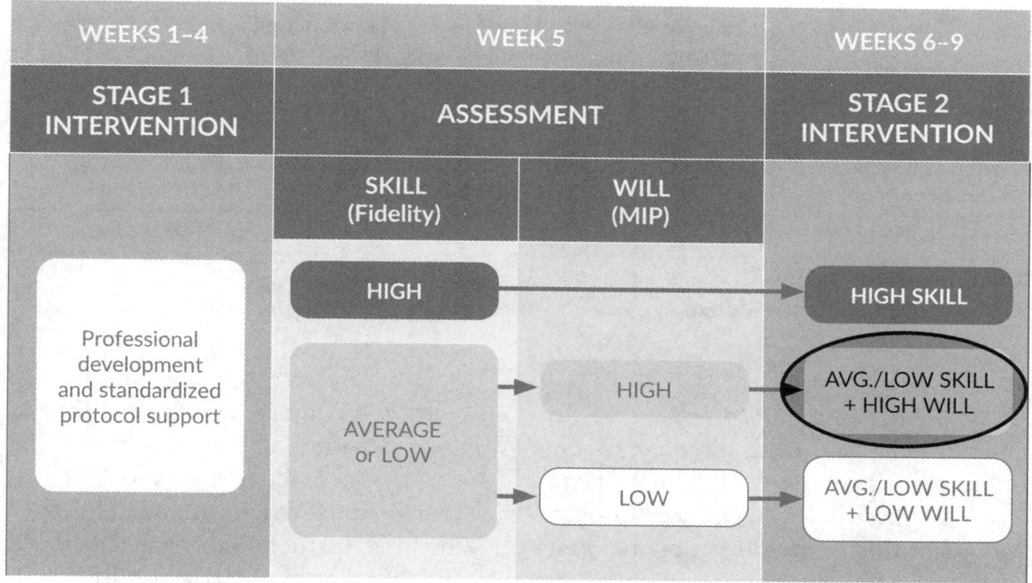

FIGURE 12.2. Stage 2 Intervention for Mr. Ryan.

The coach was glad that Mr. Ryan's MIP score and average collaborative effort score indicated that he had a high level of will. Because of his high will level, she was hopeful that he would work collaboratively with her to improve his skill.

After determining the will level of teachers with low or average skill, the next step is for the instructional coach to examine the teacher's data diagnostically. The instructional coach should examine data diagnostically for all teachers with low or average skill (whether or not they have low will) because it gives her the opportunity to understand the needs of each teacher. Here are the steps the instructional coach should take to examine low/average skill teachers' Implementation Survey data:

1. Review Part I of the teacher's Implementation Survey data by each instructional practice (e.g., Comprehension Canopy).
2. Review Part I of the teacher's Implementation Survey data by each MIP construct (e.g., motivation).
3. Review Part II of the teacher's Implementation Survey (i.e., feasibility data).
4. Conduct a follow-up interview with the teacher if more information is needed to clarify the teacher's needs.

At this point, Mr. Ryan's instructional coach put on her detective hat to examine the data she had from his Implementation Survey. Even though he had a high will level, she knew that examining his Implementation Survey data would provide diagnostic information that would allow her to tailor her support during Stage 2 Intervention. She followed these steps:

PACT Instructional Practice	I want to implement the practice in my classroom.	I want to implement the practice in my classroom.	I am willing to work hard to implement the practice.	Average per PACT Instructional Practice
Comprehension Canopy	6	6	7	19/21 = 90%
Essential Words	7	7	7	21/21 = 100%
Critical Reading	3	4	4	11/21 = 52%

FIGURE 12.3. Mr. Ryan's Implementation Survey: Part I data per PACT instructional practice.

• *Step 1: Review Part I of the teacher's Implementation Survey data by each instructional practice (e.g., Comprehension Canopy).* Was there a pattern in Mr. Ryan's data that indicated he had more MIP about one PACT instructional practice than another?

In Figure 12.3, you can see how Mr. Ryan's instructional coach examined his MIP data according to each instructional practice. When his instructional coach calculated an overall MIP score by instructional practice, she saw that his MIP scores for Comprehension Canopy and Essential Words were quite high (i.e., 90% and 100%, respectively). However, his MIP score for Critical Reading was a different story. It was only 52%. While this lower score was in the high will range (i.e., >40%), it was still much lower than his scores for Comprehension Canopy and Essential Words. His instructional coach concluded that although his overall MIP score was in the high will range (i.e., >40%), his MIP score for Critical Reading raised a red flag.

• *Step 2: Review Part I of the teacher's Implementation Survey data by each MIP construct (e.g., motivation).* Mr. Ryan's instructional coach already identified an interesting pattern in the data by looking at Mr. Ryan's MIP score according to each PACT instructional practice as illustrated in Step 1. The next step was to examine the data in a different way. This time, she broke down Mr. Ryan's score by each component of MIP: motivation, investment, and persistence. In other words, was there a common teacher profile (see Figure 11.2 for a review of teacher profiles) that matched Mr. Ryan's? For example, was he a teacher with high motivation and investment ratings but not high persistence ratings with regard to his implementation of the PACT instructional practices? In Figure 12.4, you can see how Mr. Ryan's instructional coach rearranged the MIP items, so she could easily determine if any patterns existed according to MIP component.

Mr. Ryan's instructional coach calculated an average score for the motivation, investment, and persistence items separately. Overall, Mr. Ryan's scores by MIP component did not vary by much. All scores hovered around 80%, indicating that Mr. Ryan reported approximately equal ratings of motivation, investment, and persistence when it came to implementing the PACT instructional practices. If Mr. Ryan's instructional coach had to pick a matching teacher profile, she would say he was overall equally motivated, invested, and persistent. See Figure 12.5 for the teacher profile that Mr. Ryan's instructional coach considered to be a good match.

MIP Component	Comprehension Canopy	Essential Words	Critical Reading	Average per MIP Component
I want to implement the practice in my classroom.	6	7	3	16/21 = 76%
I think that the practice is helping, or will help, my students become more proficient in reading.	6	7	4	17/21 = 81%
I am willing to work hard to implement the practice.	7	7	4	18/21 = 86%

FIGURE 12.4. Mr. Ryan's Implementation Survey: Part I data per MIP component.

Is this a teacher who . . . (M) wants to implement the practice? (I) is convinced the practice is helping, or will help, his students become more proficient in reading? (P) is willing to work hard to implement the practice?				
Teacher	**M**	**I**	**P**	**Teacher Profiles**
A	✓	✓	✓	*It is likely that this teacher will be a champion of the practice in his school. He will work hard to implement the practice with fidelity. He will likely work collaboratively with the instructional coach.*

FIGURE 12.5. Mr. Ryan's MIP profile.

To determine how to tailor her support, the instructional coach considered what stage of change Mr. Ryan was in. In AIM cycle 3, his skill levels for Comprehension Canopy and Essential Words were high and average, respectively, but his skill level for Critical Reading was relatively low. When reviewing her data for AIM cycles 1 and 2, Mr. Ryan's instructional coach noted how he consistently exhibited high will, as evidenced by his collaborative effort ratings. For Comprehension Canopy and Essential Words, the instructional coach decided that Mr. Ryan was likely in the maintenance stage of change for both Comprehension Canopy and Essential Words. AIM cycle 3 was another story. His skill level was low, and when she looked at the fidelity checklists from the monitoring sessions, it was clear that the low skill score was primarily derived from the ratings on Critical Reading (not Comprehension Canopy and Essential Words). Furthermore, his MIP score for Critical Reading was significantly lower than for the other two instructional practices, as noted above. Because his MIP score was low but not less than 40%, Mr. Ryan's instructional coach decided he was likely still in the contemplation or preparation stage of change for Critical Reading. To make a final decision about his stage of change, the instructional coach reviewed her Stage 1 Log for Mr. Ryan. Because he emailed her asking for text at one point during AIM cycle 3 but did not request any plan sessions and only participated in one reflect session, the instructional coach decided that Mr. Ryan was in the contemplation stage of change and not yet in the preparation stage.

At this point, Mr. Ryan's instructional coach began to draw conclusions from the data. Mr. Ryan had high will. However, after examining the data diagnostically, it became clear that Mr. Ryan had slightly lower MIP due to his perceptions about implementing Critical Reading. Was there something about Critical Reading that was difficult for him? This brought Mr. Ryan's instructional coach to Step 3.

• *Step 3: Review Part II of the teacher's Implementation Survey (i.e., feasibility data).* After determining that there were indeed patterns in Mr. Ryan's self-report data on the MIP items, his instructional coach examined the feasibility items from the Implementation Survey. She wanted to see if the feasibility items shed any light on the reasons for the patterns that she had uncovered. See Figure 12.6 for a copy of Mr. Ryan's completed feasibility items from the Implementation Survey.

Mr. Ryan's instructional coach considered items that he rated 3 or lower (i.e., approximately 40% of 7) and determined that Mr. Ryan did not believe he had enough materials and time to prepare for implementing Critical Reading. This aligned with the data his instructional coach had compiled, which noted that he had asked her to provide text on a topic he was hoping to teach using the Critical Reading practice. Survey items from Part II also indicated that Mr. Ryan was concerned about his students' behavior during Critical Reading. Because his instructional coach determined that he had the least amount of MIP when it came to implementing Critical Reading, she surmised that she should first target his needs in this area. Not only does Mr. Ryan's instructional coach now know that he should be receiving *average/low skill + high will support* during Stage 2 Intervention, she also has an idea of how to tailor that support to his individual needs.

Part II		1	2	3	4	5	6	7
I have enough materials to implement the practice weekly in my classroom.	**Comprehension Canopy**	☐	☐	☐	☒	☐	☐	☐
	Essential Words	☐	☐	☐	☐	☒	☐	☐
	Critical Reading	☐	☐	☒	☐	☐	☐	☐
The time preparing to implement the practice weekly in my classroom is manageable.	**Comprehension Canopy**	☐	☐	☐	☐	☐	☒	☐
	Essential Words	☐	☐	☐	☒	☐	☐	☐
	Critical Reading	☐	☐	☒	☐	☐	☐	☐
The time to implement the practice weekly in my classroom is manageable.	**Comprehension Canopy**	☐	☐	☐	☐	☐	☐	☒
	Essential Words	☐	☐	☐	☐	☒	☐	☐
	Critical Reading	☐	☐	☐	☒	☐	☐	☐
My students' behavior is good enough for me to implement the practice weekly in my classroom.	**Comprehension Canopy**	☐	☐	☐	☒	☐	☐	☐
	Essential Words	☐	☐	☐	☒	☐	☐	☐
	Critical Reading	☐	☒	☐	☐	☐	☐	☐
I have the support I need to implement the practice weekly in my classroom.	**Comprehension Canopy**	☐	☐	☐	☐	☐	☐	☒
	Essential Words	☐	☐	☐	☐	☐	☒	☐
	Critical Reading	☐	☐	☐	☒	☐	☐	☐

FIGURE 12.6. Part II of Mr. Ryan's Implementation Survey.

• *Step 4: Conduct a follow-up interview with the teacher if more information is needed to clarify the teacher's needs.* There might be a situation where the instructional coach feels that she would benefit from more information about a teacher, regardless of skill and will level, to guide her intervention support in Stage 2 Intervention. To the extent that a teacher is willing to engage in a short interview (e.g., 20–30 minutes) with the instructional coach, this is a way to gather additional information to intervene appropriately. Note that this might not be a realistic use of time for the instructional coach. Therefore, she should proceed based on her judgment of the importance of such an interview along with consideration of her time.

Should the instructional coach decide to proceed with a one-on-one interview, she can design the interview as a way to follow up on information revealed on the teacher's Implementation Survey. The instructional coach should focus the interview questions on the teacher's areas of particular need. In the case of Mr. Ryan, his instructional coach might ask about his lower MIP ratings for Critical Reading and some of the feasibility statements.

For each item of concern, the instructional coach can ask the teacher two questions: a question that allows the teacher to elaborate on his responses on the Implementation Survey and a question that helps the instructional coach identify the specific support she can provide that the teacher will be receptive to. Let's look back at the instructional coach's work with Mr. Ryan to see this in action.

Mr. Ryan's responses to the feasibility items on the Implementation Survey indicate that he feels he does not have enough text reading materials to use on a weekly basis, which may explain his lower MIP score related to Critical Reading. Because evidence-based adolescent literacy practices typically require teachers to use a variety of text for different purposes, not having access to appropriate text makes implementation on a consistent basis an added challenge and, frankly, a big headache for the teacher. If locating text is difficult for Mr. Ryan, how can the instructional coach expect him to implement the intervention consistently? The instructional coach can ask Mr. Ryan, "I noticed that, on the Implementation Survey, you answered that it is difficult for you to find an adequate amount of text reading materials to implement Critical Reading. Can you elaborate on that? Is it just one type of text that you are unable to find? Is the district-provided text too difficult for your students?" Next, the instructional coach can say, "I would like to assist you in finding text-reading materials. I have a few ideas about how to do this, but before I share my ideas, can you think of any specific ways you would like me to assist you so that you can find text-reading materials? Are there any resources that you found worked well for you and your students in the past?"

In summary, follow-up interviews can give instructional coaches even more diagnostic information that will allow them to target teachers' needs so they can intervene accordingly. These interviews also provide the instructional coach with other opportunities to offer a teacher support.

What are the instructional coach's goals for supporting Mr. Ryan during Stage 2 Intervention? What is her intervention plan? In the Stage 2 Intervention section below, you will read about the level and type of individualized support that Mr. Ryan's instructional coach will provide to Mr. Ryan: average/low skill + high will support.

STAGE 2 INTERVENTION

The final stage includes three options for different levels of intervention support: ***high skill support, average/low skill + high will support,*** and ***average/low skill + low will support.*** At this point, the instructional coach has supported teachers through Stage 1 Intervention using standardized protocol. She has also determined each teacher's skill level and some teachers' will level during the Assessment Stage. She has additionally considered Implementation Survey data diagnostically to help her target her support for teachers in Stage 2 Intervention. Some teachers have already made changes to their practice (i.e., high skill teachers). Some teachers are ready to begin or continue changing their practice (i.e., average/low skill + high will teachers). Some teachers haven't even contemplated or have just begun contemplating the idea of changing their practice (i.e., average/low skill + low will teachers). Below we provide guidance on how the instructional coach can support teachers with different levels of skill and will.

High Skill Support

High skill support is essentially a "lighter level of support" than teachers were receiving during Stage 1 Intervention. This level of support also promotes a **resource-wise** use of the instructional coach's time by lightening the burden on her. By not having to focus on high skill teachers as much, she can put more effort into teachers who have greater needs. Furthermore, it is important to not overburden teachers who demonstrate high skill. After all, who qualifies as a high skill teacher? These are teachers who are likely in the termination or maintenance stage of change, indicating that they have already changed or are well on their way to changing their practice. We intentionally set the criteria to be a high skill teacher conservatively so that our decision rule only captures the highest performers.

The instructional coach maintains a presence with each high skill teacher by continuing with a weekly check-in. The instructional coach also engages in the plan–monitor–reflect–check-in sequence on a "by request" basis. We allow teachers to request more support regardless of the intervention support they are assigned. Therefore, it is possible for the instructional coach to provide a more intensive level of support to a high skill teacher who requests it as long as the instructional coach has the time. See Figure 12.7 and the AIM Coaching Manual (under Stage 2 Support) in Appendix 10.3 for dosage guidelines for a high skill teacher in Stage 2 Intervention.

Average/Low Skill + High Will Support

For teachers who demonstrate average or low skill and high will, the instructional coach continues to deliver the same plan–monitor–reflect–check-in sequence with a

Intervention Support Level	Plan	Monitor	Reflect	Check-In
Stage 2 Intervention				
High skill	By request	By request	By request	Once a week

FIGURE 12.7. Stage 2 Intervention high skill support dosage guidelines.

more intensive required dosage for each teacher. This is the type of support that Mr. Ryan's instructional coach will provide to him. Average/low skill + high will teachers are likely in the preparation or action stage of change for at least one of the practices. We see these teachers as the ones who the instructional coach is most likely to influence. These are teachers who have room to grow skill-wise, and they demonstrate a willingness to do so. For this reason, we think it is a wise use of the instructional coach's time to put most of her efforts into supporting such teachers. After all, by adapting support for high skill teachers (i.e., reducing the dosage; see the description above), the instructional coach can direct most of her efforts to teachers who lack the appropriate amount of skill but demonstrate an adequate amount of will, likely making them receptive to the extra support. See Figure 12.8 and the AIM Coaching Manual in Appendix 10.3 for dosage guidelines for an average/low skill + high will teacher in Stage 2 Intervention. You will notice that the plan session becomes mandatory in Stage 2 Intervention, as opposed to a "by request" basis in Stage 1 Intervention. Furthermore, the number of required check-ins increases from one per week to two per week in Stage 2 Intervention.

In sum, it is likely that average and low skill teachers are willing to engage in an intensified, individualized dose of the same intervention options (i.e., plan, monitor, reflect, and check-ins) as delivered in Stage 1 Intervention *if* they also demonstrate high will. However, increasing dosage is not the only way to intensify support for teachers (Brock & Carter, 2017). To individualize and intensify intervention further, the instructional coach might think to herself: What is each teacher specifically struggling with that is preventing him from being a high skill teacher? Then she can use data collected on her fidelity checklists, anecdotal notes from her Stage 1 Log, the follow-up interview, and the Implementation Survey to determine potential barriers. Depending on the barriers revealed by the data, the instructional coach can provide support targeting these needs during the plan, monitor, and reflect sessions as well as during the check-ins. See the next section for guidance on matching intervention to teacher need.

Intervention Support Level	Plan	Monitor	Reflect	Check-In
Stage 2 Intervention				
Average or Low Skill + High Will	Once a week	Once a week	Once a week	Twice a week

FIGURE 12.8. Stage 2 Intervention low/average skill + high will support dosage guidelines.

Average/Low Skill + Low Will Support

Some teachers not only possess average or low skill but also low will. Is a low will teacher someone who doesn't want to change? Is this someone who wants to change but isn't ready? It is likely that a low will teacher falls into either the precontemplation or contemplation stage of change. Change, or at least the change that the instructional coach wants a low will teacher to make, is not necessarily on her radar. This makes "moving the needle" with such a teacher challenging. Therefore, the intervention options for this group are designed to (1) target their low and average skill *and* low will needs and (2) contribute to a resource-wise use of the instructional coach's time. As a reminder, a resource-wise use of the instructional coach's time means we want to reduce the burden on the instructional coach. We do not want him to put too much effort into teachers who do not need his support (i.e., high skill teachers) and teachers who are unlikely to engage in his support collaboratively and, thus, even more unlikely to implement the evidence-based practices with fidelity. Therefore, while we do not promote "abandoning" support for these teachers, we advise instructional coaches to choose how and how much to intervene with low will teachers cautiously. For example, instructional coaches might choose to abandon the plan–monitor–reflect–check-in sequence in exchange for a low will intervention. For expanded details and ideas for a low will intervention, see the Low Will Guide on this book's companion website (see the box at the end of the table of contents).

One way to think about the degree to which the instructional coach should support low will teachers is to consider the distribution of teachers on the skill and will continuums in the school where he is working. Do most teachers fall into the average/low skill + high will category? In this case, the instructional coach will not have a lot of time left to spend supporting teachers who demonstrate low will because he will be spending his time supporting those who have average or low skill *and* high will (since they require a more intensive dosage of the plan–monitor–reflect–check-in sequence). However, if there are just a handful of low will teachers in a school, it may behoove the instructional coach to dedicate more time to advancing these teachers into a higher skill level by targeting their will. Support for these teachers also depends on where they fall on the low will continuum and the stages of change (see Figure 12.1). Are they teachers who are in the precontemplation stage of change, or are they in the contemplation stage of change? If they are in the contemplation stage of change, they may be more willing to engage in support and, therefore, change their practices.

On the contrary, if there is a sizable group of teachers who exhibit low will, common patterns may emerge from their data that could help the instructional coach provide more targeted support and, ultimately, move the whole school closer to the goal of implementing a schoolwide adolescent literacy model. For example, if many teachers answered the feasibility items on the Implementation Survey (e.g., *I have enough text reading materials available to use PACT on a weekly basis; I have the proper administrator support that I need to implement PACT*) with 1's and 2's (on a scale of 7), it might be possible for the instructional coach to work with the administrative team to identify solutions to these feasibility challenges, which may be impacting many teachers' MIP as well as their skill.

Therefore, if there are a lot of low will teachers, it might be helpful to dedicate more time and effort to them. Ultimately, this means spending time on activities that will help the instructional coach gain a better understanding about teachers' reasons for exhibiting low will. To do this, the instructional coach can diagnostically evaluate data from low will teachers who have completed the Implementation Survey and participated in the follow-up interview, to the extent that it does not draw resources from teachers who are more likely to change (i.e., low/average skill + high will teachers). We described this process above.

MATCHING INTERVENTION TO TEACHER NEED

The question now becomes this: What can the instructional coach do for teachers whose will may be impacting their skill? There are many ways to support teachers with low scores in one or more MIP constructs (e.g., motivation). For example, the instructional coach can target teachers' perceived feasibility of the intervention. Additionally, we have added a column in Figure 12.9 to provide some general intervention ideas for each teacher profile. These are simply general ideas, but there are numerous strategies to intervene with teachers who represent each teacher profile. Note that we have explained many of these ideas in the Low Will Guide (see the companion website). Also note that most of the ideas center on supporting teachers' intrinsic motivation, rather than extrinsically motivating them. We chose this course because the instructional coach rarely has access to resources he can use to provide tangible extrinsic rewards (e.g., funds). In addition, extrinsic rewards can lead to individuals' loss of intrinsic motivation, decreasing the likelihood that they sustain a particular behavior (e.g., instructional practice) into the future (Lepper, Green, & Nisbett, 1973). Thus, directly supporting teachers' intrinsic motivation is likely to have longer-lasting effects. Finally, as a reminder, for low will teachers, we recommend abandoning the use of the plan–monitor–reflect–check-in sequence and replacing it with interventions from the Low Will Guide (see the companion website).

STAGE 2 LOG

As you know by now, Stage 2 Intervention looks different for teachers depending on their skill and will levels. To track the support the instructional coach provides to high skill teachers and average/low skill + high will teachers during this stage, the instructional coach uses a Stage 2 Log (see Appendix 12.1). At the top of the log, the instructional coach indicates each teacher's Stage 2 Intervention support status: *high skill support* or *average/low skill + high will support.* Each week, the instructional coach records the support she provides to the teacher, any relevant notes, and the teacher's fidelity and

Is this a teacher who . . . (M) wants to implement the practice? (I) is convinced the practice is helping, or will help, her students become more proficient in reading? (P) is willing to work hard to implement the practice?					
Teacher	**M**	**I**	**P**	**Teacher Profiles**	**General Intervention Ideas**
A	✓	✓	✓	*It is likely that this teacher will be a champion of the practice in her school. She will work hard to implement the practice with fidelity. She will likely work collaboratively with the instructional coach.*	N/A: This teacher does not need low will intervention; however, she could still have average/low skill.
B	✓	O	✓	*Teacher B wants to implement the practice and is willing to work hard to do so. Despite his willingness to work hard, he does not particularly value the practice. This may seem counterintuitive at first. How can he be willing to work hard at implementing a practice but not value it? Perhaps his willingness to implement the practice is due to compliance, rather than believing in the practice's value. This teacher will likely work collaboratively with the instructional coach because he is expected to do so. However, he will not go out of his way to be a champion of the practice. Simultaneously, he might push his administration to adopt other practices.*	This teacher would benefit from raising his awareness about the value of the practice. This could include showing how the practice has evidence of success with a similar population of students. This teacher might also benefit from discussing the value of the practice with a respected colleague who has more MIP.
C	✓	✓	O	*This teacher is motivated to implement the practice and thinks the practice is a worthy investment. She wants to implement the practice, perhaps due to the fact that she values it. She feels that her students will benefit from the practice. However, she is not willing to work hard to implement it. This also sounds counterintuitive. You would think that if a teacher is motivated and invested in a practice and believes it's a worthy investment, she would also be persistent. Some people might just not be willing to work hard at implementing a practice. Perhaps she has other priorities that she is also working on implementing that are taking up all of her effort. Perhaps she is getting ready to retire or change jobs, and is unwilling to change her routine at this point in order to actually translate the practice(s) into action.*	This is a teacher who needs more guidance about how to get started and how to implement the practice in her classroom. She might need an instructional coach to scaffold the steps for her. She might benefit from some modeling from the instructional coach or another colleague who teaches the same subject and/or has a similar set of students in her classroom during a peer observation.
D	✓	O	O	*This is a teacher who wants to implement the practice, perhaps due to compliance or because he believes his students need something to help improve their achievement. He does not, however, see the value of this particular practice. Maybe he sees value in a different practice or set of practices. To this end, he is not willing to work hard to implement the practices. However, he might work collaboratively with the instructional coach for compliance reasons.*	This teacher might benefit from a booster session, where the focus is raising awareness about the value of the intervention. This could include showing how the practice has evidence of success with a similar population of students. A colleague may have more success working with the teacher than an instructional coach. Therefore, this teacher might also benefit

(continued)

FIGURE 12.9. Teacher MIP profiles with intervention ideas.

Teacher	M	I	P	Teacher Profiles	General Intervention Ideas
					from working with respected staff members who have more MIP in collaborative support teams.
E	O	✓	✓	*This is an example of a teacher who does not necessarily want to change her current routine. She does not want to implement the practice. She does, however, see value in the practice, and she is willing to work hard to do so if she has to. Perhaps her lack of motivation reflects a lack of confidence when it comes to changing her current routine. Perhaps she is anticipating behavior problems in her class if she implements this practice. There is something standing in the way of her motivation; however, she is still willing to work hard to implement the practice. She might work with the instructional coach to the extent that she is required.*	If the follow-up interview reveals that this teacher's lack of motivation is due to a general work ethic issue, then the problem will be difficult to address. To do so, the instructional coach should consider working with the administration. If the teacher's lack of motivation results from a lack of confidence, perhaps the instructional coach could offer to model or co-teach a lesson with the teacher. Alternatively, the teacher could conduct a peer observation of a teacher with high skill.
F	O	✓	O	*This is a teacher who thinks that his students would benefit from the practice, which he regards as valuable. However, he does not want to implement the practice and is not willing to try. Why not? Perhaps he does not want to implement the practice because he believes he does not know what steps to take to implement it. Thus, he is unwilling to work hard to implement the practice. Perhaps he is working hard on other priorities. Because he values the practice, he might work with the instructional coach collaboratively.*	After verifying in a follow-up interview that this is a teacher who does not believe he knows the right steps to implement the practice, an instructional coach can plan to provide a booster session and/or scaffold the task for the teacher.
G	O	O	✓	*This is a teacher who does not want to implement the practice and does not value it. Why, then, is she willing to persist at the task? This is likely a teacher who is compliant. Despite her lack of motivation and perception of whether or not it is a good investment, she will attempt to implement the practice, at least according to the minimum requirements. She will not go above and beyond that. She will work with the instructional coach to the extent that it is required.*	This teacher would benefit from raising her awareness about the value of the practice. This could include showing how the practice has evidence of success with a similar population of students. This teacher might also benefit from discussing the value of the practice with a respected colleague who has more MIP, perhaps in a collaborative support team meeting.
H	O	O	O	*This teacher does not want to implement the practice. She does not value the practice. She is also not willing to work hard to implement the practice. She will likely not work collaboratively with the instructional coach.*	It will be difficult to change the will level of this teacher. The instructional coach might want to pursue an interview with the teacher and see if she can identify at least one area that might be targeted.

FIGURE 2.9. *(continued)*

collaborative effort ratings, just as she did on the Stage 1 Log. For high skill teachers, the instructional coach may only have check-in and collaborative effort information to record. That's okay since plan, monitor, and reflect sessions are all by request for high skill teachers now. Additionally, low will interventions may replace plan, monitor, and reflect sessions and check-ins for teachers with low will. That's okay as well! The instructional coach should document the support she provides to low will teachers on the Low Will Log, which can be found at the end of the Low Will Guide. No matter what, if the instructional coach has new fidelity data for *any* teacher by the end of Stage 2 Intervention, she should record the single fidelity rating or calculate the average fidelity score on the fidelity arrow at the bottom of the Stage 2 Log.

A FINAL NOTE ABOUT AIM COACHING: NEGOTIABLES AND NON-NEGOTIABLES

As you know by now, AIM Coaching is designed to help the instructional coach systematically provide professional development and ongoing instructional coaching support that is tailored to teachers' needs. AIM Coaching assists the instructional coach in making data-based decisions as he supports teachers in increasing their use of selected evidence-based practices. However, you might be wondering if there is any flexibility in the guidelines we set forth above. The answer is "yes"! We recommend several negotiables and non-negotiables for the instructional coach who is implementing AIM Coaching, which we summarize below. **Negotiables** are aspects of AIM Coaching that the instructional coach can modify based on his discretion and judgment. **Non-negotiables** are aspects that we strongly encourage the instructional coach to implement as originally intended. These are what we believe to be the "active ingredients" of AIM Coaching; therefore, they should be implemented by the instructional coach with high fidelity.

The AIM Coaching Schedule

Although we do suggest that the instructional coach implement AIM Coaching using a 9-week quarterly repeating sequence, this is flexible and adjustable based on a school's schedule and the number of practices teachers are expected to implement by the end of the school year. For example, the instructional coach in a year-round school might have to adjust the AIM sequence schedule. Perhaps a 12-week rotating AIM cycle makes more sense in this situation. A non-negotiable associated with the schedule, however, is that the instructional coach should leave enough time in each AIM cycle to be dedicated to each stage of the AIM. For example, it is necessary that there is adequate time (e.g., several weeks) allocated to Stage 1 Intervention to assure that the instructional coach can provide standard protocol support to teachers during this stage, following professional development on an evidence-based practice. Allowing for several weeks of Stage 1 Intervention is necessary to make sure that teachers have adequate time to learn a new practice.

AIM Coaching Intervention Types, Dosages, and Activities

What about the types, dosages, and activities of interventions prescribed in AIM Coaching? While we recommend that the instructional coach use a plan–monitor–reflect–check-in sequence and check-ins as types of interventions, the required dosage of these interventions during Stage 1 Intervention and Stage 2 Intervention may vary and, therefore, be negotiable. For example, in a smaller school, the instructional coach may decide to increase the required number of check-ins in Stage 1 and 2 Interventions for all teachers. While the dosage is somewhat negotiable, what is non-negotiable is the idea that the dosage should vary from Stage 1 to Stage 2 Interventions (e.g., dosages should decrease for high skill teachers and increase for average skill + high will teachers). Also, although we suggest activities that can occur during plan, monitor, and reflect sessions as well as check-ins (see Figures 10.6–10.9), these are negotiable based on teachers' specific needs.

Plan Session Participant Size

A plan session typically occurs with one teacher, but it is possible that the instructional coach conducts a plan session with multiple teachers if they are all planning the same or a similar lesson.

Tailoring Variables

While we recommend that the instructional coach use the same tailoring variables (i.e., skill and will), there might be some flexibility in the manner by which they determine a teacher's skill and will level. For example, the instructional coach may need to develop her own fidelity measures depending on the practices she adopts schoolwide, and she can establish her own cut points to categorize teachers as high, average, or low skill.

Overall, AIM Coaching should be conceptualized as a *model,* not a *program*. We encourage you to keep the non-negotiable aspects of the model intact and consider the overarching principles of adaptive interventions as described in Chapter 9 when setting the guidelines of AIM Coaching for your school. The instructional coach should consider the context and logistics inherent to her school, the amount of available resources, and the specific evidence-based practices her school is adopting.

REVIEW AND PREVIEW

In this chapter, we reviewed the stages of change and how skill and will levels can help us operationalize what stage(s) of change a teacher is in. We then provided a step-by-step guide on how to use the Implementation Survey diagnostically and how to implement Stage 2 Intervention. We also presented negotiables and non-negotiables for AIM Coaching.

Terms to Know

Average/low skill + high will support: The more intensive required dosage of intervention support that teachers displaying average or low skill and high will receive during Stage 2 intervention.

Average/low skill + low will support: The set of intervention options an instructional leader can implement to support teachers displaying average or low skill and low will.

High skill support: The lower dosage of intervention support teachers displaying high skill receive during Stage 2 intervention.

Negotiables: Aspects of the AIM that a coach can adapt based on needs specific to the school where she works.

Non-negotiables: Aspects of the AIM that we recommend a coach not attempt to adapt.

Resource-wise: Choosing coaching duties and priorities that encourage a coach to spend her time supporting teachers who will likely work collaboratively with her, thus reducing the burden on the coach.

Reflection Questions

1. What are the stages of change, and how do they align with teachers' skill and will levels? Also, how can the stages of change help the instructional coach plan for a teacher's Stage 2 support?
2. Why should an instructional coach examine data from the Implementation Survey (and other sources) diagnostically?
3. What are the four steps an instructional coach can follow to examine the Implementation Survey data diagnostically?
4. What are some reasons why an instructional coach might want to conduct a follow-up interview with a teacher? What are some reasons why an instructional coach might decide to forgo the use of follow-up interviews?
5. What are two types of questions an instructional coach can use to design a follow-up interview with a teacher?
6. In general, how does the dosage of a plan–monitor–reflect–check-in sequence differ between Stage 1 and Stage 2 Intervention for each level of Stage 2 Intervention support?
7. Can you describe the support an instructional coach might give to a high skill teacher?
8. Can an instructional coach give a high skill teacher more support should she request it?

9. Why is putting effort into average or low skill + high will teachers the wise use of an instructional coach's time?
10. Can you describe the support an instructional coach might give to an average or low skill + high will teacher?
11. What is a situation where an instructional coach might choose to support one or more low will teachers?
12. Describe the type of support an instructional coach may give to average or low skill + low will teachers. What resource presented in Appendix 12.1 can help an instructional coach match interventions to a teacher's need?
13. Where does an instructional coach record notes for average or low skill + high will teachers? Average or low skill + low will teachers?
14. What are some negotiables and non-negotiables with regard to implementing AIM Coaching?

APPENDIX 12.1

Stage 2 Log

Teacher Name: ______________________

Last Cycle Notes:

Stage 2 Intervention Support (check one):

☐ High skill (Support occurs by request; check in once per week.)

☐ Average/low skill + high will (The Plan, Monitor, and Reflect stages occur once per week; the Check In stage occurs twice per week.)

Week 6

Plan	Monitor	Reflect	Check In
☐ Review goals ☐ Review st. data ☐ Choose materials ☐ Lesson template ☐ Review fidelity ☐ Discuss/practice ☐ Discuss coach role	☐ Observe ☐ Support ☐ Model	☐ Teacher reflect ☐ Provide feedback ☐ Review student data ☐ Problem solve ☐ Set goals	☐ Feedback ☐ Question w/ support ☐ Content resources ☐ Process resources
Notes:	**Notes:**	**Notes:**	**Notes:**
	Fidelity Rating Date: ______ 1 ☐ 2 ☐ 3 ☐ 4 ☐		**Collaborative Effort** 1 ☐ 2 ☐ 3 ☐ 4 ☐

(continued)

© 2019 The University of Texas at Austin/The Meadows Center for Preventing Educational Risk. *PACT Plus Coaching Form* licensed under Creative Commons BY-NC-ND 4.0 International. Reprinted in *Literacy Coaching in the Secondary Grades: Helping Teachers Meet the Needs of All Students* by Jade Wexler, Elizabeth Swanson, and Alexandra Shelton (The Guilford Press, 2021). Permission to photocopy this material is granted to purchasers of this book for personal use or use with students (see copyright page for details). Purchasers can download enlarged versions of this material (see the box at the end of the table of contents).

APPENDIX 12.1 *(continued)*

Week 7

Plan	Monitor	Reflect	Check In
☐ Review goals ☐ Review st. data ☐ Choose materials ☐ Lesson template ☐ Review fidelity ☐ Discuss/practice ☐ Discuss coach role **Notes:**	☐ Observe ☐ Support ☐ Model **Notes:** **Fidelity Rating** Date: _____ 1 ☐ 2 ☐ 3 ☐ 4 ☐	☐ Teacher reflect ☐ Provide feedback ☐ Review student data ☐ Problem solve ☐ Set goals **Notes:**	☐ Feedback ☐ Question w/ support ☐ Content resources ☐ Process resources **Notes:** **Collaborative Effort** 1 ☐ 2 ☐ 3 ☐ 4 ☐

(continued)

APPENDIX 12.1 *(continued)*

Week 8

Plan	Monitor	Reflect	Check In
☐ Review goals ☐ Review st. data ☐ Choose materials ☐ Lesson template ☐ Review fidelity ☐ Discuss/practice ☐ Discuss coach role **Notes:**	☐ Observe ☐ Support ☐ Model **Notes:** **Fidelity Rating** Date: ______ 1 ☐ 2 ☐ 3 ☐ 4 ☐	☐ Teacher reflect ☐ Provide feedback ☐ Review student data ☐ Problem solve ☐ Set goals **Notes:**	☐ Feedback ☐ Question w/ support ☐ Content resources ☐ Process resources **Notes:** **Collaborative Effort** 1 ☐ 2 ☐ 3 ☐ 4 ☐

(continued)

APPENDIX 12.1 *(continued)*

Week 9

Plan	Monitor	Reflect	Check In
☐ Review goals ☐ Review st. data ☐ Choose materials ☐ Lesson template ☐ Review fidelity ☐ Discuss/practice ☐ Discuss coach role	☐ Observe ☐ Support ☐ Model	☐ Teacher reflect ☐ Provide feedback ☐ Review student data ☐ Problem solve ☐ Set goals	☐ Feedback ☐ Question w/ support ☐ Content resources ☐ Process resources
Notes:	**Notes:** **Fidelity Rating** Date: ____ 1 ☐ 2 ☐ 3 ☐ 4 ☐	**Notes:**	**Notes:** **Collaborative Effort** 1 ☐ 2 ☐ 3 ☐ 4 ☐

End of Stage 2 Intervention

SKILL: Consider the average fidelity score and your notes.

FIDELITY

1	2	3	4
Low ≤ 2.4		Average 2.5–3.4	High 3.5–4.0

Do your anecdotal notes override/inform the teacher's fidelity score?

CHAPTER 13

AIM Coaching Case Study

The purpose of the following case study is to provide an example of how AIM Coaching helps instructional coaches support secondary teachers as they integrate evidence-based literacy practices into their content-area instruction, building toward a schoolwide adolescent literacy model.

UNION MIDDLE SCHOOL

At the beginning of the summer, City School District held a meeting to present their literacy plan to secondary school administrators. District leaders told the school administrators that literacy would be a top priority for the upcoming school year. They explained that there are grave consequences for the individual and society that result from poor reading achievement (Biancarosa & Snow, 2006). District leaders explained that, to improve outcomes for all secondary students in the district, each middle school and high school would be responsible for rolling out a new literacy initiative—a schoolwide adolescent literacy model that prioritizes literacy instruction across content areas—not just English language arts (ELA).

The first step in building a schoolwide adolescent literacy model was for the school administrators to understand the literacy needs of their students. Therefore, district leaders walked the school administrators through the ways in which they could examine their state test data. By learning to review their data, administrators could determine the proportion of their students who were struggling readers, students with reading disabilities, and students with more intensive literacy needs. Assistant Principal (AP) Martinez from Union Middle School (UMS), who attended the meeting, brought this information back to his fellow administrative team.

Examining Reading Assessment Data

Using the information learned at the districtwide meeting, UMS administrators began reviewing their students' state standardized reading assessment data from the previous school year. They found that approximately 40% of their students were performing at the basic or below-basic level in reading comprehension (see Figure 13.1).

They knew some of their students were struggling, but they didn't realize the extent of the problem. The data made it clear that many students needed reading support. In fact, examining the data helped them realize just how important the districtwide literacy initiative was for their students. Although some students would benefit from supplemental reading intervention to focus on more foundational level skills that they lacked (e.g., decoding multisyllabic words), *all* students would benefit from enhanced Tier 1 content-area literacy instruction (e.g., explicit vocabulary and comprehension instruction). After all, most students, including students with disabilities (SWD), spend a majority of their day in the general education content-area setting (Hussar et al., 2020). This was no different at UMS. UMS administrators knew what they needed to focus on: They would build a schoolwide adolescent literacy model that included evidence-based adolescent literacy instruction across the Tier 1 content-area setting (i.e., ELA, social studies, science, math) and evidence-based adolescent literacy intervention in supplemental reading intervention classes for students with more intensive needs.

The administrative team knew that introducing the schoolwide adolescent literacy model would add to the list of expectations for teachers who were already being pulled in many different directions. However, like the district leaders, they considered this effort to be a top priority. They also knew that without all teachers contributing to this schoolwide model, it was unlikely that student achievement would improve. Therefore, the administrators needed to develop a plan to ensure that their teachers had the requisite knowledge and skills to provide students with the instruction and intervention required. The administrators needed to provide UMS teachers with high-quality professional development and follow-up support (Kretlow & Bartholomew, 2010) to help them incorporate evidence-based adolescent literacy practices into the

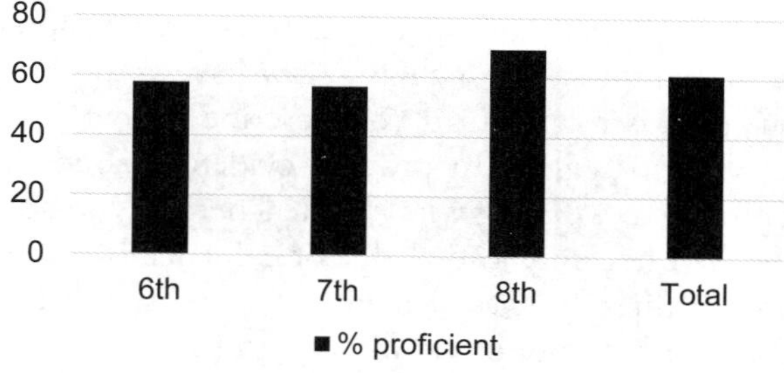

FIGURE 13.1. Union Middle School's state standardized reading assessment data.

different content areas and in supplemental reading intervention classes. But, how would they do this?

Finding an Instructional Coach

At the summer district-led meeting AP Martinez attended, district leaders explained that each secondary school was required to have a dedicated literacy instructional coach who would help guide the development of the schoolwide adolescent literacy model. Additionally, the instructional coach would help teachers adopt evidence-based adolescent literacy practices by providing them with professional development and ongoing coaching support. To fulfill these responsibilities, this instructional coach would need to be in the school for at least 20 hours a week. The instructional coach could be a member of the current administrative team, or the school administrators could choose to hire a reading specialist, budget permitting.

AP Martinez agreed that having an instructional coach was essential to supporting teachers, but the reality was that all of the administrators at UMS were already busy supporting other initiatives, leaving no administrators to serve as the instructional coach. Therefore, he decided to examine the UMS budget to determine if there were enough funds to support hiring an instructional coach for the specific purpose of promoting this new initiative. AP Martinez was pleased to discover that with the remaining professional development funds from the district, the administrative team had enough money to hire a part-time instructional coach. He knew that finding someone who had the unique skills needed for a part-time position might be challenging, but he was confident the team would be able to find someone with enough expertise to serve in this role. After all, the instructional coach would be an essential piece of the puzzle in building their schoolwide adolescent literacy model.

To get started, AP Martinez posted the position on the district website and placed ads on both general and education-specific employment websites. Additionally, AP Martinez asked UMS teachers to share the job posting with others, including current and retired reading specialists, who might be interested in and eligible for the position. From there, he interviewed several applicants with other members of the administrative team. Because the instructional coach would be working directly with teachers, having initial buy-in from some of the teachers themselves would be important, too. Therefore, a few UMS teachers participated in interviewing applicants as well. The interview committee asked questions such as "How have your past experiences in education prepared you for this role?" "Can you describe a time when you had to work with a teacher who was struggling to provide evidence-based literacy instruction?" "What was your approach to working with this teacher?" UMS administrators wanted to find someone who had not only knowledge of evidence-based literacy practices but also experience working directly with teachers of various skill levels. Eventually, AP Martinez narrowed down his pool of candidates and hired Ms. McKinney, a former reading specialist. Ms. McKinney was excited about her new position and hoped all the teachers would be, too.

MS. McKINNEY

Hiring Ms. McKinney was a necessary step in improving the reading achievement of UMS students. The administrators were clear with Ms. McKinney about her mission. First, she would help select a set of evidence-based literacy practices that the school would adopt as part of their schoolwide adolescent literacy model. Then, she would help ensure that teachers implemented these practices with high levels of fidelity by providing professional development and ongoing instructional coaching. Some instructional coaches come prepared, knowing exactly how to start on such a mission. Others might need more guidance. Ms. McKinney had prior experience as a reading specialist, but she was less skilled in how to lead an entire faculty in implementing literacy instruction and intervention. She had also been a mentor teacher to preservice teachers in the past, but she knew her new role would require a new set of skills. How would she support teachers across several content areas all at once?

Professional Development for Instructional Coaches

At the summer meeting AP Martinez attended, district leaders announced that toward the end of the summer, they would be hosting an expert from a partnership with a local university who would be providing professional development to instructional coaches on how to lead a school in its implementation of a schoolwide adolescent literacy model. The expert would provide instructional coaches with guidance on how to implement the instructional coaching model included in this book. Specifically, the book provided information essential for any secondary instructional coach: a rationale about the importance of delivering evidence-based literacy instruction and intervention across a schoolwide adolescent literacy model, clear descriptions of evidence-based adolescent literacy practices, and an adaptive intervention coaching model that instructional coaches could use to support all teachers in a school. Instructional coaches could attend the professional development meeting for a small fee and would receive a copy of the book there.

The goals of this professional development aligned with Ms. McKinney's needs, so she was happy when informed that UMS would pay the professional development fee for her. At the professional development meeting, she would learn how to select evidence-based practices to adopt *and* how to organize and deliver professional development sessions for teachers around these practices. Finally, she would learn a systematic instructional coaching model that would help her support the whole school.

In early August, Ms. McKinney attended the three-day professional development meeting for secondary literacy instructional coaches across the district. She felt fortunate to participate in the professional development meeting because she had a colleague in another school who did not have the opportunity to attend. Her school did not have enough funds to support her attendance at the in-person professional development conference, but her administrative team did give her a copy of this book.

According to the professional development agenda Ms. McKinney received, there were three overarching topics that instructional coaches would learn about during their professional development. On Day 1 of the professional development meeting, the expert, Dr. Wright, would focus on "using data to select evidence-based practices." On this day, the expert would also introduce PACT, an evidence-based intervention that focuses on building vocabulary and comprehension skills among secondary students. By using PACT, the expert would be able to provide an example of evidence-based adolescent literacy practices appropriate for schoolwide adoption. Additionally, PACT would serve as an "anchor" for Days 2 and 3 of the professional development meeting. In other words, Dr. Wright would link the PACT practices to the instructional coaching model practices throughout the rest of the professional development meeting. The focus of Day 2 would be "preparing for schoolwide adoption of evidence-based practices." Finally, Day 3 of the professional development conference would focus on teaching the adaptive intervention coaching model. See Figure 13.2 for the agenda Dr. Wright provided to attendees.

Dr. Wright explained to attendees that there were five essential outcomes of attending the professional development meeting. By its end, instructional coaches would be able to:

- Use school data to determine the school's needs and which targeted evidence-based practices to adopt;
- Develop fidelity tools or adopt existing ones to monitor adherence to the practices;
- Develop implementation plans/schedules for the target evidence-based practices;
- Deliver professional development effectively; and
- Support teachers' implementation of evidence-based practices using an adaptive intervention coaching model.

Professional Development Day 1

The goal of Professional Development Day 1 was for instructional coaches to learn how to use data to identify the literacy needs of a school and make decisions on what evidence-based practices can help address those needs. Fortunately, upon Ms. McKinney's hiring, AP Martinez had already prepped her on UMS's state-standardized reading assessment data, which the administrators had reviewed earlier in the summer. UMS had many students who required supplemental intensive intervention. However, one of UMS's ongoing challenges was a lack of resources. Specifically, the administrators were not confident that they had enough funds to buy literacy instructional materials *and* hire the personnel needed for both Tier 1 instruction in content-area classes and supplemental interventions for students with more foundation-level needs (e.g., reading interventionist). This is why AP Martinez was so eager for Ms. McKinney to provide guidance about an alternative solution.

Because of the professional development meeting she attended, Ms. McKinney now had a better idea of how to guide UMS, given the students' reading assessment data. Since most of the students at UMS spent a majority of their day in the general

PD Module	Topic	Delivery Day	Delivery Time
	Using Data to Select EBPs		
1A	Reviewing school data and adopting EBPs	1	2 hours
1B	Comprehension Canopy	1	2 hours
1C	Essential Words	1	2 hours
1D	Critical Reading of Text	1	1 hour
	Preparing for Schoolwide Adoption of EBPs		
2A	Developing or adopting existing fidelity tools	2	1 hour
2B	Developing implementation plan/schedules for PD in Target EBPs	2	1 hour
2C	Delivering effective PD	2	2 hours
	AIM		
3A	Overview of AIM	3	1 hour
3B	Stage 1 Interventions	3	2 hours
3C	Intermediate Outcomes: Using tailoring variables and applying decision rules	3	2 hours
3D	Stage 2 Interventions	3	2 hours

FIGURE 13.2. Dr. Wright's professional development agenda for instructional coaches.

education content-area setting, she decided that for the upcoming school year, UMS should prioritize providing professional development and instructional coaching to enhance teachers' Tier 1 literacy instruction. During Year 2 of its schoolwide adolescent literacy model, UMS could expand its focus by providing professional development and instructional coaching on supplemental intervention for students with more intensive needs. Ms. McKinney was confident that this would be not only feasible but also an essential step in building a platform to make future intensive intervention efforts successful. In addition, providing evidence-based adolescent literacy instruction across content-area classes might prevent some students from falling further behind by reinforcing the skills students need to read and comprehend complex text.

Ms. McKinney also decided not to include math in the schoolwide adolescent literacy model because she knew that math teachers would be working on an algebra readiness initiative that would take up a lot of their time. However, she did recommend including math as part of the model in the future. Now that she had decided to focus on Tier 1 instruction in ELA, science, and social studies, Ms. McKinney could dive into choosing which practices the school would adopt.

Dr. Wright explained that it was not necessary to adopt an extensive list of strategies for Tier 1 literacy instruction; just a few evidence-based vocabulary and comprehension strategies that teachers could use across the curriculum would suffice. She alerted teachers to this information, which is stressed in Chapter 2 of this book.

Dr. Wright also emphasized the importance of instructional coaches and teachers becoming "effective consumers of research" with regard to how to determine which practices schools should adopt. This concept was familiar to Ms. McKinney. In one of the preservice classes she took years ago when studying to become a reading specialist, she learned that being an effective consumer of research means asking questions and using resources to identify practices that are supported by rigorous evidence. Dr. Wright recommended that the instructional coaches consult several trusted resources outlined in Chapter 2 of this book when selecting practices to adopt. Although Dr. Wright did not provide time during the professional development session for the instructional coaches to review each resource in depth, she was able to familiarize them with a few that they could consult when they had more time. Ms. McKinney used the resources Dr. Wright shared and Chapter 2 of this book to outline a plan of action to complete on her own.

In the meantime, Dr. Wright introduced PACT to prepare instructional coaches for Days 2 and 3 of the professional development meeting. PACT targets both reading comprehension and content knowledge in secondary content-area classes. The instructional coaches received professional development on three PACT instructional practices: Comprehension Canopy, Essential Words, and Critical Reading of Text. Dr. Wright explained that teachers use Comprehension Canopy at the beginning of a unit to build background knowledge and motivate students to learn new content using a short, engaging visual. During Essential Words, teachers define (and later review) high-utility concepts and words that are essential to comprehending unit content. Finally, teachers facilitate Critical Reading of Text to allow students to read and discuss information from high-quality text, which promotes text-based comprehension and extends their thinking. For additional information on PACT, Dr. Wright told instructional coaches that they could read Chapter 7 of this book.

After Professional Development Day 1

In order to decide what evidence-based adolescent literacy practices to include in UMS's schoolwide literacy model, Ms. McKinney decided to review some of the resources that Dr. Wright introduced during the professional development session. First, she would complete the IRIS module called Evidence-Based Practices (Part 1): Identifying and Selecting a Practice or Program (*https://iris.peabody.vanderbilt.edu/module/ebp_01*). Second, Ms. McKinney would review the interventions evaluated on the National Center on Intensive Intervention (NCII) academic intervention tools chart (*www.intensiveintervention.org*), which provides information on the effectiveness of academic programs in reading, writing, and math. Finally, she would review the What Works Clearinghouse (WWC), which reviews studies to determine the effectiveness of different interventions. Ms. McKinney clearly had her work cut out for her, but she was glad there were resources like these that synthesized this important information and that she could review on her own time.

One of the interventions reviewed on the WWC's website was PACT, the set of instructional practices that Dr. Wright taught instructional coaches during the professional development sessions. According to the WWC (USDOE, IES, & WWC, 2013), students who receive PACT instruction improve in reading comprehension and content knowledge significantly more than students who do not receive PACT instruction. Based on the information Ms. McKinney found in the WWC report and her experience in the PACT professional development sessions, Ms. McKinney made the decision that UMS would adopt PACT instructional practices to meet the literacy needs of students in content-area classes. Ms. McKinney emailed the administrative team her decision and its underlying rationale, and the team agreed to her plan. She was one step closer to building UMS's schoolwide adolescent literacy model.

Professional Development Day 2

On the second day of the professional development conference, Dr. Wright introduced how to begin adopting evidence-based adolescent literacy practices in a schoolwide model. He explained that once a school has chosen its evidence-based practices, a good next step is for the instructional coach to select the fidelity tools to use for monitoring teachers' implementation of those practices. Each time the instructional coach observes a teacher's implementation, the instructional coach needs to complete a fidelity checklist to determine whether or not the teacher is adequately fulfilling each element of the practice. Dr. Wright provided instructional coaches with copies of the PACT fidelity checklists as examples. Ms. McKinney was happy to find out that fidelity tools already existed for PACT, since UMS was adopting PACT instructional practices. Ms. McKinney felt lucky that there was no need to reinvent the wheel. She would adopt these fidelity tools (see Appendix 8.1) and review general information about fidelity by reading Chapter 8 of this book.

After sharing information and examples of fidelity tools, Dr. Wright discussed how instructional coaches could create implementation schedules and provided them with examples for guidance on how to offer teachers professional development in a scaffolded manner. Finally, the second professional development day ended with Dr. Wright sharing how instructional coaches could deliver this professional development effectively. Not only did Dr. Wright model effective professional development delivery during this session, she also gave instructional coaches opportunities to practice professional development delivery themselves.

After Professional Development Day 2

Thanks to the choice of PACT instructional practices for UMS's schoolwide adolescent literacy model, Ms. McKinney's fidelity tools were all set. Additionally, she felt confident that she knew how to deliver professional development effectively. However, she still needed to determine when she would provide professional development to introduce the three PACT instructional practices. She wanted to avoid overwhelming the teachers and ensure that they gained a thorough understanding of PACT overall as well

PD Session	Date/Time
PD 1: Comprehension Canopy	Tuesday, August 15 All teachers: 12:45 P.M.–3:00 P.M.
PD 2: Essential Words	Thursday, October 19 Science teachers: 8:30 A.M.–10:00 A.M. Social studies teachers: 10:15 A.M.–11:45 A.M. ELA teachers: 1:45 P.M.–3:15 P.M.
PD 3: Critical Reading of Text	Friday, January 5 All teachers: 8:30 A.M.–10:00 A.M.

FIGURE 13.3. Union Middle School's PACT Plus professional development schedule.

as each instructional practice separately. Therefore, Ms. McKinney decided to hold three separate professional development sessions for each PACT instructional practice. The different professional development sessions would be held at the beginning of the fall, winter, and spring quarters. This way, Ms. McKinney could scaffold the professional development with instructional coaching support throughout the year for all teachers, and they would be implementing all of the PACT instructional practices by the middle of the second semester. Figure 13.3 depicts the professional development schedule Ms. McKinney had developed based on this plan.

Professional Development Day 3

On the final day of the professional development meeting, it was time for Dr. Wright to discuss how instructional coaches can support teachers' implementation of evidence-based practices in a schoolwide adolescent literacy model by providing them with ongoing instructional coaching. Dr. Wright explained that teachers have varying amounts of background knowledge and experience providing literacy instruction. This is one reason why some teachers are more willing than others to learn and implement new practices. Additionally, some teachers learn new skills easily, while others require more instructional coaching. Therefore, different teachers need different amounts and types of support.

How can instructional coaches ensure that *all* teachers receive ongoing, differentiated levels of support? This is one of the most important questions to ask when building a schoolwide adolescent literacy model. It is necessary to provide professional development and instructional coaching systematically to make sure that instructional coaches target teachers' individual needs. This is where AIM Coaching comes into play. AIM Coaching is a multistage process that an instructional coach can follow to determine when and how to deliver professional development and instructional coaching support on a selected set of evidence-based literacy practices.

For the remainder of the professional development day, Dr. Wright explained the steps of AIM Coaching. These steps are discussed in depth in Part III of this book.

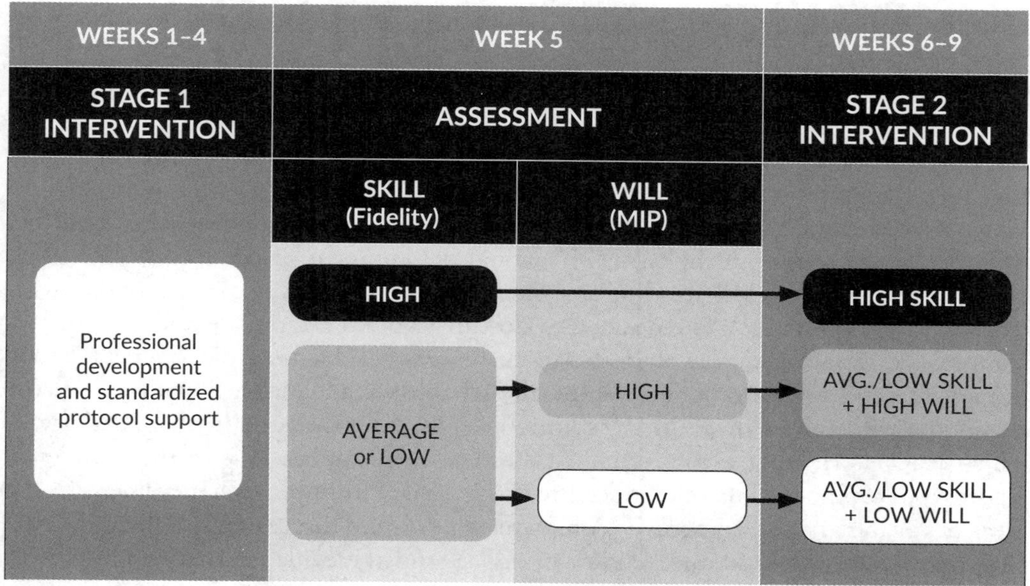

FIGURE 13.4. AIM Coaching.

After Professional Development Day 3

Ms. McKinney knew that it was her responsibility to provide teachers with individual instructional coaching to help them implement PACT instructional practices with fidelity. She believed that AIM Coaching would be the perfect model to follow in order to provide professional development and instructional coaching to content-area teachers. Each AIM cycle is 9 weeks, which would allow Ms. McKinney to deliver professional development on a different PACT instructional practice each quarter. To remind herself about the processes involved in implementing AIM Coaching, she used Part III of this book as a guide to help direct her efforts. Figure 13.4 depicts AIM Coaching.

Ms. McKinney had achieved all of the goals of the professional development meeting with regard to instructional coaching and had already begun to put what she learned into action. She used UMS's state-standardized reading assessment data to determine that teachers would integrate the PACT instructional practices into their Tier 1 content-area instruction to support students' literacy needs. Additionally, she was prepared to support teachers' implementation using the 9-week AIM cycles throughout the school year. Ms. McKinney was now ready to focus on Stage 1 Intervention of the first AIM cycle.

Stage 1 Intervention

Once again, Ms. McKinney consulted Part III of this book to plan her efforts during Stage 1 Intervention of AIM Coaching. During week 1, Ms. McKinney delivered the first PACT professional development session to all ELA, science, and social studies general education and special education co-teachers. Ten teachers were in attendance (see Figure 13.5).

As you can see in Figure 13.3, Professional Development 1 was scheduled for the longest amount of time. This is because Ms. McKinney decided that she would provide teachers with an overview of both PACT and AIM Coaching before introducing the first PACT instructional practice (Comprehension Canopy). This would help teachers know what to expect from this literacy initiative and also what their role would be. Ms. McKinney also used the first professional development of the school year as an opportunity to share UMS's reading assessment data from the previous school year with teachers (see Figure 13.1). She decided to do this to build a rationale and gain buy-in from teachers. She knew it would be difficult to get full buy-in from teachers if they did not understand the rationale behind the schoolwide adolescent literacy model. To share data with the teachers, Ms. McKinney facilitated a think–pair–share activity in which teachers thought about and then discussed the implications of their students' reading performance. The data indeed revealed a need to improve achievement in the areas of vocabulary and comprehension. After sharing and discussing student data, Ms. McKinney then provided an overview of PACT and the evidence that supports it to show teachers how implementing PACT instructional practices would support student improvement in reading.

Next, Ms. McKinney explained that she and the teachers would be working together as partners to implement PACT in content-area classes as part of their schoolwide adolescent literacy model. Ms. McKinney shared the professional development and instructional coaching calendar with teachers, as well as expectations for and roles of the teachers and herself as the instructional coach, and the overall instructional coaching plan, as based on AIM Coaching.

Teacher Name	Subject Area	Grade
Ms. Lee	Physical Science	8
Dr. Washington	U.S. History	8
Ms. Perry	English Language Arts	8
Mr. Beamer	Life Science	7
Mr. Johnson	World History	7
Ms. Rodriguez	English Language Arts	7
Ms. Yang	Earth Science	6
Ms. Connelly	Geography	6
Ms. Neil	English Language Arts	6
Ms. Zern	Special Education	6–8

FIGURE 13.5. Union Middle School's attendance list for Professional Development 1: Comprehension Canopy.

In Part 2 of initial professional development, Ms. McKinney introduced Comprehension Canopy to UMS teachers. First, Ms. McKinney explained the purpose of Comprehension Canopy. She then discussed each step of the instructional practice in detail and provided examples of each step for different content areas. Next, Ms. McKinney shared tips for successful implementation of a Comprehension Canopy lesson. She also shared the Criteria for Success sheet with teachers. Criteria for Success sheets are teacher-friendly versions of the fidelity checklist that teachers can refer to in order to self-assess their lesson and plan future lessons (see Appendix 10.2). Additionally, Ms. McKinney could use a completed fidelity checklist to fill out the Criteria for Success sheet and share it with each teacher as a way to provide feedback during reflect sessions and help set goals to improve implementation.

After discussing the Criteria for Success sheet, Ms. McKinney modeled Comprehension Canopy using a sample unit. She then answered any remaining questions teachers had. At the end of the professional development session, Ms. McKinney provided teachers with time to plan their first lesson that would incorporate Comprehension Canopy. Before teachers left the meeting, they completed a survey to provide Ms. McKinney with feedback on their perceptions of the professional development session so that she could make any necessary changes for future sessions. By administering a survey, examining the data, and adapting her professional development delivery based on the survey data, Ms. McKinney was modeling the same practices she expected to see from the teachers: using data to drive instruction.

After the first professional development session, Ms. McKinney was ready to begin providing teachers with Stage 1 standardized protocol support. Next, we will learn how Ms. McKinney implemented AIM Coaching with Mr. Johnson.

MR. JOHNSON

Mr. Johnson is a seventh-grade World History teacher. He has 6 years of teaching experience, but this is his third year at UMS. For the remainder of the case study, you will read about Ms. McKinney's work with Mr. Johnson. First, you will learn about Mr. Johnson's participation in Stage 1 Intervention of AIM cycle 1. We will then examine the data from the week 5 Assessment Stage. These data will help Ms. McKinney make decisions about how to tailor her support of Mr. Johnson during Stage 2 Intervention. Finally, we will describe how Ms. McKinney supports Mr. Johnson's implementation during Stage 2 Intervention and how he responds to that assistance.

Stage 1 Intervention

Mr. Johnson attended Ms. McKinney's first PACT professional development session. During it, Ms. McKinney presented UMS's standardized reading assessment data to teachers, as explained above; provided teachers with an overview of PACT; and explained that she would be supporting teachers' implementation of three PACT instructional practices in their content-area classes.

After the professional development session, Ms. McKinney offered to help all teachers plan their first Comprehension Canopy lesson. However, Mr. Johnson did not request any assistance. Therefore, Ms. McKinney continued with the Stage 1 Intervention support plan that required her to conduct monitor sessions. Ms. McKinney conducted Comprehension Canopy monitor sessions during Mr. Johnson's third period once a week during weeks 2–4 of Stage 1 Intervention. Because Ms. McKinney did not plan anything with Mr. Johnson, they did not decide before monitor sessions what her role would be. Therefore, rather than model the practice or support Mr. Johnson's implementation during monitor sessions, Ms. McKinney simply observed Mr. Johnson's implementation of Comprehension Canopy and completed the fidelity checklist. Ms. McKinney recorded Mr. Johnson's weekly fidelity ratings along with other standardized protocol support data, such as weekly collaborative effort ratings, on his Stage 1 Log (see Figure 13.6 for this example).

Assessment Stage

At week 5 of AIM cycle 1, Ms. McKinney was ready for the Assessment Stage. Specifically, Ms. McKinney reviewed the fidelity ratings she recorded on each teacher's Stage 1 Log. Based on Mr. Johnson's fidelity checklist ratings, Mr. Johnson's average fidelity score was 2.0 (see Figure 13.7). According to the fidelity arrow, Mr. Johnson exhibited low skill during Stage 1 Intervention. Additionally, there were no anecdotal notes to override Mr. Johnson's low skill level.

Because Mr. Johnson demonstrated low skill during Stage 1 Intervention, Ms. McKinney needed to assess his will level. To do this, Ms. McKinney asked Mr. Johnson to complete the Implementation Survey. On a scale of 1–7, Mr. Johnson rated his motivation a 2, his investment a 4, and his persistence a 2. Therefore, Mr. Johnson's total

Teacher Name: Mr. Johnson

Last Cycle Notes:

STAGE 1 EBP: Comprehension Canopy

Week 2

Plan (by request)	**Monitor** (1/week)	**Reflect** (1/week)	**Check In** (1/week)
☐ Review goals	☒ Observe	☒ Teacher reflect	☐ Feedback
☐ Review st. data	☐ Support	☒ Provide feedback	☐ Question w/ support
☐ Choose materials	☐ Model	☐ Review st. data	☐ Content resources
☐ Lesson template		☒ Problem solve	☒ Process resources
☐ Review fidelity		☒ Set goals	
☐ Discuss/practice			
☐ Discuss coach role			
Notes: Mr. Johnson didn't request any plan sessions.	Notes:	Notes: Virtual reflect session	Notes:
	Fidelity Rating Date: 9/2 — 1 ☐ 2 ☒ 3 ☐ 4 ☐		Collaborative Effort 1 ☐ 2 ☒ 3 ☐ 4 ☐

FIGURE 13.6. Example of Mr. Johnson's week 2 standardized protocol support data.

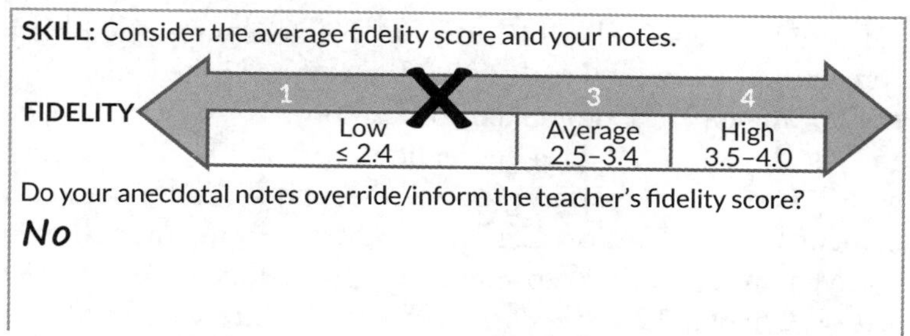

FIGURE 13.7. Mr. Johnson's AIM cycle 1 skill data.

MIP score was 8 out of 21, equaling 38% (see Figure 13.8). Ms. McKinney recorded Mr. Johnson's MIP score onto the MIP arrow, which indicated that Mr. Johnson had a low MIP score (i.e., less than 40%).

Ms. McKinney also used Mr. Johnson's collaborative effort ratings from the Stage 1 Log to determine whether the data would inform or override his MIP score. Thus, Mr. Johnson's collaborative effort wasn't very high. Mr. Johnson's average collaborative effort score was 2.33 out of 4 (see Figure 13.8). Neither his MIP score nor his average collaborative effort score was very high. Therefore, there was no need for Ms. McKinney to override Mr. Johnson's MIP score. Mr. Johnson's low MIP and average collaborative effort scores reinforced to Ms. McKinney that his low skill may be a result of his low will.

Gathering Diagnostic Information

Next, Ms. McKinney examined Mr. Johnson's Implementation Survey data diagnostically in hopes that his survey responses would reveal key ways to target his will. Mr. Johnson's responses to the Part II feasibility items were especially telling. Although Mr. Johnson believed he had enough materials and time to prepare for Comprehension Canopy, he did not believe he had enough time to implement the instructional

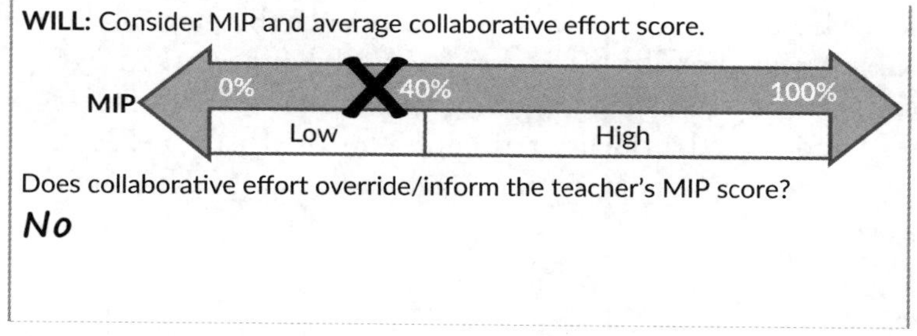

FIGURE 13.8. Mr. Johnson's AIM cycle 1 will data.

practice. He also didn't believe that his students' behavior supported his implementation of Comprehension Canopy. Finally, Mr. Johnson indicated that he did not have enough support to implement Comprehension Canopy.

Although Ms. McKinney had a better idea of what was hindering Mr. Johnson's skill, she still had some remaining questions, such as "Why doesn't Mr. Johnson want to implement Comprehension Canopy?" In order to uncover the answers to her questions, Ms. McKinney decided to conduct a short follow-up interview with Mr. Johnson, based on Chapter 12 of this book. When she interviewed Mr. Johnson, Ms. McKinney learned that Mr. Johnson's main barrier to implementing Comprehension Canopy was his students' behavior. For example, Mr. Johnson's class is so large (more than 30 students) that he doesn't believe his students can realistically participate in academically focused turn-and-talk activities without getting distracted. Based on all that she learned, Ms. McKinney decided that the key to improving Mr. Johnson's will, and eventually his skill, was to help Mr. Johnson improve his behavior management skills.

Stage 2 Intervention

During Stage 2 Intervention (i.e., weeks 6–9 of the AIM cycle), Ms. McKinney stopped implementing weekly monitor and reflect sessions with teachers who have average/low skill + low will, like Mr. Johnson. Instead, Ms. McKinney would use interventions found in the Low Will Guide available on this book's companion website (see the box at the end of the table of contents) to increase Mr. Johnson's will. She believed that peer mentorship would be the best intervention approach for Mr. Johnson. Peer mentorship targets motivation, persistence, and perceived feasibility—all areas of support for Mr. Johnson. Peer mentorship will allow Mr. Johnson to observe a high skill teacher's implementation of Comprehension Canopy, seeing firsthand the teacher's delivery and the students' responses. Observing students' responses, in particular, would give Mr. Johnson an opportunity to take stock of another teacher's behavior management system. Therefore, Mr. Johnson will have the chance to see that with the proper behavior management support, he *can* implement Comprehension Canopy effectively. Ms. McKinney noted this plan on Mr. Johnson's Low Will Log for the upcoming weeks (see Figure 13.9).

By week 8, Mr. Johnson expressed more confidence that he could implement Comprehension Canopy successfully. Therefore, Ms. McKinney asked Mr. Johnson if he would be willing to try implementing Comprehension Canopy during week 9. Mr. Johnson agreed and earned a fidelity rating of 3 for the first time! He was now implementing Comprehension Canopy with average skill. Ms. McKinney recorded this on the Stage 2 Log.

What's Next?

Ms. McKinney's first AIM cycle had now ended. Although Mr. Johnson's skill had improved, according to his single fidelity rating, he still had not yet implemented

Week 6
Intervention(s) Planned
☐ Raising Awareness
☐ Incentives to Change
☒ Peer Mentorship
☐ Collaborative Support Teams
☐ Booster Session
☐ Intervention Adjustments
☐ Other (please specify) ________________

FIGURE 13.9. Mr. Johnson's Low Will Log.

Comprehension Canopy with high skill. Therefore, Ms. McKinney decided that during AIM cycle 2, which would focus on Essential Words, she would use check-ins to continue to target Mr. Johnson's Comprehension Canopy needs. By providing him with this differentiated support, Ms. McKinney believed she might be able to help guide Mr. Johnson to successful implementation of both Comprehension Canopy and Essential Words.

MS. YANG

Ms. Yang teaches sixth-grade Earth Science at UMS. Because Ms. Yang is a first-year teacher, she receives support from both Ms. McKinney, Union's instructional coach, and Mr. Beamer, Union's science department chair and seventh-grade science teacher. In this case study, you will read about Ms. McKinney's work with Ms. Yang throughout Stage 1 and Stage 2 Interventions to support her implementation of PACT during the first AIM cycle.

Stage 1 Intervention

Ms. McKinney's PACT professional development meeting on Comprehension Canopy was the first professional development session Ms. Yang attended as an inservice teacher. Afterward, Ms. McKinney offered to help teachers plan their first Comprehension Canopy lesson. Because Ms. Yang was feeling a bit anxious about implementing Comprehension Canopy, she requested a "plan" session with Ms. McKinney. During their plan session, Ms. Yang and Ms. McKinney worked together to plan how Ms. Yang would introduce the first unit of the year. At the end of the plan session, Ms. McKinney asked Ms. Yang what role she wanted Ms. McKinney to play during her first monitor session. Ms. Yang decided that because it was the beginning of the school year and she wanted her students to get to know her teaching style, she would like to be observed during her first monitor session. Ms. Yang assured Ms. McKinney, however, that she was open to all of her feedback and would welcome support in the form of modeling or co-teaching during future monitor sessions if Ms. McKinney believed it was necessary.

During Ms. Yang's monitor sessions, Ms. McKinney used the PACT fidelity checklist to document whether or not Ms. Yang completed each step of Comprehension Canopy. At the end of each monitor session, Ms. McKinney rated Ms. Yang's fidelity on a scale of 1–4 and then transferred the rating onto the Stage 1 Log Ms. McKinney was using to keep track of Ms. Yang's progress. Ms. McKinney also recorded information about Ms. Yang's reflect sessions, check-ins, and collaborative effort on her Stage 1 Log (see Figure 13.10 for an example).

Assessment Stage

At week 5 of the first AIM cycle, Ms. McKinney was ready to complete the Assessment Stage activities for all teachers. She started with Ms. Yang. First, Ms. McKinney evaluated Ms. Yang's skill by averaging the fidelity ratings she received on the fidelity checklists during Stage 1 Intervention (recorded on the Stage 1 Log). As you can see in Figure 13.11, Ms. Yang's average Comprehension Canopy fidelity score was 3.67, which indicates high skill. Additionally, upon reviewing her monitor session notes, Ms. McKinney determined that there was no anecdotal information that would override her status.

Because Ms. Yang was in the high skill range, Ms. McKinney did not need to assess Ms. Yang's will. Ms. McKinney shared Ms. Yang's average fidelity score with her and explained that because she had high ratings on the fidelity checklist, Ms. McKinney would proceed directly to providing her with high skill support during Stage 2 Intervention.

Teacher Name: Ms. Yang

Last Cycle Notes:

STAGE 1 EBP: Comprehension Canopy

Week 2

Plan (by request)	**Monitor** (1/week)	**Reflect** (1/week)	**Check In** (1/week)
☒ Review goals	☒ Observe	☒ Teacher reflect	☒ Feedback
☐ Review st. data	☐ Support	☒ Provide feedback	☐ Question w/ support
☒ Choose materials	☐ Model	☐ Review st. data	☐ Content resources
☐ Lesson template		☒ Problem solve	☐ Process resources
☒ Review fidelity		☒ Set goals	
☒ Discuss/practice			
☒ Discuss coach role			
Notes:	**Notes:**	**Notes:**	**Notes:**
	Fidelity Rating Date: 9/1 — 1 ☐ 2 ☐ 3 ☒ 4 ☐		**Collaborative Effort** 1 ☐ 2 ☐ 3 ☐ 4 ☒

FIGURE 13.10. Example of Ms. Yang's week 2 standardized protocol support data.

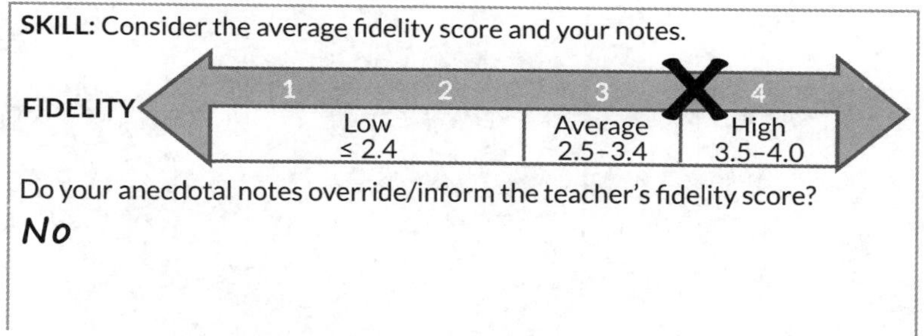

FIGURE 13.11. Ms. Yang's AIM cycle 1 skill data.

Stage 2 Intervention

According to the Stage 2 Log, Ms. McKinney only needed to provide Ms. Yang with plan, monitor, and reflect sessions if she requested them. However, Ms. Yang was still expected to implement Comprehension Canopy (although without face-to-face support from Ms. McKinney), and Ms. McKinney now conducted only one "check-in" with Ms. Yang each week of Stage 2 Intervention. Ms. Yang felt confident that the support she had received during Stage 1 Intervention gave her the foundation she needed to implement Comprehension Canopy without any plan, monitor, or reflect sessions. Therefore, by the end of Stage 2 Intervention, Ms. Yang hadn't requested any support from Ms. McKinney.

What's Next?

Because Ms. Yang received high skill support during Stage 2 Intervention, Ms. McKinney did not conduct any formal "monitor" sessions with Ms. Yang. Therefore, she did not need to recalculate her average fidelity score at the end of the AIM cycle. Ms. Yang was ready for the next AIM cycle on Essential Words.

References

Abrami, P. C., Poulsen, C., & Chambers, B. (2004). Teacher motivation to implement an educational innovation: Factors differentiating users and non-users of cooperative learning. *Educational Psychology, 24*(2), 201–216.

Adams, G., & Engelmann, S. (1996). *Research on direct instruction: 25 years beyond DISTAR*. Seattle, WA: Educational Achievement Systems.

Alan, F. (2013). Average mobile phone user will send 2 million words via text in their lifetime. Retrieved from *www.phonearena.com/news/Average-mobile-phone-user-will-send-2-million-words-via-text-in-their-lifetime_id46101.*

Alfieri, L., Brooks, P. J., Aldrich, N. J., & Tenenbaum, H. R. (2011). Does discovery-based instruction enhance learning? *Journal of Educational Psychology, 103,* 1–18.

Archer, A. L., & Hughes, C. A. (2011). *Explicit instruction: Effective and efficient teaching.* New York: Guilford Press.

Arum, R., & Roksa, J. (2011). *Academically adrift: Limited learning on college campuses.* Chicago: University of Chicago Press.

August, D., & Shanahan, T. (2006). *Developing literacy in second-language learners: Report of the National Literacy Panel on Language-Minority Children and Youth.* Mahwah, NJ: Erlbaum.

Baker, S. K., Chard, D. J., Ketterlin-Geller, L. R., Apichatabutra, C., & Doabler, C. T. (2009). Teaching writing to at-risk students: The quality of evidence for self-regulated strategy development. *Exceptional Children, 75,* 303–320.

Baker, S., Gersten, R., & Graham, S. (2003). Teaching expressive writing to students with learning disabilities: Research-based applications and examples. *Journal of Learning Disabilities, 36*(2), 109–123.

Balfanz, R., Bridgeland, J. M., Moore, L. A., & Fox, J. H. (2010). *Building a grad nation: Progress and challenges in ending the high school dropout epidemic.* Washington, DC: Civic Enterprises, Everyone Graduates Center at Johns Hopkins University, and America's Promise Alliance.

Balfanz, R., Herzog, L., & Mac Iver, D. J. (2007). Preventing student disengagement and keeping students on the graduation path in urban middle-grades schools: Early identification and effective interventions. *Educational Psychologist, 42*(4), 223–235.

Barlow, A. T., Frick, T. M., Barker, H. L., & Phelps, A. J. (2014). Modeling instruction: The impact of professional development on instructional practices. *Science Educator, 23*(1), 14–26.

Barre, E. (2013). How much should we assign?: Estimating out of class workload. Retrieved from *http://cte.rice.edu/blogarchive/2016/07/11/workload.*

Barron, K. E., & Hulleman, C. S. (2015). Expectancy-value-cost model of motivation. In J. D. Wright (Ed.), *International encyclopedia of the social and behavioral sciences* (pp. 503–509). New York: Elsevier.

Becker, K. D., Bradshaw, C. P., Domitrovich, C., & Ialongo, N. S. (2013). Coaching teachers to improve implementation of the good behavior game. *Administration and Policy in Mental Health and Mental Health Services Research, 40,* 482–493.

Belfield, C., & Levin, H. M. (Eds.). (2007). *The price we pay: Economic and social consequences of inadequate education.* Washington, DC: Brookings Institution Press.

Benjamin, A. S., & Tullis, J. (2010). What makes distributed practice effective? *Cognitive Psychology, 61*(3), 228–246.

Berkeley, S., Bender, W. N., Peaster, L. G., & Saunders, L. (2009). Implementation of response to intervention: A snapshot of progress. *Journal of Learning Disabilities, 42,* 85–95.

Berkeley, S., & Riccomini, P. J. (2011). QRAC-the-Code: A comprehension monitoring strategy for middle school social studies textbooks. *Journal of Learning Disabilities, 46,* 154–165.

Berkeley, S., Scruggs, T. E., & Mastropieri, M. A. (2010). Reading comprehension instruction for students with learning disabilities, 1995–2006: A meta-analysis. *Remedial and Special Education, 31,* 423–436.

Bhattacharya, A., & Ehri, L. C. (2004). Graphosyllabic analysis helps adolescent struggling readers read and spell words. *Journal of Learning Disabilities, 37*(4), 331–348.

Biancarosa, G., & Snow, C. (2006). *Reading next: A vision for action and research in middle and high school literacy: A report to the Carnegie Corporation of New York* (2nd ed.). Washington, DC: Alliance for Excellent Education.

Bierman, K. L., Nix, R. L., Maples, J. J., & Murphy, S. A. (2006). Examining clinical judgment in an adaptive intervention design: The Fast Track Program. *Journal of Consulting and Clinical Psychology, 74*(3), 468.

Blazar, D., & Kraft, M. A. (2015). Exploring mechanisms of effective teacher coaching: A tale of two cohorts from a randomized experiment. *Educational Evaluation and Policy Analysis, 37*(4), 542–566.

Bloom, H. S., Hill, C. J., Black, A. R., & Lipsey, M. W. (2008). Performance trajectories and performance gaps as achievement effect-size benchmarks for educational interventions. *Journal of Research on Educational Effectiveness, 1*(4), 289–328.

Bottge, B. A., Cohen, A. S., & Choi, H. (2018). Comparisons of mathematics intervention effects in resource and inclusive classrooms. *Exceptional Children, 84,* 197–212.

Brock, M. E., & Carter, E. W. (2017). A meta-analysis of educator training to improve implementation of interventions for students with disabilities. *Remedial and Special Education, 38*(3), 131–144.

Bryk, A. S., Sebring, P. A., Allensworth, E., Luppescu, S., & Easton, J. Q. (2010). *Organizing schools for improvement: Lessons from Chicago.* Chicago: University of Chicago Press.

Bulgren, J. A., Graner, P. S., & Deshler, D. D. (2013). Literacy challenges and opportunities for students with learning disabilities in social studies and history. *Learning Disabilities Research and Practice, 28*(1), 17–27.

Burke, K. (2018). How many texts do people send every day? Retrieved from *www.textrequest.com/blog/many-texts-people-send-per-day.*

Burns, M. K., Riley-Tillman, T. C., & VanDerHeyden, A. M. (2012). *RTI applications: Vol. 1. Academic and behavioral interventions.* New York: Guilford Press.

Cantrell, S. C., Almasi, J. F., Carter, J. C., & Rintamaa, M. (2013). Reading intervention in middle and high schools: Implementation fidelity, teacher efficacy, and student achievement. *Reading Psychology, 34*(1), 26–58.

Cantrell, S. C., Burns, L. D., & Callawaay, P. (2008). Middle- and high school content area teachers' perceptions about literacy teaching and learning. *Literacy Research and Instruction, 48*(1), 76–94.

Carnevale, A. (2001). *Help wanted . . . college required* (ETS Leadership 2000 Series). Princeton, NJ: Educational Testing Service.

Catts, H. W. (2018). The simple view of reading: Advancements and false impressions. *Remedial and Special Education, 39*(5), 317–323.

Center on Instruction. (2008). *Synopsis of "The Power of Feedback."* Portsmouth, NH: RMC Research Corporation.

Chall, J. S. (1996). *Stages of reading development* (2nd ed.). Fort Worth, TX: Harcourt-Brace.

Chall, J. S., & Jacobs, V. A. (1983). Writing and reading in the elementary grades: Developmental trends among low SES children. *Language Arts, 60*(5), 617–626.

Chambers Cantrell, S., David Burns, L., & Callaway, P. (2008). Middle- and high-school content area teachers' perceptions about literacy teaching and learning. *Literacy Research andInstruction, 48*(1), 76–94.

Ciullo, S., Lembke, E. S., Carlisle, A., Thomas, C. N., Goodwin, M., & Judd, L. (2016). Implementation of evidence-based literacy practices in middle school Response to Intervention. *Learning Disability Quarterly, 39,* 44–57.

Clancy, E., & Wexler, J. (2017, October). *A synthesis of co-teaching literature with student outcomes.* Poster presented at the annual meeting of the Council for Learning Disabilities, Baltimore, MD.

Cohen, J. (1988). *Statistical power analysis for the behavioral sciences* (2nd ed.). Hillsdale, NJ: Erlbaum.

Connell, A. M., Dishion, T. J., Yasui, M., & Kavanagh, K. (2007). An adaptive approach to family intervention: Linking engagement in family-centered intervention to reductions in adolescent problem behavior. *Journal of Consulting and Clinical Psychology, 75*(4), 568.

Conradi, K., Jang, B. G., Bryant, C., Craft, A., & McKenna, M. C. (2013). Measuring adolescents' attitudes toward reading. *Journal of Adolescent and Adult Literacy, 56*(7), 565–576.

Cook, B. G., Cook, L., & Landrum, T. J. (2013). Moving research into practice: Can we make dissemination stick? *Exceptional Children, 79*(3), 163–180.

Cook, L., & Friend, M. (1995). Co-teaching: Guidelines for creating effective practices. *Focus on Exceptional Children, 28,* 1–16.

Cortiella, C., & Horowitz, S. H. (2014). *The state of learning disabilities: Facts, trends and emerging issues.* New York: National Center for Learning Disabilities.

Darling-Hammond, L., Wei, R. C., Andree, A., Richardson, N., & Orphanos, S. (2009). *Professional learning in the learning profession: A status report on teacher development in the United States and abroad.* Stanford, CA: National Staff Development Council.

Denton, C. A., Bryan, D., Wexler, J., Reed, D., & Vaughn, S. (2007). *Effective instruction for middle school students with reading difficulties: The reading teacher's sourcebook.* Austin: University of Texas System/Texas Education Agency.

Denton, C. A., Wexler, J., Vaughn, S., & Bryan, D. (2008). Intervention provided to linguistically diverse middle school students with severe reading difficulties. *Learning Disabilities Research and Practice, 23*(2), 79–89.

Desimone, L. M. (2009). Improving impact studies of teachers' professional development: Toward better conceptualizations and measures. *Educational Researcher, 38*(3), 181–199.

Desimone, L. M., & Garet, M. S. (2015). Best practices in teachers' professional development in the United States. *Psychology, Society and Education, 7*(3), 252–263.

Dexter, D. D., & Hughes, C. A. (2011). Graphic organizers and students with learning disabilities: A meta-analysis. *Learning Disability Quarterly, 34*(1), 51–72.

Dijkstra, E. M., Walraven, A., Mooij, T., & Kirschner, P. A. (2017). Factors affecting intervention fidelity of differentiated instruction in kindergarten. *Research Papers in Education, 32*(2), 151–169.

District of Columbia Public Schools. (2017). Support for English Learners (ELs). Retrieved from *https://dcps.dc.gov/service/english-language-learner-ell-support.*

Duckworth, A. L. (2009). (Over and) Beyond high-stakes testing. *American Psychologist, 64,* 279–280.

Duke, N. K. (2000). 3.6 minutes per day: The scarcity of informational texts in the first grade. *Reading Research Quarterly, 35,* 202–224.

Edmonds, M. S., Vaughn, S., Wexler, J., Reutebuch, C., Cable, A., Tackett, K. K., et al. (2009). A synthesis of reading interventions and effects on reading comprehension outcomes for older struggling readers. *Review of Educational Research, 79,* 262–300.

Edwards, R., Hanson, A., & Thorpe, M. (Eds.). (2013). *Culture and processes of adult learning* (Vol. 1). New York: Routledge.

Every Student Succeeds Act. (2015). Public Law No. 114-95 § 114 Stat. 1177.

Feldman, K. (2016). Actionable feedback for teachers: The missing element in school improvement. Retrieved May 9, 2019, from *www.mnasa.org/cms/lib6/MN07001305/Centricity/Domain/44/Feldman%20Actionable%20Feedback%20for%20Teachers.pdf.*

Flynn, R. J., Marquis, R. A., Paquet, M. P., Peeke, L. M., & Aubry, T. D. (2012). Effects of individual direct-instruction tutoring on foster children's academic skills: A randomized trial. *Children and Youth Services Review, 34,* 1183–1189.

Fogarty, M., Oslund, E., Simmons, D., Davis, J., Simmons, L., Anderson, L., et al. (2014). Examining the effectiveness of a multicomponent reading comprehension intervention in middle schools: A focus on treatment fidelity. *Educational Psychology Review, 26*(3), 425–449.

Friend, M. (2000). Myths and misunderstandings about professional collaboration. *Remedial and Special Education, 21*(3), 130–160.

Fuchs, L. S., & Fuchs, D. (1998). Treatment validity: A unifying concept for reconceptualizing the identification of learning disabilities. *Learning Disabilities Research and Practice, 13*(4), 204–219.

Fuchs, L. S., Fuchs, D., & Compton, D. L. (2010). Rethinking response to intervention at middle and high school. *School Psychology Review, 39,* 22–28.

Fuchs, L. S., Fuchs, D., Hosp, M. K., & Jenkins, J. R. (2001). Oral reading fluency as an indicator of reading competence: A theoretical, empirical, and historical analysis. *Scientific Studies of Reading, 5*(3), 239–256.

Fuchs, L. S., Fuchs, D., & Malone, A. S. (2017). The taxonomy of intervention intensity. *Teaching Exceptional Children, 50*(1), 35–43.

Fuchs, L. S., & Vaughn, S. (2012). Responsiveness-to-intervention: A decade later. *Journal of Learning Disabilities, 45*(3), 195–203.

Gabriel, R., Allington, R., & Billen, M. (2012). Middle schoolers and magazines: What teachers can learn from students' leisure reading habits. *The Clearing House: A Journal of Educational Strategies, Issues and Ideas, 85*(5), 186–191.

Gajria, M., Jitendra, A. K., Sood, S., & Sacks, G. (2007). Improving comprehension of expository text in students with LD: A research synthesis. *Journal of Learning Disabilities, 40,* 210–225.

Garet, M. S., Cronen, S., Eaton, M., Kurki, A., Ludwig, M., Jones, W., et al. (2008). *The impact of two professional development interventions on early reading instruction and achievement* (NCEE Report 2008-4031). Washington, DC: National Center for Educational Evaluation and Regional Assistance, Institute of Education Sciences, U.S. Department of Education.

Garet, M. S., Heppen, J., Walters, K., Smith, T., & Yang, R. (2016). *NCEE evaluation brief: Does content-focused teacher professional development work?: Findings from three Institute of Education Science studies.* Washington, DC: Institute of Education Sciences.

Garet, M., Wayne, A., Stancavage, F., Taylor, J., Walters, K., Song, M., et al. (2010). *Middle school mathematics professional development impact study: Findings after the first year of implementation* (NCEE Report 2010-4009). Washington, DC: National Center for Education Evaluation and Regional Assistance, Institute of Education Sciences, U.S. Department of Education.

Gatweway Courses. (n.d). Texas Middle School Fluency Assessment: Administering and interpreting results. Retrieved from *www.texascourses.org/courses/course-v1:TexasGateway+TMSFA+2016/about.*

Gelzheiser, L. M., & Meyers, J. (1991). Reading instruction by classroom, remedial, and resource room teachers. *Journal of Special Education, 24*(4), 512–526.

George Washington Papers. (1778). Series 4, *General Correspondence: George Washington to George Clinton, February 16, 1778.* Washington, DC: Manuscript Division, Library of Congress. Retrieved from *www.loc.gov/item/mgw449501.*

Gersten, R., Compton, D., Connor, C. M., Dimino, J., Santoro, L., Linan-Thompson, S., et al. (2008). *Assisting students struggling with reading: Response to intervention and multi-tier intervention for reading in the primary grades: A practice guide* (NCEE Report 2009-4045). Washington, DC: National Center for Education Evaluation and Regional Assistance, Institute of Education Sciences, U.S. Department of Education. Retrieved from *http://ies.ed.gov/ncee/wwc/publications/practiceguides.*

Gersten, R., Fuchs, L. S., Williams, J. P., & Baker, S. (2001). Teaching reading comprehension strategies to students with learning disabilities: A review of research. *Review of Educational Research, 71*(2), 279–320.

Gough, P., & Tunmer, W. (1986). Decoding, reading, and reading disability. *Remedial and Special Education, 7,* 6–10.

Griffiths, J. M., Luhanga, U., McEwen, L. A., Schultz, K., & Dalgarno, N. (2016). Promoting high-quality feedback: Tool for reviewing feedback given to learners by teachers. *Canadian Family Physician, 62*(7), 600–602.

Guthrie, J. T., & Coddington, C. S. (2009). Reading motivation. In K. R. Wentzel & A. Wigfield (Eds.), *Handbook of motivation at school* (pp. 503–525). New York: Routledge.

Haager, D., Gersten, R., Baker, S., & Graves, A. (2003). The English-Language Learner Classroom Observation Instrument: Observations of beginning reading instruction in urban schools. In S. R. Vaughn & K. L. Briggs (Eds.), *Reading in the classroom: Systems for observing teaching and learning* (pp. 111–144). Baltimore MD: Brookes.

Hairrell, A., Rupley, W. H., Edmonds, M., Larsen, R., Simmons, D., Wilson, V., et al. (2011). Examining the impact of teacher quality on fourth-grade students' comprehension and content-area achievement. *Reading and Writing Quarterly, 27,* 239–260.

Hairrell, A., Rupley, W., & Simmons, D. (2011). The state of vocabulary research. *Literacy Research and Instruction, 50*(4), 253–271.

Hall, L. A. (2012). The role of reading identities and reading abilities in students' discussions about texts and comprehension strategies. *Journal of Literacy Research, 44*(4), 239–272.

Hanover Research. (2016). *Early skills and predictors of academic success.* Arlington, VA: Author.

Harmon, J. M., Hendrick, W. B., & Wood, K. D. (2005). Research on vocabulary instruction in the content areas: Implications for struggling readers. *Reading and Writing Quarterly, 21,* 261–280.

Hasbrouck, J., & Denton, C. (2005). *The reading coach: A how-to manual for success.* Longmont, CO: Sopris West.

Hattie, J. (2009). *Visible learning: A synthesis of over 809 meta-analyses relating to achievement.* New York: Routledge.

Henk, W. A., Marinak, B. A., & Melnick, S. A. (2012). Measuring the reader self-perceptions of adolescents: Introducing the RSPS2. *Journal of Adolescent and Adult Literacy, 56*(4), 311–320.

Hernandez, D. J. (2012). Double jeopardy: How third-grade reading skills and poverty influence high school graduation. Retrieved from *https://files.eric.ed.gov/fulltext/ED518818.pdf.*

Hill, H. C. (2007). Learning in the teaching workforce. *The Future of Children, 17*(1), 111–127.

Honig, B., Diamond, L., & Gutlohn, L. (2000). *Teaching reading sourcebook.* Novato, CA: Arena Press.

Hughes, P. (2011). *Five 4ths of July.* New York: Viking.

Hughes-Hassell, S., & Rodge, P. (2007). The leisure reading habits of urban adolescents. *Journal of Adolescent and Adult Literacy, 51*(1), 22–33.

Hussar, B., Zhang, J., Hein, S., Wang, K., Roberts, A., Cull, J., et al. (2020). *The condition of education 2020* (NCES Report 2020-144). Washington, DC: U.S. Department of Education, National Center for Education Statistics. Retrieved from *https://nces.ed.gov/pubs2020/2020144.pdf.*

Individuals with Disabilities Education Improvement Act of 2004. 20 U.S.C. 1400 et seq. Retrieved from *www.congress.gov/bill/108th-congress/house-bill/1350.*

IRIS Center. (2014). Evidence-based practices (Part 1): Identifying and selecting a practice or program. Retrieved from *https://iris.peabody.vanderbilt.edu/module/ebp_01.*

Ivey, G., & Broaddus, K. (2001). Just plain reading: A survey of what makes students want to read in middle school classrooms. *Reading Research Quarterly, 36*(4), 350–377.

Joyce, B., & Showers, B. (2002). *Student achievement through staff development* (3rd ed.). Alexandria, VA: Association for Supervision and Curriculum Development.

Kaldenberg, E. R., Watt, S. J., & Therrien, W. J. (2015). Reading instruction in science for students with learning disabilities: A meta-analysis. *Learning Disability Quarterly, 38*(3), 160–173.

Kamil, M. L., Borman, G. D., Dole, J., Kral, C. C., Salinger, T., & Torgesen, J. (2008). *Improving adolescent literacy: Effective classroom and intervention practices. A practice guide* (NCEE Report 2008-4027). Washington, DC: National Center for Education Evaluation and Regional Assistance, Institute of Education Sciences, U.S. Department of Education. Retrieved from *https://ies.ed.gov/ncee/wwc/PracticeGuide/8.*

Kickmeier-Rust, M. D., Peirce, N., Conlan, O., Schwarz, D., Verpoorten, D., & Albert, D. (2007). *Immersive digital games: The interfaces for next-generation E-learning?* Berlin: Springer.

Kilbourne, A. M., Goodrich, D. E., Lai, Z., Post, E. P., Schumacher, K., Nord, K. M., et al. (2013). Randomized controlled trial to reduce cardiovascular disease risk for patients with bipolar disorder: The Self-Management Addressing Heart Risk Trial (SMAHRT). *Journal of Clinical Psychiatry, 74*(7), e655.

Klauda, S. L. (2009). The role of parents in adolescents' reading motivation and activity. *Educational Psychology Review, 21*(4), 325–363.

Klingner, J. K., Urbach, J., Golos, D., Brownell, M., & Menon, S. (2010). Teaching reading in the 21st century: A glimpse at how special education teachers promote reading comprehension. *Learning Disability Quarterly, 33,* 59–74.

Klingner, J. K., Vaughn, S., Boardman, A., & Swanson, E. (2012). *Now we get it!: Boosting comprehension with collaborative strategic reading.* San Francisco: Jossey-Bass.

Knoester, M. (2009). Inquiry into urban adolescent independent reading habits: Can Gee's theory of discourses provide insight? *Journal of Adolescent and Adult Literacy, 52*(8), 676–685.

Knowles, M. (1980). *The modern practice of adult education: From pedagogy to andragogy* (rev. ed.). Englewood Cliffs, NJ: Cambridge Adult Education.

Knowles, M. S. (1984). *Andragogy in action: Applying principles of adult learning.* San Francisco: Jossey-Bass.

Knowles, M. S. (1989). *The making of an adult educator: An autobiographical journey.* San Francisco: Jossey-Bass.

Knowles, M. S., Holton, E. F., & Swanson, R. A. (2012). *The adult learner.* London: Routledge.

Kraft, M. A., Blazar, D., & Hogan, D. (2018). The effect of teacher coaching on instruction and achievement: A meta-analysis of the causal evidence. *Review of Educational Research, 88,* 547–588.

Kretlow, A. G., & Bartholomew, C. C. (2010). Using coaching to improve fidelity of evidence-based practices: A review of studies. *Teacher Education and Special Education, 33,* 279–299.

LaBerge, D., & Samuels, S. J. (1974). Toward a theory of automatic information processing in reading. *Cognitive Psychology, 6,* 293–323.

Lane, K. L., Carter, E. W., Pierson, M. R., & Glaeser, B. C. (2006). Academic, social and behavioral characteristics of high school students with emotional disturbances or learning disabilities. *Journal of Emotional and Behavioral Disorders, 14,* 108–117.

Lee, C. D., & Spratley, A. (2010). *Reading in the disciplines: The challenges of adolescent literacy.* New York: Carnegie Corporation of New York. Retrieved from *www.carnegie.org/media/filer_public/88/05/880559fd-afb1–49ad-af0e-e10c8a94d366/ccny_report_2010_tta_lee.pdf.*

Lee, H. (1982). *To kill a mockingbird.* New York: Warner Books.

Lei, H., Nahum-Shani, I., Lynch, K., Oslin, D., & Murphy, S. A. (2012). A "SMART" design for building individualized treatment sequences. *Annual Review of Clinical Psychology, 8,* 21–48.

Lepper, M. R., Green, D., & Nisbett, R. E. (1973). Undermining children's intrinsic interest with extrinsic rewards: A test of the overjustification hypothesis. *Journal of Personality and Social Psychology, 28,* 129–137.

Lester, J. H. (2000). Secondary instruction: Does literacy fit in? *High School Journal, 83*(3), 10–16.

Lobel, A. (1970). *Frog and toad are friends.* New York: Harper & Row.

Lofthouse, R., Leat, D., Towler, C., Hallet, E., & Cummings, C. (2010). *Improving coaching: Evolution not revolution* (Research report). London: CfBT Education Trust.

Logan, G. D. (1988). Automaticity, resources and memory: Theoretical controversies and practical implications. *Human Factors, 30,* 583–598.

Lynch, M. (2018). Academic rigor: You're doing it wrong and here's why. Retrieved from *http://static.pdesas.org/content/documents/m1-slide_21_4_myths_of_rigor.pdf.*

Maehr, M. L. (1991). The "psychological environment" of the school: A focus for school leadership. In P. Thurston & P. Zodhiates (Eds.), *Advances in educational administration* (Vol. 2, pp. 51–81). Greenwich, CT: JAI Press.

Magiera, K., & Zigmond, N. (2005). Co-teaching in middle school classrooms under routine conditions: Does the instructional experience differ for students with disabilities in co-taught and solo-taught classes? *Learning Disabilities Research and Practice, 20,* 79–85.

Marlowe, D. B., Festinger, D. S., Arabia, P. L., Dugosh, K. L., Benasutti, K. M., Croft, J. R., et al. (2008). Adaptive interventions in drug court: A pilot experiment. *Criminal Justice Review, 33*(3), 343–360.

Maxwell, J. (2011). *The 360-degree leader.* Nashville, TN: Author.

McCray, A. D., Vaughn, S., & Neal, L. V. I. (2001). Not all students learn to read by third grade:

Middle school students speak out about their reading disabilities. *Journal of Special Education, 35*(1), 17–30.

McFarland, J., Hussar, B., Zhang, J., Wang, X., Wang, K., Hein, S., et al. (2019). *The condition of education 2019* (NCES Report 2019-144). Washington, DC: National Center for Education Statistics. Retrieved from *https://nces.ed.gov/pubsearch/pubsinfo.asp?pubid=2019144.*

McKay, J. R. (2005). Is there a case for extended interventions for alcohol and drug use disorders? *Addiction, 100*(11), 1594–1610.

McKenna, M. C., Conradi, K., Lawrence, C., Jang, B. G., & Meyer, J. P. (2012). Reading attitudes of middle school students: Results of a U.S. survey. *Reading Research Quarterly, 47*(3), 283–306.

Meadows Center. (n.d.). PACT Plus. Retrieved from *www.meadowscenter.org/projects/detail/pact-plus.*

Meadows Center for Preventing Educational Risk. (2018). *PACT Plus reading interest survey.* Austin, TX: Author.

Moje, E. B. (2008). Foregrounding the disciplines in secondary literacy teaching and learning: A call for change. *Journal of Adolescent and Adult Literacy, 52*(2), 96–107.

Murawski, W. W., & Lochner, W. W. (2011). Observing co-teaching: What to ask for, look for, and listen for. *Intervention in School and Clinic, 46*(3), 174–183.

Murawski, W. W., & Swanson, H. L. (2001). Meta-analysis of co-teaching research: Where are the data? *Remedial and Special Education, 22*(5), 258–267.

Nahum-Shani, I., Qian, M., Almirall, D., Pelham, W. E., Gnagy, B., Fabiano, G. A., et al. (2012). Experimental design and primary data analysis methods for comparing adaptive interventions. *Psychological Methods, 17*(4), 457.

National Center on Intensive Intervention. (2014). *Designing intensive interventions for students with significant and persistent academic needs.* Washington, DC: Author.

National Center on Intensive Intervention. (n.d.-a). Academic progress monitoring tools chart. Retrieved from *https://charts.intensiveintervention.org/chart/progress-monitoring.*

National Center on Intensive Intervention. (n.d.-b). DBI Professional Learning Series. Retrieved from *https://intensiveintervention.org/implementation-support/dbi-training-series.*

National Center on Intensive Intervention. (n.d.-c). Example diagnostic tools. Retrieved from *https://intensiveintervention.org/intensive-intervention/diagnostic-data/example-diagnostic-tools.*

National Governors Association Center for Best Practices & Council of Chief State School Officers. (2010a). *Common Core State Standards.* Washington, DC: Authors. Retrieved from *www.corestandards.org.*

National Governors Association Center for Best Practices & Council of Chief State School Officers. (2010b). *Common Core State Standards; English language arts; reading: informational text; kindergarten.* Washington, DC: Authors. Retrieved from *www.corestandards.org/ELA-Literacy/RI/K.*

National Governors Association Center for Best Practices & Council of Chief State School Officers. (2010c). *Common Core State Standards; English language arts; reading: informational text; grades 11–12.* Washington, DC: Authors. Retrieved from *www.corestandards.org/ELA-Literacy/RI/11-12.*

National Reading Panel. (2000). *Teaching children to read: An evidence-based assessment of the scientific research literature on reading and its implications for reading instruction: Reports of the subgroups (00-4754).* Washington, DC: U.S. Government Printing Office.

Ness, M. K. (2016). Reading comprehension strategies in secondary content area classrooms: Teacher use of and attitudes towards reading comprehension instruction. *Reading Horizons: A Journal of Literacy and Language Arts, 49*(2), 5.

Newman, L. (2006). *Facts from NLTS2: General education participation and academic performance of students with learning disabilities.* Menlo Park, CA: SRI International. Retrieved from *www.nlts2.org/fact_sheets/nlts2_fact_ sheet_2006_07.pdf.*

Next Generation Science Standards. (2013). *Next Generation Science Standards: For states, by states.* Washington, DC: National Academies Press.

Norcross, J. C., Krebs, P. M., & Prochaska, J. O. (2011). Stages of change. *Journal of Clinical Psychology: In Session, 67,* 143–154.

Parsad, B., Lewis, L., & Farris, E. (2001). *Teacher preparation and professional development: 2000* (NCES Report 2001-088). Washington, DC: Institute of Education Sciences, National Center for Education Statistics. Retrieved from *https://nces.ed.gov/pubs2001/2001088.pdf.*

Pelletier, L. G., Dion, S. C., Slovinec-D'Angelo, M., & Reid, R. (2004). Why do you regulate what you eat?: Relationships between forms of regulation, eating behaviors, sustained dietary behavior change, and psychological adjustment. *Motivation and Emotion, 28*(3), 245–277.

Penuel, W. R., Fishman, B. J., Yamaguchi, R., & Gallagher, L. P. (2007). What makes professional development effective?: Strategies that foster curriculum implementation. *American Educational Research Journal, 44*(4), 921–958.

Petscher, Y., & Kim, Y.-S. (2011). The utility and accuracy of oral reading fluency score types in predicting reading comprehension. *Journal of School Psychology, 49*(1), 107–129.

Pierce, J. D. (2014). Effective coaching: Improving teacher practice and outcomes for all learners. Retrieved from *www.air.org/sites/default/files/NCSI_Effective-Coaching-Brief-508.pdf.*

Pitcher, S. M., Albright, L. K., DeLaney, C. J., Walker, N. T., Seunarinesingh, K., Mogge, S., et al. (2007). Assessing adolescents' motivation to read. *Journal of Adolescent and Adult Literacy, 50*(5), 378–396.

Pressley, M. (2004). The need for research on secondary literacy education. In T. L. Jetton & J. A. Dole (Eds.), *Adolescent literacy research and practice* (pp. 415–432). New York: Guilford Press.

Ramani, S., & Krackov S. K. (2012). Twelve tips for giving feedback effectively in the clinical environment. *Medical Teacher, 34,* 787–791.

RAND Reading Study Group. (2002). Reading for understanding: Towards an R&D program in reading comprehension. Retrieved from *www.rand. org/multi/achievementforall/reading/readreport.html.*

Raynor, H. A., & Champagne, C. M. (2016). Position of the academy of nutrition and dietetics: Interventions for the treatment of overweight and obesity in adults. *Journal of the Academy of Nutrition and Dietetics, 116*(1), 129–147.

Reading Rockets. (2021, January 12). We hear a lot about fidelity of implementation when talking about RTI: What does this really mean? Retrieved from *www.readingrockets.org/faqs/we-hear-lot-about-fidelity-implementation-when-talking-about-rti-what-does-really-mean.*

Reddy L. A., & Dudek, C. M. (2014). Teacher progress monitoring of instructional and behavioral management practices: An evidence-based approach to improving classroom practices. *International Journal of School and Educational Psychology, 2,* 71–84.

Reed, D. K., Swanson, E., Petscher, Y., & Vaughn, S. (2014). The effects of teacher read-alouds and student silent reading on predominantly bilingual high school seniors' learning and retention of social studies content. *Reading and Writing, 27,* 1119–1140.

Reed, D. K., & Wexler, J. (2014). "Our teachers . . . don't give us no help, no nothin'": Juvenile offenders' perceptions of academic support. *Residential Treatment for Children and Youth, 31,* 188–218.

Reed, D. K., Wexler, J., & Vaughn, S. (2012). *RTI for reading at the secondary level: Recommended literacy practices and remaining questions.* New York: Guilford Press.

Reed, D. K., Zimmerman, L., Reeger, A., Aloe, A. M., & Folsom, J. S. (2018). *An investigation of two approaches to fluency instruction in the general education classroom: Repeated reading versus varied practice reading.* Iowa City: Iowa Reading Research Center. Retrieved from *https://iowareadingresearch.org/sites/iowareadingresearch.org/files/irrc_fluency_study_report.pdf.*

Robertson-Kraft, C., & Duckworth, A. L. (2014). True grit: Trait-level perseverance and passion for long-term goals predicts effectiveness and retention among novice teachers. *Teachers College Record (1970), 116*(3). Retrieved from *www.ncbi.nlm.nih.gov/pmc/articles/PMC4211426.*

Robinson, V. M. J., Lloyd, C. A., & Rowe, K. J. (2008). The impact of leadership on student outcomes: An analysis of the differential effects of leadership types. *Educational Administration Quarterly, 44,* 635–674.

Rotermund, S., DeRoche, J., & Ottem, R. (2017). *Teacher professional development: By selected teacher and school characteristics: 2011–12* (NCES Report 2017-200). Washington, DC: Institute of Education Sciences, National Center for Education Statistics.

Sáenz, L. M., & Fuchs, L. (2002). Examining the reading difficulty of secondary students with learning disabilities: Expository versus narrative text. *Remedial and Special Education, 23,* 31–41.

Scammacca, N. K., Fall, A.-M., & Roberts, G. (2015). Benchmarks for expected annual academic growth for students in the bottom quartile of the normative distribution. *Journal of Research on Educational Effectiveness, 8*(3), 366–379.

Scammacca, N., Roberts, G., Vaughn, S., Edmonds, M. S., Wexler, J., Reutebuch, C. K., et al. (2007). *Reading interventions for adolescent struggling readers: A meta-analysis with implications for practice.* Portsmouth, NH: RMC Research Corporation, Center on Instruction.

Scammacca, N. K., Roberts, G., Vaughn, S., & Stuebing, K. K. (2015). A meta-analysis of interventions for struggling readers in grades 4–12: 1980–2011. *Journal of Learning Disabilities, 48*(4), 369–390.

Scheeler, M. C., Ruhl, K. L., & McAfee, J. K. (2004). Providing performance feedback to teachers: A review. *Teacher Education and Special Education, 27,* 396–407.

Shanahan, T., & Shanahan, C. (2008). Teaching disciplinary literacy to adolescents: Rethinking content-area literacy. *Harvard Educational Review, 78,* 40–59.

Shannon, T. M. (2019). Historic peacemakers: Learning A–Z. Retrieved from *www.readinga-z.com.*

Silverstein, S. (1964). *The giving tree.* New York: Harper & Row.

Simmons, D., Hairrell, A., Edmonds, M., Vaughn, S., Larsen, R., Willson, V., et al. (2010). A comparison of multiple-strategy methods: Effects on fourth-grade students' general and content-specific reading comprehension and vocabulary development. *Journal of Research on Educational Effectiveness, 3,* 121–156.

Smarter Balanced Assessment Consortium. (2019). Smarter Balanced Assessment Consortium: 2016–17 Technical report. Retrieved from *http://portal.smarterbalanced.org/library/en/2016–17-summative-assessment-technical-report.pdf.*

Smith, J. L. M., Doabler, C. T., & Kame'enui, E. J. (2016). Using explicit and systematic instruction across academic domains. *Teaching Exceptional Children, 48*(6), 273–274.

Snow, C. E., Porche, M. V., Tabors, P. O., & Harris, S. R. (2007). *Is literacy enough?: Pathways to academic success for adolescents.* Baltimore: Brookes.

Stanovich, K. (1986). Matthew effects in reading: Some consequences of individual differences in the acquisition of literacy. *Reading Research Quarterly, 22,* 360–407.

Stanovich, P. J., & Jordan, A. (1998). Canadian teachers' and principals' beliefs about inclusive education as predictors of effective teaching in heterogeneous classrooms. *The Elementary School Journal, 98*(3), 221–238.

Stanovich, P. J., & Stanovich, K. E. (2003). *Using research and reason in education: How teachers can use scientifically based research to make curricular and instructional decisions.* Portsmouth, NH: RMC Research Corporation.

Stevens, E., Vaughn, S., & Swanson, E. (2020). Examining the effects of a tier 2 reading comprehension intervention aligned to tier 1 instruction for fourth-grade struggling readers. *Exceptional Children, 86*(4), 430–448.

Stewart, A. A., & Swanson, E. (2019). *Turn and talk: An evidence-based practice. Teacher's guide.* Austin, TX: Meadows Center for Preventing Educational Risk.

Stormont, M., & Reinke, W. M. (2014). Providing performance feedback for teachers to increase treatment fidelity. *Intervention in School and Clinic, 49,* 219–224.

Swanson, E., Hairrell, A., Kent, S., Ciullo, S., Wanzek, J. A., & Vaughn, S. (2014). A synthesis and meta-analysis of reading interventions using social studies content for students with learning disabilities. *Journal of Learning Disabilities, 47*(2), 178–195.

Swanson, E., Stevens, E. A., & Wexler, J. (2019). Engaging students with disabilities in text-based discussions: Guidance for general education social studies classrooms. *Teaching Exceptional Children, 51,* 305–312.

Swanson, E., Vaughn, S., & Roberts, G. (2015). *Examining the efficacy of differential levels of professional development for teaching content area reading strategies* (R305A150407). Washington, DC: Institute of Education Sciences, U.S. Department of Education.

Swanson, E., & Wanzek, J. (2014). Applying research in reading comprehension to social studies instruction for middle and high school students. *Intervention in School and Clinic, 49*(3), 142–147.

Swanson, E., Wanzek, J., McCulley, L., Stillman-Spisak, S., Vaughn, S., Simmons, D., et al. (2016). Literacy and text reading in middle and high school social studies and English language arts classrooms. *Reading and Writing Quarterly, 32*(3), 199–222.

Swanson, E., Wanzek, J., Vaughn, S., Fall, A., Roberts, G., Hall, C., et al. (2017). Middle school reading comprehension and content learning intervention for below-average readers. *Reading and Writing Quarterly, 33*(1), 37–53.

Swanson, E., Wanzek, J., Vaughn, S., Roberts, G., & Fall, A. (2015). Improving reading comprehension and social studies knowledge among middle school students with disabilities. *Exceptional Children, 81*(4), 426–442.

Swanson, E., & Wexler, J. (2017). Using the Common Core State Standards guidelines to select appropriate text for adolescents with learning disabilities. *Teaching Exceptional Children, 49*(3), 160–167.

Swanson, E., Wexler, J., Shelton, A., Kurz, L. A., & Vaughn, S. (2018). *Partner reading: An evidence-based practice: Teacher's guide.* Austin, TX: Meadows Center for Preventing Educational Risk.

Taylor, P. (2008). *How to give quality feedback.* Sydney, Australia: Macquarie University.

Texas Center for Learning Disabilities. (2012). Essential characteristics of reading instruction and interventions in middle school. Retrieved from *www.texasldcenter.org/files/projects/Summary_P3.pdf.*

Texas Education Agency. (2019). TEA brochures. Retrieved from *https://tea.texas.gov/communications/brochures.aspx.*

Thompson, D. (2013). The 10 most-common (and 10 least-common) jobs in America today. Retrieved from *www.theatlantic.com/business/archive/2013/04/the-10-most-common-and-10-least-common-jobs-in-america-today/274526.*

Thoonen, E. E. J., Sleegers, P. J. C., Oort, F. J., Peetsma, T. T. D., & Geijsel, F. P. (2011). How to improve teaching practices: The role of teacher motivation, organizational factors and leadership practices. *Educational Administration Quarterly, 47,* 496–536.

Torgesen, J. K., Houston, D. D., Rissman, L. M., Decker, S. M., Roberts, G., Vaughn, S., et al. (2007). *Academic literacy instruction for adolescents: A guidance document from the Center on Instruction*. Portsmouth, NH: RMC Research Corporation, Center on Instruction.

Torgesen, J. K., Wagner, R. K., & Rashotte, C. A. (2012). *Test of word reading efficiency* (2nd ed.; TOWRE-2). Austin, TX: PRO-ED.

Ungemah, L. D. (2012). What is academic rigor?! Retrieved from *http://static.pdesas.org/content/documents/m1-slide_21_4_myths_of_rigor.pdf.*

University of Oregon Center on Teaching and Learning. (2018a). *Dynamic Indicators of Basic Early Literacy Skills (DIBELS®*; 8th ed.). Eugene: Author. Retrieved from *http://dibels.uoregon.edu.*

University of Oregon Center on Teaching and Learning. (2018b). *Understanding the research behind DIBELS®* (8th ed.; Technical Report 1801). Eugene, OR: Author.

U.S. Bureau of Labor Statistics. (2018). Labor force statistics from the current population survey. Retrieved from *www.bls.gov/cps/aa2018/cpsaat07.htm.*

U.S. Department of Education. (2011). National report on the condition of education. Retrieved from *http://nces.ed.gov/pubs2011/2011033.pdf.*

U.S. Department of Education. (2017). Total number of homeless students enrolled in LEAs with or without McKinney-Vento subgrants—Total: 2014–2015. Retrieved May 1, 2017, from *https://eddataexpress.ed.gov/data-element-explorer.cfm.*

U.S. Department of Education, Institute of Education Sciences, National Center for Education Statistics. (2016). Digest of education statistics, 2015 (NCES Report 2016-014). Retrieved from *https://nces.ed.gov/fastfacts/display.asp?id=59.*

U.S. Department of Education, Institute of Education Sciences, National Center for Education Statistics. (2017). Digest of education statistics, 2016 (NCES Report 2017-094). Retrieved from *https://nces.ed.gov/fastfacts/display.asp?id=59.*

U.S. Department of Education, Institute of Education Sciences, National Center for Education Statistics, National Assessment of Educational Progress. (2009). *The nation's report card: Reading 2009.* Washington, DC: Authors.

U.S. Department of Education, Institute of Education Sciences, National Center for Education Statistics, National Assessment of Educational Progress. (2011). *The nation's report card: Reading 2011.* Washington, DC: Authors.

U.S. Department of Education, Institute of Education Sciences, National Center for Education Statistics, National Assessment of Educational Progress. (2013). *The nation's report card: A first look 2013 mathematics and reading.* Washington, DC: Authors.

U.S. Department of Education, Institute of Education Sciences, National Center for Education Statistics, National Assessment of Educational Progress. (2015). *The nation's report card: Reading 2015.* Washington, DC: Authors.

U.S. Department of Education, Institute of Education Sciences, National Center for Education Statistics, National Assessment of Educational Progress. (2017). *The nation's report card: Reading 2017.* Washington, DC: Authors.

U.S. Department of Education, Institute of Education Sciences, National Center for Education Statistics, National Assessment of Educational Progress. (2018). *2017 NAEP mathematics and reading assessments: Highlighted results at grades 4 and 8 for the nation, states, and districts.* Washington, DC: Authors. Retrieved from *www.nationsreportcard.gov.*

U.S. Department of Education, Institute of Education Sciences, National Center for Education Statistics, National Assessment of Educational Progress. (2019). 2019 reading grades 4 and 8 assessment report cards: Summary data tables for national and state average scores and NAEP achievement level results. Retrieved from *www.nationsreportcard.gov/reading/supportive_files/2019_Results_Appendix_Reading_State.pdf.*

U.S. Department of Education, Institute of Education Sciences, What Works Clearinghouse. (2013, August). WWC review of the report: Improving reading comprehension and social studies knowledge in middle school. Retrieved from *http://whatworks.ed.gov.*

Vadasy, P. F., & Sanders, E. A. (2009). Supplemental fluency intervention and determinants of reading outcomes. *Scientific Studies of Reading, 13*(5), 383–425.

Vadasy, P. F., Sanders, E. A., & Nelson, J. R. (2015). Effectiveness of supplemental kindergarten vocabulary instruction for English learners: A randomized study of immediate and longer-term effects of two approaches. *Journal of Research on Educational Effectiveness, 8*(4), 490–529.

Vaughn Gross Center for Reading & Language Arts. (2005). *Introduction to the 3-tier reading model: Reducing reading difficulties for kindergarten through third grade students* (3rd ed.). Austin, TX: Author.

Vaughn, S., Cirino, P. T., Wanzek, J., Wexler, J., Fletcher, J., Denton, C. D., et al. (2010). Response to Intervention for middle school students with reading difficulties: Effects of a primary and secondary intervention. *School Psychology Review, 39*(1), 3–21.

Vaughn, S., Fall, A.-M., Roberts, G., Wanzek, J. Swanson, E., & Martinez, L (2018). Class percentage of students with reading difficulties on content knowledge and comprehension. *Journal of Learning Disabilities, 52,* 120–134.

Vaughn, S., Fletcher, J. M., Francis, D. J., Denton, C. A., Wanzek, J., Wexler, J., et al. (2008). Response to intervention with older students with reading difficulties. *Learning and Individual Differences, 18,* 338–345.

Vaughn, S., Klingner, J. K., Swanson, E., Boardman, A. G., Roberts, G., Mohammed, S. S., et al. (2011). Efficacy of collaborative strategic reading with middle school students. *American Educational Research Journal, 48*(4), 938–964.

Vaughn, S., Linan-Thompson, S., & Hickman, P. (2003). Response to intervention as a means of identifying students with reading/learning disabilities. *Exceptional Children, 69,* 391–409.

Vaughn, S., Roberts, G., Klingner, J. K., Swanson, E. A., Boardman, A., Stillman-Spisak, S. J., et al. (2013). Collaborative strategic reading: Findings from experienced implementers. *Journal of Research on Educational Effectiveness, 6*(2), 137–163.

Vaughn, S., Roberts, G., Schnakenberg, J. B., Fall, A.-M., Vaughn, M. G., & Wexler, J. (2015). Improving reading comprehension for high school students with disabilities: Effects for comprehension and school retention. *Exceptional Children, 82,* 117–131.

Vaughn, S., Roberts, G., Swanson, E. A., Wanzek, J., Fall, A.-M., & Stillman-Spisak, S. J. (2014). Improving middle school students' knowledge and comprehension in social studies: A replication. *Educational Psychology Review, 27*(1), 31–50.

Vaughn, S., Roberts, G., Wexler, J., Vaughn, M. G., Fall, A. M., & Schnakenberg, J. B. (2015). High school students with reading comprehension difficulties: Results of a randomized control trial of a two-year reading intervention. *Journal of Learning Disabilities, 48*(5), 546–558.

Vaughn, S., Swanson, E., Roberts, G., Wanzek, J., Stillman-Spisak, S. J., Solis, M., et al. (2013). Improving reading comprehension and social studies knowledge in middle school. *Reading Research Quarterly, 48*(1), 77–93.

Vaughn, S., Swanson, E., Wexler, J., & Roberts, G. (2015–2019). *Adolescent literacy model for students with disabilities: Improving instruction and intervention to enhance reading* (CFDA 84.326M). Washington, DC: Office of Special Education and Rehabilitative Services, U.S. Department of Education.

Vaughn, S., Wanzek, J., Murray, C. S., & Roberts, G. (2012). *Intensive interventions for students struggling in reading and mathematics: A practice guide.* Portsmouth, NH: RMC Research, Center on Instruction.

Vaughn, S., Wanzek, J., Wexler, J., Barth, A., Cirino, P. T., Fletcher, J. M., et al. (2010). The relative effects of group size on reading progress for older students with reading difficulties. *Reading and Writing: An Interdisciplinary Journal, 23,* 931–956.

Vaughn, S., Wexler, J., Leroux, A., Roberts, G., Denton, C. A., Barth, A., et al. (2012). Effects of an intensive reading intervention for eighth grade students with persistently inadequate response to intervention. *Journal of Learning Disabilities, 45*(6), 515–525.

Vaughn, S., Wexler, J., Roberts, G., Barth, A. A., Cirino, P. T., Romain, M. A., et al. (2011). Effects of individualized and standardized interventions on middle school students with reading disabilities. *Exceptional Children, 77*(4), 391–407.

Vellutino, F. R., Scanlon, D. M., Small, S., & Fanuele, D. P. (2006). Response to Intervention as a vehicle for distinguishing between reading disabled and non-reading disabled children: Evidence for the role of kindergarten and first grade intervention. *Journal of Learning Disabilities, 38*(6), 157–169.

Wanzek, J., Kent, S. C., Vaughn, S., Swanson, E. A., Roberts, G., & Haynes, M. (2015). Implementing team-based learning in middle school social studies classes. *Journal of Educational Research, 108,* 331–344.

Wanzek, J., Otaiba, S. A., Rivas, B. K., Jones, F. G., Schatschneider, C., Petscher, Y., et al. (2017). Effects of a year long supplemental reading intervention for students with reading difficulties in fourth grade. *Journal of Educational Psychology, 109*(8), 1103–1119.

Wanzek, J., Swanson, E., Vaughn, S., Roberts, G., & Fall, A. (2016). English learner and non-English learner students with disabilities: Content acquisition and comprehension. *Exceptional Children, 82*(4), 428–442.

Wanzek, J., & Vaughn, S. (2007). Research-based implications from extensive early reading interventions. *School Psychology Review, 36*(4), 541–561.

Wanzek, J., & Vaughn, S. (2008). Response to varying amounts of time in reading intervention for students with low response to intervention. *Journal of Learning Disabilities, 41,* 126–142.

Wanzek, J., & Vaughn, S. (2011). Is a three-tier reading intervention model associated with reduced placement in special education? *Remedial and Special Education, 32,* 167–175.

Wanzek, J., Vaughn, S., Kent, S. C., Swanson, E. A., Roberts, G., Haynes, M., et al. (2014). The effects of team-based learning on social studies knowledge acquisition in high school. *Journal of Research on Educational Effectiveness, 7,* 183–204.

Wanzek, J., Wexler, J., Vaughn, S., & Ciullo, S. (2010). Reading interventions for struggling readers in the upper elementary grades: A synthesis of 20 years of research. *Reading and Writing, 23*(8), 889–912.

Waters, T., Marzano, R., & McNulty, B. (2003). *Balanced leadership: What 30 years of research tells us about the effect of leadership on student achievement.* Working paper.

Weingarten, Z., Bailey, T. R., & Peterson, A. (2018). *User guide for sample reading lessons.* Washington, DC: National Center on Intensive Intervention, Office of Special Education Programs, U.S. Department of Education.

Welch, M., Brownell, K., & Sheridan, S. M. (1999). What's the score and game plan on teaming in schools?: A review of the literature on team teaching and school-based problem-solving teams. *Remedial and Special Education, 20*(1), 36–49.

Wexler, J. (2009, March). *Remediation of older students with reading difficulties: Response to Intervention through classroom instruction and interventions.* Paper presented at the annual meeting of the Society for Research on Educational Effectiveness, Washington, DC.

Wexler, J. (2016). *Targeting the 2% brief 7: Fluency.* Austin, TX: Meadows Center for Preventing Educational Risk.

Wexler, J., Kearns, D. M., Lemons, C. J., Mitchell, M., Clancy, E., Davidson, K. A., et al. (2018).

Reading comprehension and co-teaching practices in middle school English language arts classrooms. *Exceptional Children, 84*(4), 384–402.

Wexler, J., Mitchell, M. A., Clancy, E. E., & Silverman, R. D. (2017). An investigation of literacy practices in high school science classrooms. *Reading and Writing Quarterly, 33*(3), 258–277.

Wexler, J., Reed, D. K., Barton, E. E., Mitchell, M. A., & Clancy, E. (2014, February). The effect of enhanced comprehension for incarcerated adolescents. Paper presented at the annual meeting of the Pacific Coast Research Conference, San Diego, CA.

Wexler, J., Reed, D. K., Pyle, N., Mitchell, M., & Barton, E. E. (2015). A synthesis of peer-mediated academic interventions for secondary struggling learners. *Journal of Learning Disabilities, 48,* 451–470.

Wexler, J., Reed, D. K., & Sturges, K. M. (2015). Reading practices in the juvenile correctional facility setting: Incarcerated adolescents speak out. *Exceptionality, 23*(2), 100–123.

Wexler, J., Wanzek, J., & Vaughn, S. (2009). Preventing and remediating reading difficulties for elementary and secondary students. In G. D. Sideridis (Ed.), *Strategies in reading for struggling learners* (pp. 15–35). Weston, MA: Learning Disabilities Worldwide.

Wexler, J., Wanzek, J., & Vaughn, S. (2018). Spotting problems before they grow: Preventing and remediating reading difficulties for elementary and secondary students. In N. D. Young, C. N. Michael, & T. Citro (Eds.), *From floundering to fluent: Reaching and teaching the struggling reader* (pp. 17–40). Lanham, MD: Rowman & Littlefield.

Williamson, R., & Blackburn, B. R. (2010). *Four myths about rigor in the classroom*. Larchmont, NY: Eye on Education. Retrieved from *http://static.pdesas.org/content/documents/m1-slide_21_4_myths_of_rigor.pdf.*

Wilson, S. M. (1993). The self-empowerment index: A measure of internally and externally expressed teacher autonomy. *Educational and Psychological Measurement, 53*(3), 727–737.

Wolgemuth, J. R., Abrami, P. C., Helmer, J., Savage, R., Harper, H., & Lea, T. (2014). Examining the impact of ABRACADABRA on early literacy in northern Australia: An implementation fidelity analysis. *Journal of Educational Research, 107*(4), 299–311.

Yoon, K. S., Duncan, T., Lee, S. W.-Y., Scarloss, B., & Shapley, K. (2007). *Reviewing the evidence on how teacher professional development affects student achievement* (Issues & Answers Report, REL 2007-No. 033). Washington, DC: U.S. Department of Education, Institute of Education Sciences, National Center for Education Evaluation and Regional Assistance, Regional Educational Laboratory Southwest. Retrieved from *http://ies.ed.gov/ncee/edlabs.*

Yoshino, A., Sawamura, T., Kobayashi, N., Kurauchi, S., Matsumoto, A., & Nomura, S. (2009). Algorithm-guided treatment versus treatment as usual for major depression. *Psychiatry and Clinical Neurosciences, 63*(5), 652–657.

Zumeta Edmonds, R., Gruner Gandhi, A., & Danielson, L. (2019). *Essentials of intensive intervention.* New York: Guilford Press.

Index

Note. *f* or *t* following a page number indicates a figure or a table.

D

E

H

I

K

L

M

N

O

P

Q

R